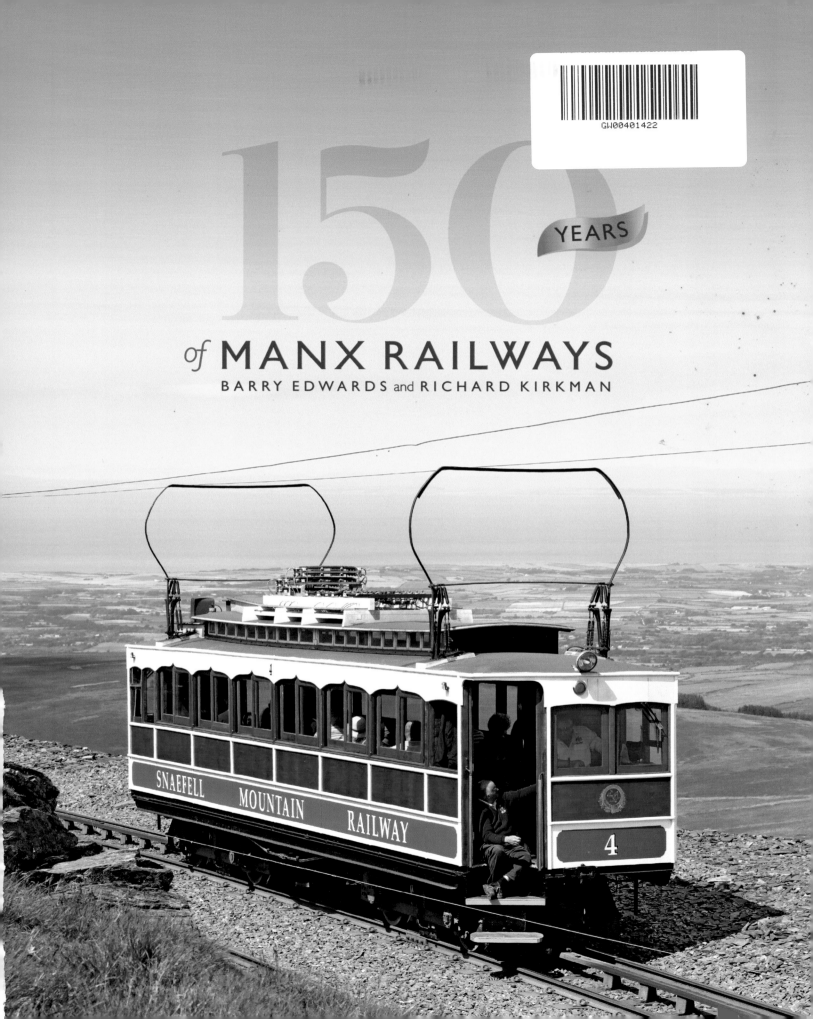

150 YEARS

of MANX RAILWAYS

BARRY EDWARDS and RICHARD KIRKMAN

CONTENTS

Published by and copyright
© 2023 Lily Publications
(IOM) Ltd. 2nd edition.
All rights reserved.
ISBN 978-1-911177-94-4

Title page: Tram No.4 has
departed the Summit
station and begun its
descent towards
Bungalow and Laxey on
18th July 2021. It is
passing what is known as
the North Shoulder, with
the northern plains of
the Island, and mountains
of Scotland, visible
behind. *Barry Edwards*

This book is dedicated to the late Alan Corlett. Alan was the chief architect of the 1993 'Year of Railways' celebrating the centenary of the Manx Electric Railway. The events of that year put the Island and its unique railways firmly back on the enthusiasts map, and hence re-launched them as a vital tourist attraction. That we are about to celebrate the 150th anniversary of the Steam Railway and the 130th birthday of the Manx Electric, stems from the exciting programme devised by Alan around 30 years ago.

Barry Edwards

Barry Edwards was born and brought up in Southwest London. His interest in railways stems from his Father who spent his entire working life with British Railways. He made his first visit to the Isle of Man in 1976, returning at regular intervals.

An interest in photography and in 1981, the acquisition of a Mamiya 645 medium format film camera, soon led to the first published photograph, a class 31 diesel locomotive at London Paddington station, soon followed by others in magazines. All black and white film processing and printing was done in a home built darkroom.

The visits to the island became ever more frequent and the collection of monochrome negatives grew, eventually leading to the first book 'The Railways and Tramways of the Isle of Man' in 1993, published to mark the centenary of the Manx Electric Railway. This was followed by further titles, and then in 1998, the probably inevitable move to the Island.

Being resident allowed a more extensive coverage of the railways, initially with the film camera. A second hand digital camera was purchased in 2006, the digital age eventually embraced with the purchase of a Nikon DSLR in 2008. The original DSLR has been upgraded a couple of times and the move to full frame came in 2018.

This is his 20th book and the 8th for Lily Publications, these have included previous titles about the railways, the various airlines that have served the Island and the story of the Peel Cars. He is also a contributor to the quarterly magazine, Ferry & Cruise Review, published by Ferry publications.

Richard Kirkman

Richard Kirkman divided his career between the railway and ferry industries. Born in Bury, his interest in the Isle of Man was kindled by family holidays on the island, where he travelled the length and breadth of the railway system in 1959 and 1960, albeit at too young an age to remember much detail.

His interest in railways was strengthened by visits to, and working as a volunteer on, the Ravenglass & Eskdale Railway. He began his career with British Rail in northwest England, joining Sealink just before privatisation, and spent time with P&O European Ferries. Richard moved to the island in 1990 to join the Isle of Man Steam Packet Company as Passenger Manager and served on the Marketing Committee for the 1993 Year of Railways.

Returning to the 'other island', he spent the remainder of his career with Railtrack and Network Rail. Now in semi-retirement, he is editor of the quarterly magazine, Ferry & Cruise Review. He met and married his wife Christina on the island and remains a regular visitor.

He is the author of twelve books, including the award winning 'Lakeland Waterways' in 2015. He co-authored 'Isle of Man Railways – a celebration' with Peter van Zeller to mark the centenary of the Manx Electric Railway in 1993 and has contributed to a wide range of publications on railways and ferry services.

INTRODUCTION: A BRIEF HISTORY OF THE ISLE OF MAN'S RAILWAYS

The Isle of Man is just 32½ miles long by 13½ wide, with a total area of 227 square miles, set in the middle of the Irish Sea. It is a nation in miniature, unique and distinct from the adjacent islands. Like the mountainous landscape and the native people, the island's railway network has managed to preserve its distinct identity in a changing world. Rarely can a small island have sustained such a plethora of different railway systems, where the modern visitor can still experience authentic Victorian rolling stock operating on its original routes. The island recognises and values this heritage, and the future of the network is now more secure than at any time in the recent past.

Railways on the island began long before the growth of Victorian tourism. The first 2ft gauge wooden rails were laid in the 18th century lead mines of Bradda Head and the mines at Laxey utilised a wagonway from 1823, the prelude to an extensive network of railways and tramways in the valley. Horse traction was used on the lengthy tramway from Contrary Head quarry to Peel in the middle of the century, with the 3ft gauge wagons negotiating steep inclines at each end of the route.

After April 1866 the island was allowed to keep surplus revenues to fund local improvements. The construction of a breakwater at Port Erin employed a short 7ft gauge line with a steam locomotive named after Lieutenant-Governor Henry Loch. Completed in 1876, the breakwater was short-lived and did not survive a ferocious storm in 1881.

The Victorian era saw the growth of mass tourism and the island became an exclusive holiday resort, linked by an expanding network of shipping services. The town of Douglas grew rapidly along its fine seafront, with classic seaside attractions supplemented with excursions to visit the Glens and the beautiful, varied Manx scenery, Snaefell mountain was only 2,036ft high, but enough for the seven kingdoms to be visible on a clear day.

Several railway schemes were prospected and proposed for the island from 1847 onwards, but these came to naught. The Isle of Man Railway Company (IoMR) was formed in 1871 and sought £200,000 capital to connect Douglas, with Castletown, Peel and Ramsey. The company chose the 3ft gauge recommended for routes that did not justify standard gauge construction. The necessary finance was not available on the island but enthusiasts for railway development soon became involved in the project. The third Duke of Sutherland, a relative of Loch, became Chairman; he had experience of underwriting construction of the Highland line from Inverness to Wick and Thurso.

Construction started at twenty sites on routes from Douglas to Peel and Port Erin in June 1872. Contractors Watson & Smith used an 0-4-0 loco *Mona*, but progress slowed when local Manx labour deserted the works for the herring fishing season,

requiring Irish and Welsh labour to be brought in. The line from Douglas to Peel followed two river valleys and was easy to construct, but the northern section of the Port Erin line cut across the grain of the land, imposing heavy earthworks and structures.

The IoMR ordered direct copies of a Beyer Peacock 2-4-0 design for its first three locos, and several four wheeled coaches. The first train to Peel ran behind locomotive No 1 *Sutherland* with all due ceremony, accompanied by the band of the Royal Bengal Fusiliers in an open wagon; the Isle of Man Times reported: "On Thursday 1 July, the Isle of Man was en fete, and good cause it had for excitement and revelry, for on this

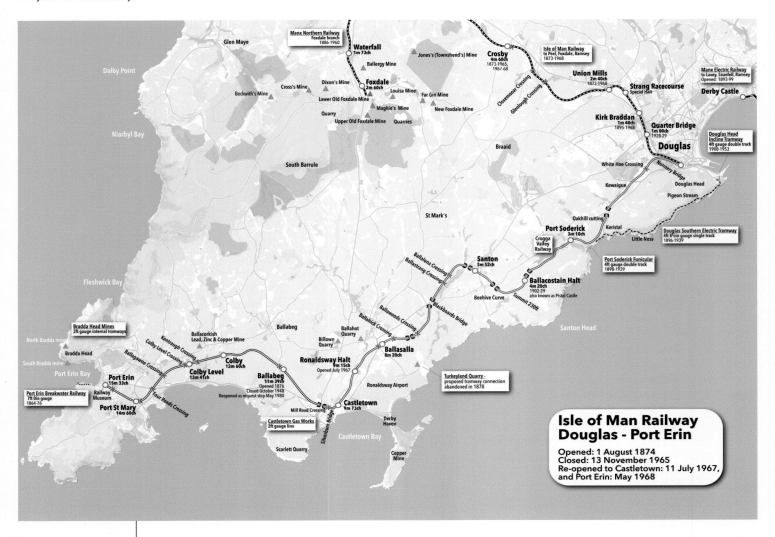

Manx Northern Railway
Foxdale branch
1886-1960

Isle of Man Railway
to Peel, Foxdale, Ramsey
1873-1968

Manx Electric Railway
to Laxey, Snaefell, Ramsey
Opened: 1893-99

Derby Castle

Glen Maye

Waterfall
1m 73ch

Ballergy Mine

Jones's (Townshend's) Mine

Crosby
4m 60ch
1873-1965,
1967-68

Union Mills
2m 40ch
1873-1968

Strang Racecourse
Special Halt

Dalby Point

Niarbyl Bay

Beckwith's Mine

Cross's Mine

Dixon's Mine

Foxdale
2m 60ch

Louisa Mine

Far Gin Mine

Kirk Braddan
1m 40ch
1895-1968

Quarter Bridge
1m 00ch
1928-29

Douglas Head
Incline Tramway
4ft gauge double track
1900-1953

Lower Old Foxdale Mine

Maghie's Mine

New Foxdale Mine

Douglas

Quarry

Upper Old Foxdale Mine

Quarries

Braaid

White Hoe Crossing

Douglas Head

South Barrule

St Mark's

Kewaigue

Pigeon Stream

Fleshwick Bay

Oakhill cutting

Port Soderick
3m 10ch

Keristal

Douglas Southern Electric Tramway
4ft 8½in gauge single track
1896-1939

Crogga
Valley
Railway

Little Ness

Santon
5m 52ch

Ballalona Crossing

Ballastrang Crossing

Ballacostain Halt
4m 20ch
1902-29
also known as Pistol Castle

Port Soderick Funicular
4ft gauge double track
1898-1939

Bradda Head Mines
2ft gauge internal tramways

North Bradda mine

Beehive Curve

Summit 230ft

Santon Head

Bradda Head

South Bradda mine

Ballagawne Crossing

Kentraugh Crossing

Colby Level Crossing

Ballacorkish
Lead, Zinc & Copper Mine

Ballabeg

Ballahick Crossing

Ballawoods Crossing

Blackboards Bridge

Port Erin Bay

Port Erin
15m 33ch

Colby
12m 60ch

Ballahot
Quarry

Ballasalla
8m 20ch

Port Erin Breakwater Railway
7ft 0in gauge
1864-76

Railway
Museum

Four Roads Crossing

Colby Level
13m 41ch

Ballabeg
11m 39ch
Opened 1876
Closed October 1948
Reopened as request stop May 1980

Billown
Quarry

Ronaldsway Halt
9m 15ch
Opened July 1967

Turkeyland Quarry -
proposed tramway connection
abandoned in 1878

Port St Mary
14m 60ch

Ronaldsway Airport

Mill Road Crossing

Castletown
9m 73ch

Derby
Haven

Castletown Gas Works
2ft gauge line

Silverburn Bridge

Scarlett Quarry

Castletown Bay

Copper
Mine

**Isle of Man Railway
Douglas - Port Erin**

Opened: 1 August 1874
Closed: 13 November 1965
Re-opened to Castletown: 11 July 1967,
and Port Erin: May 1968

day those who had the island's welfare really at heart saw their hopes at last come true."

The line to Peel was an immediate success, but completion of the southern line was hampered when the contractors ran out of money. The company was forced to finish the route to Port Erin itself and started services without ceremony on 1st August 1874. Two additional locomotives with larger water tanks suitable for the heavier grades of the southern line were obtained from Beyer Peacock, followed by another locomotive and bogie coaches with a much-improved ride. Both single track routes were sparsely equipped at first, with loops, sidings and station buildings added as funds permitted.

The number of tourists grew dramatically after the completion of Victoria Pier in Douglas that allowed ships to berth at any stage of the tide. In 1875 Governor Loch opened the promenade bearing his name, and Thomas Lightfoot proposed running a two-mile horse drawn tramway along it. This was built as a single track with passing loops, also on a 3ft gauge, and opened on 7th August 1876.

Construction of a railway to Ramsey was beyond the resources of the IoMR. Loch's influence obtained a government guarantee for dividends on some shares, so local directors formed a new company, the Manx Northern Railway (MNR), in March 1877. The chosen route skirted west of the central mountains and crossed two viaducts to link up with the

IoMR at St John's. At Ramsey an extension to the harbour was approved.

The MNR spared no expense on its buildings and facilities. Although the IoMR had agreed to work the line, the MNR obtained its own rolling stock – locomotives from Sharp Stewart, similar to the Beyer Peacock designs, and superior six-wheeled Cleminson-type coaches. Trial trips revealed problems with couplings and wheel standards that were different to the IoMR, and the delayed new line opened without formality or advertising on 23rd September 1879.

Relationships between the two railway companies were fraught, and the IoMR banned MNR wagons from their tracks; through passenger running was only introduced when the MNR agreed to make no charge for the use of their stock beyond St John's. By early 1883 track was laid on Ramsey Quay, partly with the aim of securing the lucrative Foxdale lead mine traffic then moved over the IoMR to Douglas, under an exclusive agreement with the Isle of Man Mining Co that expired in 1884. MNR directors formed a new company to build the 2½ mile Foxdale Railway from St John's to the mines. This project was fought bitterly by the IoMR who sought powers for their own Foxdale line and a Douglas harbour tramway. Eventually the MNR-sponsored Foxdale Railway Bill was passed, which allowed for a future extension to Ballasalla or Castletown.

The Isle of Man Mining Co was unwilling to fund the new line following depression in the mining industry, whilst the Foxdale Railway Company was legally bound to build it. The MNR agreed to lease the Foxdale Railway for 50 years and guaranteed a 5% return on capital from income generated by Foxdale traffic. Freight services began in June 1886 and celebrations took place on 16th August, two days after passenger services began.

Passengers were the mainstay of future railway schemes on the island. George Noble Fell surveyed a Douglas, Laxey & Snaefell Railway to run one mile of its eight-mile route on viaducts and climb to the summit using his patent centre rail for traction and braking. This bold proposal was authorised in part, but no building work began.

In Douglas, an extension of the promenade to the Derby Castle dance hall mentioned "electric… tramcars". An offshore company proposed the Douglas, Laxey & Maughold Head Marine Drive and Tramway in 1890, while the highly speculative Douglas Head Suspension Bridge and Tower Company became involved in another Marine Drive project along the cliffs south of Douglas. This company built an ornate gateway, and 1½ miles of carriage drive cut into the rock-face before creditors and bankruptcy caught up in 1892.

The development of pleasure grounds on the Howstrake Estate north of Douglas also had legal provisions for an electric tramway. Promoted chiefly by Alexander Bruce, general manager of Dumbell's Banking Co and town treasurer of Douglas, this took shape in early 1893. As the 3ft gauge track was being laid from Derby Castle to the northern boundary of the estate at Groudle, the scheme was transmuted into a new company with greater aspirations in March 1893. Electric traction enabled the Douglas & Laxey Coast Electric Tramway to surmount the gradients necessary to cross the difficult east coast terrain avoided by the MNR. By May the power station and car sheds were being erected at Derby Castle and a single track laid. By 8th August the bogie cars had arrived from G F Milnes & Co. Ltd of Birkenhead but there were difficulties with current collection from the first form of bow collector; but by 26th August the first car reached Groudle, and regular services began on 7th September; over 20,000 passengers were carried in just 19 days.

Not content with its more impressive scenery, the Douglas Head Marine Drive opened on 7th August 1893 and announces another electric tramway project. Although the drive was completed to Keristal by November, it was to be another 2½ years before standard gauge trams ran on this route.

The Douglas & Laxey Coast Electric Tramway meanwhile successfully bid for the horse tramway with the aim of extending their services along the Douglas seafront to reach the

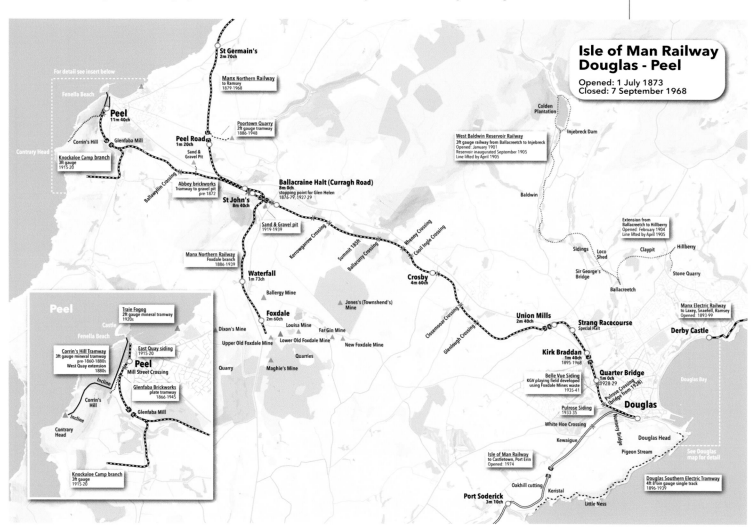

harbour and railway station. Changing its name to the Isle of Man Tramways & Electric Power Co (IoMT&EP) on 30th April 1894, it hoped to sell electricity for domestic and commercial use, in addition to transport. The line to Groudle was doubled in the spring and the Laxey extension opened on 28th July. This proved immediately popular and became a must with visitors; summer traffic on the steam-worked lines suffered in consequence. The following winter, the railways proved their worth when the island was brought to a stand by the Great Blizzard of February 1895; it took over a week for *Caledonia* to plough its way from Ramsey to St John's.

Bruce and his colleagues were not yet finished. They completed a private venture railway from Laxey to the top of Snaefell in only seven months and opened the first mountain line in Britain on 21st August 1895. The Snaefell Mountain Railway Association leased the site and laid the track to 3ft 6in gauge to allow Fell's centre rail to be used with overhead electric traction. The group then sold the line to the IoMT&EP for double the cost of construction.

New lines were appearing thick and fast. 1896 saw a 2 ft gauge line opened in Groudle Glen in May as the first 'miniature railway' in the British Isles; a Bagnall 2-4-0 *Sea Lion* took visitors from the attractions at the top of the Glen to a small zoo on the cliffs. On 7th August the Douglas Southern Electric Tramway (DSET) opened much of its three-mile

standard gauge tramway along the Douglas Head Marine Drive. With American expertise from William Graff Baker, the DSET was equipped with a technically advanced overhead wire and trolley poles, which also became the standard for the extension of the IOMT&EP beyond Laxey. In contrast, the tramway that opened from the seafront and around the town centre on 15th August was worked by the largely obsolete cable system.

Some two million passengers were carried on the route mileage of the IOMT&EP in 1896, but a rival group engaged Fell to survey a route from Laxey to Ramsey. The IOMT&EP promoted its own line to complete the east coast route and protect its monopoly. This was enacted as a separate undertaking and built by the IOMT&EP, which hired IoMR and MNR locomotives during construction. From Laxey the route ran along the cliff tops at Bulgham before looping inland. At Ramsey, the route crossed Ballure Glen by a tall viaduct instead of the original proposal for a line along the promenade. The tramway opened to Ballure on 2nd August 1898 and reached the present terminus at Ramsey on 24th July 1899.

The IoMR fought the upstart tramway by investing in new station buildings and rolling stock and co-operated with the MNR to improve schedules to Ramsey – 26½ miles in 68 minutes including a locomotive change at St John's. Meanwhile, the MNR approached the IoMT&EP hoping to sell its line for

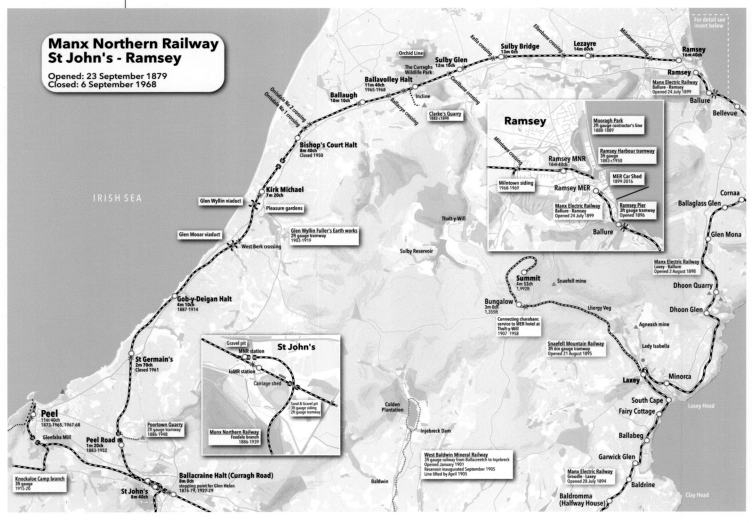

electrification, but the latter was too heavily committed to the Ramsey extension.

The IoMT&EP had its own problems; the tramway had cost £500k to build and only a third of this sum had been raised. Dividends were being paid from capital. The fragile finances collapsed alongside Dumbell's Banking Co in February 1900. Bruce died soon after, the auditors were jailed, and their entire rail and tramway network was liquidated. On 2nd January 1902, Douglas Corporation acquired the horse and cable tramways for £50,000; they had already operated another 3ft gauge railway to construct a dam across the West Baldwin valley from 1899.

The electric lines fetched a further £252,000, and the Manx Electric Railway (MER) was formed. The new management found many shortcomings; the line needed 20,000 tons of ballast, new rail and sleepers, and a new electricity supply system. The MER sought to expand operations, converting early passenger cars to a cattle van and a goods motor, acquiring a locomotive and bogie wagons for stone, and four wheeled vans for mail traffic.

Meanwhile the MNR needed to recapitalise government loans after the Dumbell's Bank collapse, and was absorbed by the IoMR, along with the FR, after a brief flirtation with the MER and the passing of an Act in April 1905.

The 1906 season broke records across the island railways. The following year, the MER inaugurated a charabanc service from the Bungalow to Tholt-y-Will, and in 1908 bid to acquire and electrify Douglas Corporation Tramways. The IoMR instituted a 60-minute express to Ramsey but inherited liabilities from the MNR and FR, with a non-standard locomotive fleet, and a requirement for bridge and viaduct reconstruction. Meanwhile the Isle of Man Mining Co was liquidated in 1911, turning Foxdale into a ghost town and sealing the fate of the branch.

The outbreak of the First World War at the height of the 1914 season saw traffic on the IoMR fall by 30% while that on the MER fell by 79%. A new railway from near Peel to Knockaloe Farm was built and operated for the UK Government in 1915 to serve a camp housing 23,000 internees.

After the war peace was celebrated with 12 coach trains to Peel and 14 to Ramsey. Traffic soared with IoMR passengers first topped a million a season, and freight reaching 56,000 tons in 1924. Heavy cattle traffic from Ramsey still demanded lengthy trains, but the last new wagon was delivered in 1925 and the final coach and locomotive the year after. Designed with the power to avoid double heading, No 16 *Mannin* was considerably larger than No 1 *Sutherland* but from the same Beyer Peacock stable.

Road competition grew when a five-year programme of highway improvements began in 1924, the IoMR and local charabanc operators formed Manx Motors to compete with Manxland Bus Services. With AM Sheard as manager, rail fares were slashed, services improved and speeded up, and a Road Services operation begun. The IoMR absorbed their road competitors, but local passenger traffic switched to buses as an integrated bus/train timetable was introduced.

In Douglas the cable trams ran an increasingly shorter season, losing money until 19th August 1929. The Isle of Man Times commented "What a strange quiet place Douglas has

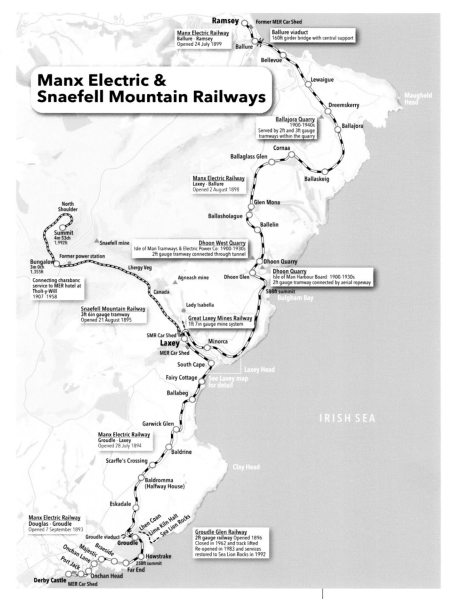

become, the clanking noise had gone, the cable trams had stopped!" The tracks were last used by buses hauling horse trams for winter storage. From 1927 the horse trams ran only in summer but, made a steady profit which was put into track renewals.

The MER lost local traffic to buses, but on 5th April 1930, the Laxey car sheds caught fire with the loss of four power cars and seven trailers. Then on 17th September a cloudburst filled the power station weir in the river below with debris, flooding lower Laxey, and damaging the power plant and village. The MER encountered financial problems throughout the thirties, although passenger numbers climbed back to over half a million, whilst summer crowds on the IOMR compensated for decreasing winter carryings. Public work schemes led to the removal of mine spoil by rail from Foxdale to Douglas for the King George V playing fields, which accounted for over half the freight revenue. In a steady drive to improve the efficiency of operations on the IOMR, Sheard considered oil fired locos and diesel railcars.

The Douglas Head Marine Drive tramway closed on 15th

September 1939 after the outbreak of the Second World War. The last Foxdale passenger train ran on 1st July, although mine waste became valuable for airfield construction. This traffic and services for military and aliens' camps, caused IoMR receipts to soar by 1941. The MER profited from conveying work parties of aliens to cut peat on Snaefell and moved lead mine 'deads' from Laxey to Ramsey for Jurby airfield. 1944 saw the second-best season's figures ever on the IoMR.

Post-war plans for new 2-6-2 and 2-4-2 designs were prepared by Beyer Peacock, but three new boilers were bought instead to help move 1,312,780 passengers in the first summer of peace. But economies followed; evening and Sunday trains ceased, buses substituted for winter trains, and locomotives went into permanent storage.

George Howden of the Great Northern Railway of Ireland reported to the government that the Ramsey line was expensive to maintain and never paid its way, steam services should be limited to the South line and the electrics to Laxey and Snaefell, although he saw the historic value of rolling stock. But the IoMR chairman told shareholders "by no other means can the traffic be dealt with as by the Isle of Man Railway and the Isle of Man Road Services in conjunction and co-operation".

The end of petrol rationing in 1950, precipitated decline; passenger numbers had dropped below a million for good within seven years. The Marine Drive was sold to the Harbour Board who removed track and overhead wires in 1947, the stock remaining in isolation until car No 1 was preserved and the rest scrapped in 1951. The MER sought winter closure on its own line with the rising operating losses and debt to debenture holders.

In 1955 the MER was offered for sale, and British Railways'

consultants recommended total bus replacement. As over 70% of island visitors rode the line, Tynwald refused to allow abandonment and indemnified losses, while nationalisation was negotiated for £50,000 in 1957. This enabled gradual improvements, and a modern image green and white livery was applied to some stock.

The Foxdale line was last inspected in January 1961, although it remained in existence if not in use, and the Groudle Glen Railway ceased to run in 1962. That same year the IoMR steam loco situation became critical and two County Donegal railcars were purchased. Sheard died in June 1965 and his successor, William Lambden, saw the company's future completely dependent on buses, without rail. The Ramsey line closed for the winter in September, but other services were suspended for 'track repairs` on 15th November, before the IoMR admitted it was seeking an abandonment bill.

Meanwhile services continued on the MER despite the loss of goods traffic on 1st April 1966. A government commission proposed closure north of Laxey, and the decision was almost made for them when the embankment wall collapsed at Bulgham above a 550ft sheer drop to the sea. The line continued to operate in two sections while substantial repairs were made, before the first through passenger car ran on 10th July.

The commission also recommended that the Peel line be retained for tourists. The IoMR arranged for the Marquis of Ailsa to lease the line for 21 years from April 1967. There was a great ceremony at Douglas on 3rd June and reopening to Peel was followed by trains to Ramsey the next day and Castletown on 11th July. A new halt was opened at Ronaldsway Airport, while the newly formed Isle of Man Steam Railway Supporters Association (IoMSRSA) repainted disused locos for display at St

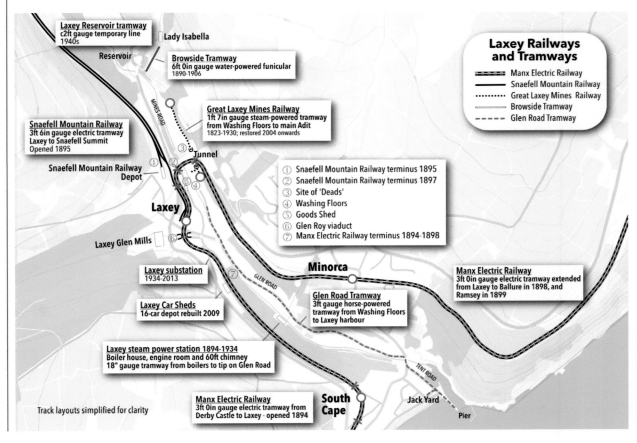

Laxey Reservoir tramway
c2ft gauge temporary line
1940s

Lady Isabella

Reservoir

Browside Tramway
6ft 0in gauge water-powered funicular
1890-1906

MINES ROAD

Great Laxey Mines Railway
1ft 7in gauge steam-powered tramway
from Washing Floors to main Adit
1823-1930; restored 2004 onwards

Snaefell Mountain Railway
3ft 6in gauge electric tramway
Laxey to Snaefell Summit
Opened 1895

Snaefell Mountain Railway
Depot

③ Tunnel

Laxey Railways and Tramways

═════ Manx Electric Railway
─────── Snaefell Mountain Railway
··········· Great Laxey Mines Railway
─────── Browside Tramway
- - - - - Glen Road Tramway

Laxey

① Snaefell Mountain Railway terminus 1895
② Snaefell Mountain Railway terminus 1897
③ Site of 'Deads'
④ Washing Floors
⑤ Goods Shed
⑥ Glen Roy viaduct
⑦ Manx Electric Railway terminus 1894-1898

Laxey Glen Mills

Laxey substation
1934-2013

GLEN ROAD

Minorca

Glen Road Tramway
3ft gauge horse-powered
tramway from Washing Floors
to Laxey harbour

Manx Electric Railway
3ft 0in gauge electric tramway extended
from Laxey to Ballure in 1898, and
Ramsey in 1899

Laxey Car Sheds
16-car depot rebuilt 2009

Laxey steam power station 1894-1934
Boiler house, engine room and 60ft chimney
18" gauge tramway from boilers to tip on Glen Road

TENT ROAD

Track layouts simplified for clarity

Manx Electric Railway
3ft 0in gauge electric tramway from
Derby Castle to Laxey - opened 1894

South Cape

Jack Yard

Pier

Johns. This bold revival of the main system was commercially unsound despite innovations like the Man-tainor service to Castletown and fuel oil tanks for Ramsey power station. Douglas works just managed to restore loco No 4 *Loch* in time to haul one of the last trains to Peel on 7th September 1968. All lines closed again to traffic by the end of the month.

A subsidy from Tynwald enabled the group to continue operating the south line as the Isle of Man Victorian Steam Railway, before the IoMR took over its own line again. On 2nd August 1972 the Queen travelled on the line. The south line celebrated its centenary of 1st August 1974 with greater style than its opening, but the next year services ran only between Castletown and Port Erin, and then from Ballasalla to Port Erin, with repair facilities still maintained in Douglas.

Tynwald acquired the IoMR surplus land on the Peel and Ramsey lines and the metals were sold for scrap for £149,100. Demolition work spread from St John's, while the MER used the loco from Ramsey Pier to lift some five miles of rail near Ballaugh. Its own future was still less than clear – Tynwald was indecisive with only the Lord Bishop positively supporting the MER. A bill allowing winter closure in 1975 meant that, for the first time since 1873, no trains ran on the island and the MER mail contract was lost.

The Ramsey-Laxey section remained closed for the 1976 season, though Tynwald voted monies to rebuild the Snaefell cars, still running with the original motors, using equipment from German tramcars. In the following election campaign, the fate of the railways became a real political issue after a Ramsey resident presented a Petition of Grievance. As a result, the MER reopened back to Ramsey with panache in 1977, and steam train services returned to Douglas once again.

Douglas Corporation Transport and Isle of Man Road Services Ltd were nationalised in October 1976, while the Port Erin line was sold to the government for £250,000 on 13th January 1978, coming under the existing Manx Electric Railway Board. Considerable improvement works were in progress on both systems, while plans to single the track from Laxey to Ramsey were shelved and a celebration of the century of electric railways was commemorated by a procession at Laxey. Winter services recommenced on the MER in 1980.

The IoMSRSA now saw a reduced role with the IoMR gaining the security of nationalisation and sought a new venture. The site of the former Groudle Glen Railway was inviting, although overgrown and inaccessible. The volunteer workforce re-laid track to the passing loop and restarted services with diesel power on 18th December 1985. This success was followed by the complete rebuilding and return to steam of *Sea Lion* in 1987 and the reopening of the route to Sea Lion Rocks in May 1992.

The modern era has seen the rail and tram network prosper as a key visitor attraction. The promotion of 1993 as the Year of Railways, commemorating the centenary of the electric railway to Groudle, affirmed that the system was an inalienable part of Manx Heritage. The Steam Railway, Manx Electric Railway, and Snaefell Mountain Railway have seen extensive investment, with new storage facilities for their vintage rolling stock collection. The Douglas Horse Tramway has been re-laid as part of the extensive promenade works, albeit on a truncated section at present. The Groudle Glen Railway has undergone

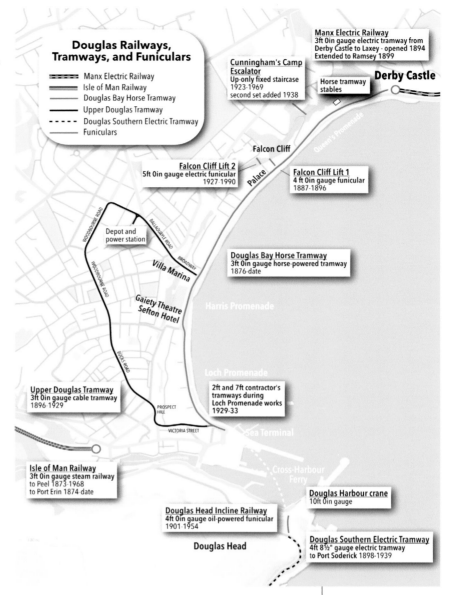

continuous improvement with the restoration of facilities at Lhen Coan and Sea Lion Rocks. Meanwhile, new railways have opened at the Orchid Line and Crogga, and the Great Laxey Mines Railway has been revived with two new replica steam locomotives in operation.

Every opportunity has been taken to promote the railway systems by appropriate celebration of the successive anniversaries that followed the first Year of Railways, and this volume commemorates the milestone of 150 years of Steam Railway operation. An innovative and popular range of dining opportunities drives business on the Steam and Snaefell Railway, and enthusiasts' events are now a core part of the annual programme. The Isle of Man's railways can face the future with confidence – there is no better place to enjoy such a broad range of differing traction, gauge, or scenery, on a system which is fully appreciated by the local community.

Barry Edwards, Ballasalla, Isle of Man.
Richard Kirkman, Seaford, East Sussex.
November 2022

THE STEAM RAILWAY

We begin our steam railway journey at the southern end on the system and this fine view of Port Erin station, likely taken in the 1920's. A pair of busy trains occupy the two platforms, only one of them has a locomotive attached. The platform on the left has been shortened to about where the far end of the train is. The wonderful telegraph pole adds interest. *Barry Edwards Collection*

Proposals for a railway linking Douglas with Peel were made in 1860 and 1863, but neither project succeeded, nor did a scheme registered with Tynwald in 1865. Eventually, a meeting was called for any interested parties in Douglas in April 1870, to produce a plan that would not suffer the fate of previous attempts. Agreement was reached in principle to form a railway company to build a route linking Douglas with Peel, Ramsey, and Castletown, with a projected extension to Port Erin, to connect with a proposed steamer service to Holyhead from the new breakwater, then under construction.

The Isle of Man Railway Company was registered in December 1870 with a capital of £200,000 but, following a survey of the routes, it was realised that this sum was insufficient. Approaches for funding were made further afield, and the company was soon supported by The Duke of Sutherland and John Pender. The Duke became company chairman for the first seven years, being later followed by Mr Pender.

Tenders were invited to construct a 3′0″ gauge railway from Douglas to both Peel and Port Erin in 1872. Four replies were received, and the contract was awarded to Messrs Watson & Smith of London. Construction started at 20 sites on both routes in June 1872, with an 0-4-0 locomotive *Mona* used to assist in the works.

Three locomotives were ordered from Beyer, Peacock of Gorton Foundry, Manchester in 1872. They were identical 2-4-0T locomotives with copper-capped chimneys, brass domes, and brass numerals on the chimneys. Eventually 15 such locomotives were delivered to the railway, a decision that proved useful in later years as it allowed for interchange of most parts between locomotives. The livery was to be green with a black smokebox. Locomotive 1 *Sutherland* arrived in March 1873 and 2 *Derby* and 3 *Pender*, followed in June. Rolling stock was delivered from the Metropolitan Carriage & Wagon Co. of Saltley, comprising of 29 four-wheeled coaches including two guard's vans, and several items of freight stock were procured.

The first train ran from Douglas to Peel on 1st May 1873,

with the Duke of Sutherland on the footplate of 1 *Sutherland*, the train formed of open wagons specially fitted out with seating. Unfortunately, 1 *Sutherland* left the rails at Peel, and the construction contractor's locomotive was summoned to take the train back to Douglas. The Duke of Sutherland returned to the railway on 1st July 1873 to take his seat in the directors' saloon that formed part of the 12-coach official opening train, which included the band of the Royal Bengal Lancers in an open wagon. Locomotive 1 *Sutherland* hauled the train, sporting suitable decoration and a banner reading 'Douglas and Peel United'. Huge crowds turned out to welcome the railway to the Island and watch the train clatter past at speeds of up to 25 mph, faster than any islander had seen before.

Meanwhile, over 400 men were busy pushing on with the Port Erin line, which was proving a more difficult task with its steep gradients, sharper curves, and multiple bridges. The contractor pulled out in June 1874, leaving the railway company to complete the line, which in the end cost £9,875 per mile to build. This prompted economies to be made on stations, with only simple wooden structures being provided. The line opened without ceremony on 1st August 1874.

Two further locomotives with larger water tanks, 4 *Loch* and 5 *Mona,* were delivered in 1874 to work the new line and the rolling stock fleet was increased to 56 coaches, still all four-wheeled. Locomotives 6 *Peveril* and 7 *Tynwald*, were delivered in 1875 and 1880 respectively. Bogie coaches with much improved riding were added by 1876.

The residents in the north of the Island thought they would be next to get a railway but, despite its initial intentions, the company had neither plans nor funds for such an extension. Governor Loch helped obtain a government guarantee for share dividends and local directors formed the Manx Northern Railway Company in March 1877. A 16-mile route from St Johns to Ramsey, running west of the island's central mountains, was given government consent in 1878. An extension to Ramsey Harbour was also approved.

The construction contract, that included several viaducts, was awarded to J. & W. Grainger of Glasgow, with completion due by 1st July 1879. Although the Isle of Man Railway initially agreed to operate the line, the Manx Northern ordered two locomotives from Sharp, Stewart & Company of Manchester – 1 *Ramsey* and 2 *Northern*. Coaches were provided by the Swansea Wagon Company, based on a Cleminson-type patent six-wheel chassis. A third locomotive, 3 *Thornhill* was ordered for delivery in 1880, this time from Beyer, Peacock, like those supplied to the Isle of Man Railway. In contrast to the Isle of Man Railway, the Manx Northern spared no expense on its station facilities. The new railway opened without ceremony on 23rd September 1879.

↑A later image of Port Erin, taken in the 1960s shows No. 5 *Mona* arriving in the bay platform with a four-coach train and open wagon. *Barry Edwards Collection*

←Locomotive No. 10 *G H Wood* with van G17 in the siding opposite the platform at Port Erin. *E Paget Tomlinson*

Relationships between the two companies were fractious, and the Isle of Man Railway banned Manx Northern wagons from running on their tracks; through passenger services were only introduced when the Manx Northern agreed to make no charge for the use of their stock beyond St John's.

The small mining village of Foxdale was producing 4,000

↑Another 1960s view of Port Erin station, it's not clear what the train is doing, although the guard does appear to be checking tickets. This view has changed completely in the 60 or so years since the image was taken. *Peter Kirkman*

→Schoema diesel No.17 *Viking* captured shortly after arrival at Port Erin with a lengthy train banked by one of the steam locomotives. *Barry Edwards*

tons of ore annually, and the idea of a two and a half miles railway to the other lines at St Johns was actively considered. The Foxdale Railway Company was formed by Manx Northern directors in 1882 but faced strong opposition from the Isle of Man Railway when construction powers were sought at Tynwald. The Foxdale Railway Bill, which included powers to extend to Ballasalla and Castletown, eventually passed. The depressed state on the mining industry left the Isle of Man Mining Company unable to support funding of the line, but the Foxdale Railway Company was committed to build it; the Manx Northern agreed to lease the Foxdale Railway for 50 years and guaranteed a 5% return on capital.

Stations at Foxdale and St Johns were constructed by Hugh Kennedy & Sons of Glasgow, and the line opened to freight traffic in June 1886, with passenger services following on 14th August. A fourth locomotive was delivered to the Manx Northern, this time an 0-6-0T from Dubs & Co., Scotland, 4 *Caledonia*.

The final years of the nineteenth century saw the Isle of Man Railway go from strength to strength, 26 bogie coaches being delivered by 1896 and locomotives 8 *Fenella* and 9 *Douglas* arriving in 1894 and 1896. Douglas station was rebuilt with the impressive forecourt that still exists today, the carriage shed was built, and extensions were added to the locomotive sheds and workshops.

Port Erin, Port St. Mary, Peel and Castletown stations were also rebuilt, as was Port Soderick where a passing loop was added. The tourist boom had not gone unnoticed by other railway promoters and the opening of the Derby Castle to Groudle electric railway, which eventually reached Ramsey in 1899, provided some interesting competition. The Isle of Man Railway cooperated with the Manx Northern to advertise a 68-minute journey from Douglas to Ramsey, including a locomotive change at St John's, whilst the electric railway offered 70 minutes.

The Foxdale Railway went into voluntary liquidation in 1891, leaving the Manx Northern to carry out the requirements of the remaining lease, although the company found itself in financial difficulties after the collapse of Dumbell's Bank in 1900. The Isle of Man Railway was approached and an Act of Tynwald in 1905 enabled the purchase of the Manx Northern for £60,000 and the Foxdale Railway for £7,000. New coaches were ordered, and the four Manx Northern Railway locomotives were taken into Isle of Man Railway stock; they were renumbered as 14 *Thornhill* and 15 *Caledonia*, with *Ramsey* and *Northern* never carrying their

←←No.12 *Hutchinson* awaits departure from Port Erin with a mixed train during 1959. Apart from the names above the shops, this scene is little changed today. *Peter Kirkman*

←Once the Covid situation allowed, locomotives 5 and 9 were towed south on 2nd June 2020, for removal of asbestos. No.9 was left at Port St Mary, where it is seen a week later, No.5 was taken to Port Erin and stored in the carriage shed. The work was completed in the Port St Mary Goods Shed, a space that allowed all the necessary precautions to be taken. *Barry Edwards*

allocated numbers and being scrapped in 1923 and 1912. Two more locomotives arrived from Beyer, Peacock in 1905, 10 *G.H. Wood* and 11 *Maitland*, and a further two, in 1908 and 1910, 12 *Hutchinson* and 13 *Kissack*.

A record season in 1906 prompted more investment and Peel station building was rebuilt in 1908, Port Erin enlarged in 1911, and platform canopies were added at Douglas. One million passengers were carried for the first time in 1913. The Foxdale mines closed in 1914, but the passenger service continued, usually comprising a locomotive and just one coach.

The outbreak of war in 1914 reduced the number of visitors to the Island and brought an immediate 30% reduction in traffic. From 1915, the railway was called upon to operate trains between Peel and Knockaloe over a specially constructed line serving a camp for 23,000 inhabitants. The former Manx Northern locomotive, 4 *Caledonia*, worked the line as it was the best to cope with the steep gradients.

Peace was celebrated with 12-coach trains to Peel and 14 to Ramsey. Visitors returned to the Island in volume after the war and the railway continued to flourish despite the rising costs of materials and wages, and the introduction of the eight-hour working day. Overtime kept the frequent service operating, with attention turning to the maintenance of locomotives, rolling stock and track each winter.

Cattle traffic still generated 40-wagon trains from Ramsey. The last new wagon was delivered in 1925, 16 *Mannin*, a

much larger Beyer Peacock locomotive, was delivered in 1926 as the last locomotive ordered new by the railway, and the last completely new coach, F49 also arrived. Cumberland Motor Services' subsidiary Manxland Bus Services were granted permission to operate motor bus services on a range of routes from Douglas in 1924. The railway response was to cut fares, reduce journey times and increase the number of timetabled trains, particularly during the evening. The early bus competition culminated in the railway establishing Manx Motors in co-operation between charabanc operators, 'Freedom of the Island' tickets being offered jointly. The latter years of the 1930s saw an annual rail passenger level of around 750,000. Public works schemes saw Foxdale mine

↙Departing from Port St Mary with just a couple of minutes of its journey from Douglas left, is No.4 *Loch* with a well loaded five-coach train on 17th July 2021. The track in the foreground leads to the goods shed. *Barry Edwards*

↓On 2nd June 2020 diesel locomotive 18 *Ailsa* hauled steam locomotives 9 and 5 from Douglas to Port St Mary for asbestos removal. Here the train is seen approaching Port St Mary, making an unusual sight. *Barry Edwards*

→Ballagawne Crossing is situated on Mount Gawne Road. Approaching the crossing on 20th September 2019 is No.8 *Fenella*. The houses of Colby Level are seen to the left of the train. *Barry Edwards*

↓Approaching Kentraugh crossing, a small farm track between Colby Level and Colby, is No.11 *Maitland* with five coaches on 4th June 2022. *Maitland* returned to service at the beginning of the season, after several years stored. *Barry Edwards*

→A slightly different view of No.13 *Kissack* steaming through Ballabeg station on 29th July 2019. Taken with a 500mm lens from the road bridge. *Barry Edwards*

waste being transported to Douglas to build the King George V playing fields, accounting for over half the freight revenues.

The Second World War brought more work for the railway but, as the Knockaloe camp had been demolished, hotels were commandeered to house prisoners of war. Although the last passenger train to Foxdale ran on 1st July 1939, but the railway carried mine waste for the construction of airfields. Training camps at Jurby and Castletown took passenger numbers above those of peacetime, and school journeys came back from the buses because of shortages of tyres and fuel. Over 14,000 special trains had operated by the end of hostilities in 1945.

Visitors once again returned in large numbers in 1946, with 1,312,780 passengers carried. However, the steam locomotives were all in need of overhaul, several requiring completely new boilers, of which three were ordered and fitted. During 1945, 7 *Tynwald* had been cannibalised for much needed spares and 2 *Derby* went the same way in 1951. Locomotives 3 *Pender*, 4 *Loch* and 9 *Douglas* were also withdrawn from service, in need of new boilers.

The post-war boom ended in 1956 with over a million passengers carried for the last time, the numbers steadily declining thereafter as air travel took holidaymakers off to other parts of the world. Costs continued to rise, receipts fell, and service cuts started. Sunday services were withdrawn, and winter services reduced to school traffic levels without much loss of revenue. 11 *Maitland* received a badly needed new boiler in 1959, but replacements for 1 *Sutherland*, 6 *Peveril*, 13 *Kissack* and 16 *Mannin* were considered unnecessary. More cuts followed and winter services became virtually non-existent.

Two former County Donegal diesel railcars were obtained at £160 each in 1961 and were refurbished in time to work the winter Peel service. The situation on the railway was now serious and the outlook bleak.

On 7th July 1963 Her Majesty Queen Elizabeth the Queen Mother arrived on the Island and travelled on the railway from Douglas to Kirk Braddan in coach F36, with 11 *Maitland* doing the honours.

A loss of £8,000 was made in 1965 and all winter services were cancelled to carry out much needed maintenance; this too was later cancelled without warning. No trains ran in 1966 but a report into the future of the line recognised the importance of the railway to the community. The Isle of Man Railway Supporters' Association was formed, offering to assist in any way it could. Relief arrived from the Marquis of Ailsa, who agreed to lease the line for 21 years with an opt-out clause after five years. Hundreds of people turned out on 3rd June 1967, the occasion of the railway's reopening. Five special trains ran to Peel, with services to Ramsey and Castletown as well, and a frequent daytime service operated across the network for the rest of that season. A new halt opened at Ronaldsway Airport.

Innovations like a Man-tainor service to Castletown and fuel oil tanks for Ramsey power station boosted winter traffic, but mounting losses again caused the 1968 season to be cut short, the final train from Ramsey running on 6th September and the last from Peel the next day. The Peel and Ramsey lines never reopened. Yet, 4 *Loch* received a new boiler in 1968, returning to service on the last day of the season. Tynwald acquired the Isle of Man Railway surplus land, and the metals were sold for £149,00. Demolition work spread outward from St John's.

The Tourist Board agreed in 1968 to assist in keeping the Port Erin line open for three years. Locomotive 13 *Kissack* received a new boiler and passenger numbers increased slightly but the Marquis was still losing money and

←Diesel locomotive No.21 was used as the south locomotive for a short period towards the end of the 2019 season. It is seen here passing Ballabeg with the 10:00 Port Erin to Douglas on 20th October 2019. *Barry Edwards*

↓In Indian red livery, No.13 *Kissack* passes Ballabeg, temporarily renamed Sulby Glen for the 2015 Transport Festival. Photographed on 1st August 2015. *Barry Edwards*

announced that he would take the five-year exit option. It is estimated that he lost around £43,000 during his stay but, without him, the railway would almost certainly have closed and been lost forever.

In 1971 the Tourist Board offered the railway company further support for another three years and costs were reduced by only operating a Monday to Friday service. Her Majesty the Queen travelled on the line from Castletown to

↑Running as No.5 *Mona*, No.10 *G H Wood* is seen passing Ballabeg station with a northbound train, during the 2015 Summer Transport Festival, a feature of which was the temporary renaming of the Port Erin Line stations to replicate a journey from St John's to Ramsey. *Barry Edwards*

→A bus drivers' strike in December 2012, resulted in the construction of a temporary station at School Hill, adjacent to the Castletown bypass, to enable Castle Rushen High School pupils to get to school from both directions. On the morning of 20th December 2012, No.12 *Hutchinson* has arrived from Port Erin with the first train to use the station. *Barry Edwards*

The A7 road between Ballabeg and Colby affords the photographer this view of trains running round the curve between Ballabeg and the long straight section towards Colby Level. No.8 *Fenella* is in charge of four coaches on 13th September 2020. *Barry Edwards*

↑During the reconstruction of the Top Shed at the Manx Electric Derby Castle depot, open power car 33 was stored at Douglas Steam sheds. The opportunity was taken as part of the Steam 125 event, to operate the tram on the Steam Railway, using a generator van to provide the power. Here No.33 approaches Malew Road bridge with a northbound working on 3rd May 1998. *Barry Edwards*

↘Looking the other way from the same bridge as the previous image, we have locomotive No.4 *Loch* accelerating away from Castletown with the 15:50 Douglas to Port Erin on 9th August 2021. *Barry Edwards*

→→On 22nd April 2019, locomotive No.8 *Fenella* crosses the Silverburn river as it approaches Castletown station with a mixed train. This train had worked from Douglas and was shunting around the station area for photographers as part of the annual rush hour event. *Barry Edwards*

Douglas on 2nd August 1972, the total number of passengers carried that year being the best for some time.

The centenary of the opening of the Peel line on 1st July 1973 was marked by a special train on the Port Erin line, which celebrated its own centenary in style the following year. On 1st August 1974 4 *Loch*, also celebrating 100 years and having completed 2,000,000 miles, hauled a special train from Douglas, stopping at every station to pick up guests to attend a fete in Port Erin.

Tynwald debated the future of the line in 1974 and, after much discussion, the railway company was supported from 1975 to run four trains daily between Port Erin and Castletown, except Saturdays. These were extended to Ballasalla in 1976, efforts then being concentrated on a return to Douglas, still the island's main tourist centre. The Government was persuaded to purchase the line in 1977, following the election of several new members of Tynwald at

the Manx General election of 1976. The steam railway became part of the Manx Electric Railway Board's responsibility, under the title 'Isle of Man Railways'. The full Port Erin line re-opened in 1977, coincidentally the same year as the Manx Electric Railway returned to Ramsey.

This positive development was accompanied by a drive to reduce costs and tidy up the railway. Douglas lost its station canopies, signals, and the eleven tracks were reduced to five to reduce loan costs, and the station building at Port Soderick was sold. Surplus land at Ballasalla, was sold for office development in return for a new station building on the other side of the line. Santa specials were introduced and now form an important part of the railway calendar. New boilers were obtained for Nos. 11 *Maitland* and 12 *Hutchinson*, extensive track repairs carried out and coaches renovated.

In 1983 the Manx Electric Railway Board became The Isle of Man Passenger Transport Board and this in turn became part of the Department of Tourism and Transport in 1986.

Plans for the 1993 'Year of Railways' included an attempt to bring an American Baldwin 4-4-0 to the line but sadly this did not come about. The day before the official launch of the year of railways, diesel 17 was named *Viking* at Douglas station. The County Donegal railcars gave rides around Douglas station to a group of Irish rail fans. 4 *Loch* visited the Manx Electric for public runs from Laxey to Dhoon Quarry as part of the celebrations, and spent, the intervening time on its own line, unusually facing Douglas instead of Port Erin. One of the highlights of the year was the return to service on 20th June of 10 *G. H. Wood*, using the boiler of 13 *Kissack* and painted in an attractive Brunswick Green livery. Locomotive *6 Peveril* was cosmetically restored by the IOMSRSA.

Two accidents marred 1993. 11*Maitland* collided with a Metro car on the crossing at White Hoe on 4th June. The car, driven by a district nurse was pushed 40 yards along the track by the train but although having to be cut free the nurse was not seriously injured. A second incident occurred between Ballabeg and Colby when a tractor and trailer were in collision, again with 11 *Maitland*. The locomotive sustained minimal damage while some damage was caused to grab rails on the coaches as they brushed past the road trailer whilst the train came to a stop.

The Duchess of Kent travelled from Douglas to Port Erin on 22nd September with a stop at Ballasalla for refreshments, the train using F45, F36 and F29 and hauled by locomotive 10.

New crossing lights were installed at Ballasalla, and the station track work was re-laid during the winter of 1993/94,

as was most of the line between Port Erin and Port St. Mary. The wooden canopy at Castletown was demolished during the restoration of the brick building. Level crossing lights were also installed at White Hoe following the incident earlier in the year.

The success of the 'Year of Railways' led to ideas being collated for the forthcoming Snaefell Mountain Railway centenary in 1995. Former MNR locomotive 15 *Caledonia* was removed from Port Erin Museum for inspection and made a triumphant return to steam in time for the 1995 season, the highlight being its return to the Snaefell line, operating on a specially laid 3ft 0in gauge section between the Bungalow and the Summit with Manx Electric trailers 57 and 58. The locomotive made an impressive sight on the island's highest mountain.

Shortly after the close of the 1995 season a special train was operated for the emergency services into the Nunnery cutting for a simulated car collision in the deep cutting. 10 and four coaches made up the collision train while 17 and a flat were used as an ambulance train to bring out the wounded.

During the 1995/96 winter Tynwald approved the building of a new transport headquarters at Banks Circus adjacent to the railway station in Douglas. The development included a new bus maintenance facility which required the signal box to be moved from its original position and the demolition of the former Mirn & Co. carriage shed, the last survivor of the three originally built to serve the railway. Work on the signal box move and demolition of the shed was completed in time for the new building to be started early in 1997.

Following the success of the reinstatement of *Caledonia*, plans for the 125th anniversary of the opening of the Douglas to Peel line in 1998 began to include the return to steam of locomotive 1 *Sutherland*. The locomotive was removed from the Port Erin Museum in October 1996 and towed to Douglas. The body of coach F57 was scrapped creating an additional flat runner, while 4 *Loch* was withdrawn from service pending a full overhaul at the end of the 1996 season. A batch of second-hand wagons from the Lochaber

Railway at Fort William were acquired to augment the permanent way fleet.

A series of speed restrictions were imposed for the 1997 running season, a high number of broken spring incidents occurring because of the poor track. A major rebuild and refurbishment project for the Port Erin Museum began with the framework being stripped of its old cladding. The former locomotive shed was returned to its proper use and the goods shed, used as a locomotive shed in recent years was incorporated into the new museum. The water tower was also rebuilt. Partial height platforms were installed at Castletown station during 1997/98, although preliminary work had

Having crossed the river, the line runs through a tree tunnel on the final approach to Castletown station. No.8 *Fenella* arrives with an early season three-coach train forming the 10.00 Port Erin to Douglas on 9th April 2019. *Barry Edwards*

←A 1959 picture of No.12 *Hutchinson* coming to a stand at Castletown. The friends of Castletown Station are currently re-creating the advertising hoardings on the up platform, the adverts make an interesting addition to this image. *Peter Kirkman*

←A specially commissioned headboard was carried on a number of trains on 27th July during the 2022 Summer Transport Festival. The board was the work of David Archer and commissioned by Andy Taylor. It is seen here on No.11 *Maitland* while awaiting departure form Castletown with the 12:50 Douglas to Port Erin. *Barry Edwards*

↑Approaching Castletown from the north is No.13 *Kissack* on 11th October 2021 with the 15:50 Douglas to Port Erin. The houses of Brookfield Avenue form a backdrop. *Barry Edwards*

→A view from the same bridge 34 years earlier. Square cabbed and blue liveried No.12 *Hutchinson* is arriving with a four-coach train from Douglas, during August 1988. *Ray Hulock*

begun the previous winter. Douglas station was completely re-laid during the winter, using new rail, sleepers, and ballast, partly in preparation for the building of the new integrated bus parking, workshops, and transport headquarters.

The Government advertised for expressions of interest from contractors to build two new sheds, at Douglas and Port Erin. It was also planned to fill the gap between the existing locomotive sheds and paint shop/carriage works at Douglas to provide more undercover storage. Plans to restore the two former County Donegal railcars were also developed. Work on the Castletown platforms continued and completed by the beginning of the 1998 season. Meanwhile in the sheds, work on the rebuild of 1 *Sutherland* was progressing well, while during March 1998 4 *Loch* was loaded onto a lorry and taken to Laxey for track tests. On its return to Douglas a unique photographic opportunity was created at the Sea Terminal

Having left Castletown northbound, the next station is the request stop at Ronaldsway Halt. Captured with a long lens set at 360mm, No.4 *Loch* passes with the 12:00 Port Erin to Douglas on 7th May 2022. *Barry Edwards*

↖A further image of Manx Electric tram 33 having a holiday on the Steam Railway. It is passing Ronaldsway Halt with its generator van behind on 3rd May 1998. The tram is being driven by the late Colin Goldsmith, for many years Workshop Manager at Douglas. *Barry Edwards*

↑Ronaldsway Halt is just about a ten-minute walk from Ronaldsway Airport, although this mixed train has not stopped, the station being on request only. No.8 *Fenella* makes a fine sight as she passes on 4th April 2015. *Barry Edwards*

←Taken from the other side of the line, No.12 *Hutchinson* storms past with the 13:50 Douglas to Port Erin on 28th March 2016. The white pole visible above the locomotive is all that remains of a small prototype wind turbine. *Barry Edwards*

↙With a young enthusiast watching from the front coach, No.8 *Fenella* passes with the 16:00 Douglas to Port Erin on 31st August 2019. The provision of the station makes Ronaldsway Airport unique in being served by a timetabled steam hauled service. *Barry Edwards*

↓Shortly after passing Ronaldsway, the line runs adjacent to the Silverburn river. No.10 *G H Wood* is passing with a southbound train on 3rd June 2006. *Barry Edwards*

The same location as the previous photograph but earlier in 1985, with considerably less foliage, shows No.4 *Loch* passing with a southbound train. The leading coach is F26. *Ray Hulock*

↓Ballasalla is the next stop, where we see No.5 *Mona* with a southbound train, passing a northbound train, while a brake coach occupies the siding. This view has changed completely since this image was taken in 1964. *Barry Edwards Collection*

↘Local railway contractors operate two former Bord na Mona locomotives. Seen at Ballasalla on 17 February 2019, is *Otter*, with a flat wagon containing a small digger and concrete castings. *Barry Edwards*

with the locomotive being posed alongside the world record holding car Thrust SSC, that was making a brief publicity trip to the Island.

The restored locomotive 1 *Sutherland*, with boiler from 8 *Fenella* was officially inaugurated at Douglas on 2nd May. Celebrations of the 125th anniversary of the opening of the Peel line took place on 1st July when, after a short ceremony, 1 *Sutherland* departed for Port Erin with a nine-coach train banked by 11 *Maitland*.

The IOMSRSA officially handed over a replica M wagon M79; a replica H wagon was completed by July 2000. The society entered into a 21-year lease agreement to raise

£30,000 to restore 4 *Loch* to working condition. 9 *Douglas* was the subject of a similar appeal in 1977 but the government takeover thwarted the attempt, and it was sold to a rival group. Meanwhile, the railcar restoration was well under way, with the body of 19 dismantled whilst that of 20 was being used to create working drawings for the rebuild of both cars.

Peel saw its first steam locomotive for 30 years on 8th July when 1 *Sutherland* was transported by road to the city and operated on a short demonstration track laid in the car park of Manx National Heritage's House of Manannan. The loco returned to Peel on 22nd August; the opportunity was taken to pose the loco on its road trailer under the Foxdale line bridge east of St. John's station during the return road trip to Douglas. Construction of the new carriage sheds continued through the summer, with Douglas shed first used just after the Santa train weekend at the end of 1998. The Port Erin

shed had its first occupants on 16th December.

1999 saw coach F21 repatriated from the Cavan and Leitrim Railway in Ireland. The relocation of Douglas signal box was completed at the start of the season, with the main structure refurbished and fully repainted and a new set of steps provided. Completion of the new sheds allowed demolition of the old one to take place between 6th and 8th June. The 125th anniversary of the south line was celebrated with a special train on 1st August followed by the official opening of the new museum adjacent to Port Erin station. The railway featured as a location for the filming of 'Thomas and the Magic Railroad' during 1999; Castletown station was clad in timber and renamed Shining Time, whilst the goods shed at Port St. Mary was used for indoor work and had a wooden extension added at one end.

The line entered its third century as the year 2000 dawned and was treated to a new timetable for the summer with six trains each way during the peak season and the normal four train off peak service times amended to allow longer days in Douglas and Port Erin. In a break with recent tradition, trains passed at Castletown instead of Ballasalla. The timetable also required some trains to pass at Santon and consequently a stationmaster was employed. Santon became the latest station to receive half-height platforms during the 1999/2000 winter; it also became a base for the permanent way gang.

Work on the rebuild of the Donegal railcars was halted after a considerable cost overrun with a great deal of work remaining. Meanwhile, fully rebuilt F54 returned to service on 9th March, a tribute to the talent of the railway craftsman involved. The body of former Manx Northern Railway coach N41 was removed from its long-term home outside Douglas shed and put in store in early May. New mess facilities for the train crews were provided by a portable cabin nearby.

Following restoration at Ramsey Shipyard, van Gr12 was moved to display adjacent to the restored Lezayre station. 1 *Sutherland* was repainted into the now standard Indian red livery during the latter part of 2000 and the bodies were removed from coaches F41 and F70. Meanwhile the body of C1 (part of F64) was moved from storage at Douglas to Peel in June 2001 for restoration by Peel Heritage Trust and display alongside the station's former water tower. HRH Prince Edward and his royal party travelled from Douglas to Santon to attend the Santon Fayre on 7th July 2001.

Plans were unveiled by the Department of Transport to improve the road at Kewaigue by building a new railway overbridge with greater clearance for high road vehicles.

↖On 29th March 2019 the wastewater pipe that runs along under the track began leaking just to the north of Ronaldsway Halt. Trains ran to and from Ballasalla and Castletown with a bus link between the two stations. No.15 *Caledonia* runs through the rarely used loop at Ballasalla, before departing towards Douglas. *Barry Edwards*

↑Manx Electric tram No.33 pauses at Ballasalla while working south during August 1998. The down platform has been installed as part of the construction of the new station building, the opposite platform has now been added. *Barry Edwards*

↓Locomotives 11 *Maitland* and 13 *Kissack* at Ballasalla with the Royal Jubilee Double Header, celebrating the platinum jubilee of the now late Queen Elizabeth II. The leading locomotive displays a special commemorative headboard and flag standard. *Mike Buttell*

↓↓On 1st August 2014, a special train operated, conveying a selection of Peel Engineering fibreglass cars. The cars were manufactured in Peel in the 1960's. Diesel locomotive No.21 is seen at Ballasalla, No.15 *Caledonia* is on the rear of the train. *Barry Edwards*

←A 1960's view of No.5 *Mona* arriving at Ballasalla with a southbound train. Housing now occupies the land on the left, and very soon on the right as well. *Barry Edwards Collection*

↑A view that has changed completely over the recent couple of years, with a new housing estate now occupying the fields behind the train. No.8 *Fenella* is slowing for the Ballasalla stop. *Barry Edwards*

↓Locomotive No.10 is seen here climbing hard with its six-coach load, as it passes Ballaquaggan Farm on the approach to Blackboards on 12th April 2009. *Barry Edwards*

↑In recent years the long proposed Ballasalla bypass has begun to materialise, albeit with around 300 new homes that will be situated on both sides of the railway just to the north of the village. The bypass crosses the railway over a bridge, this view taken from the bridge on 4th June 2022, shows No.4 *Loch* leading the 15:50 Douglas to Port Erin, passenger numbers requiring a six-coach train. *Barry Edwards*

→Blackboards is where the main A5 road crosses the railway and provides this fine view of the railway. No.15 *Caledonia* is passing with the 12:00 Douglas to Port Erin on 25th July 2019, displaying celebratory headboards for the 140th anniversary of the Manx Northern Railway. The boards made by David Archer are now on display in the Port Erin Museum. *Barry Edwards*

←Diesel locomotive No.21 approaches Blackboards with a test train on 20th August 2019. The dining train was used to provide a load, as it would have been spare at the time. *Barry Edwards*

↙Manx Electric Diesel Electric No.34 approaches Blackboards with an open MER trailer on 1st May 2010. The duo were undergoing tests ahead of operating enthusiast trips during the summer event. *Barry Edwards*

↓The dining train operates a significant period of Christmas themed trains through December and into early January. On 29th December 2020 No.13 *Kissack* approaches Ballaglonney crossing with a Xmas Lunch train heading for Castletown. *Barry Edwards*

↑During December, Santon station is used as Santa's Grotto for the Santa trains. It is therefore well decorated, as seen in this evening image of No.15 *Caledonia* passing with the Manx Radio Carnaby Street dining train on 12th December 2020. *Barry Edwards*

←As the line approaches Santon from the south, it curves round past the Santon Burn on a short embankment. The location was chosen for this view of No.15 *Caledonia* with an eleven-coach train, banked by No.4 *Loch* on 19th April 2014. The front half of the train is the dining set accommodating a wedding and the service train on the rear. *Barry Edwards*

↑A close-up of the superb headboard made by David Archer for the Manx radio train. *Barry Edwards*

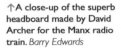

↗An empress van, 'G' van and an 'M' wagon occupy the siding at Santon station, taken in 1986. *Ray Hulock*

→An interesting view at Santon, looking towards the main A5 road bridge, from about where the station building is situated. There is no siding but there is an 'H' wagon parked just beyond the heap of tree, adjacent to the old cattle dock, also visible. *Barry Edwards Collection*

Following agreement between the IOMSRSA and Isle of Man Transport, 4 *Loch* left the Island on 6th March 2001 for a full overhaul at Chatham Steam, including a new boiler. The access road to the new IRIS sewage processing plant at Meary Veg required a new bridge over the line just south of the Crogga woods. The bridge, built of concrete and faced with stone, was completed by August 2001.

The season concluded on 28th October 2001 with the last trains running very full. The reason for this was once again the IRIS scheme. A new underground pipeline was to be laid along the length of the line from Meary Veg to Port Erin over the next two years, with the steam railway only operating over part of its length. So, just about every local enthusiast and a large contingent of interested residents and, no doubt, a few visitors, took the opportunity to make one last complete trip before the end of the season, the last complete trips until the start of the 2004 season. On the last day the 14:00 departure from Douglas and the 16:35 return carried a commemorative headboard marking the retirement of long-standing driver John Elkin. John was due to retire before the complete line would reopen and so this would be his last full round trip as a driver.

Immediately after the last train the track between Meary Veg and Santon station was lifted in preparation for the laying of the new pipeline. This short stretch needed to be finished in time for the start of the 2002 season.

↑A 1993 image of Santon station, before the addition of platforms on both tracks. Nowadays, unless there is a need for trains to pass here, all trains use the track nearest to the camera. The palm trees remain but are now among a good deal of other foliage. *Richard Kirkman*

←On 17th August, the railway operated 'The Veterans Express' as part of their Island at War weekend. No.15 *Caledonia* passes Santon, adorned by another of Mr Archer's superb headboards. The station building is hidden behind the tree towards the rear of the train, and unusually the siding is empty. *Barry Edwards*

↖Shortly after leaving Santon the trains pass under a small bridge that carries a footpath and farm track over the line. No.13 *Kissack* is working hard as it takes its lengthy train up towards the summit of the line, on 18th March 2022. *Barry Edwards*

↑After a lengthy period out of service, locomotive No.11 *Maitland* re-entered traffic for the 2022 season. An official launch was included in the Summer Transport Festival on 28th July. The locomotive was launched by the current Speaker of the House of Keys, the Manx Parliament. Dalrymple Maitland, after whom the locomotive was named, was the speaker between 1909 and 1919 and indeed a railway director. The launch train is seen passing Meary Veg, with another superb headboard. *Barry Edwards*

←No.13 *Kissack* passes the same location on 21st October 2019, the changing seasons creating a completely different image. *Barry Edwards*

←An earlier picture of No.4 *Loch* passing under the road that leads to the shooting range. *Barry Edwards Collection*

←←No.13 *Kissack* passing the Crogga Estate and the Crogga Valley Railway as it heads south with a combined dining and passenger train on Saturday 26th June 2021. The miniature railway features elsewhere in this book. *Barry Edwards*

↙On 31st July 2022, the final day of the Summer Transport Festival, the 09:50 from Douglas carried a headboard celebrating the Platinum Jubilee of the now late Queen Elizabeth II. The train is seen here easing into Port Soderick station, displaying another of David Archer's superb creations and a full flag display. *Les Ward*

←Port Soderick station seen in the 1960's, with a southbound train arriving. The station building has now been fully restored and is in use as a private dwelling. *Barry Edwards Collection*

↑ The unusual sight of a Manx Electric tram at Port Soderick, along with Schoema diesel locomotive No.17 *Viking*, makes for an interesting image. The tram has made use of a generator van to provide the power up from Douglas. *Barry Edwards*

↗ Complete with painted face and headboard, No.4 *Loch* approaches Port Soderick with a Santa Special bound for Santon during December 1992. An interesting mix of coaches make up the train, all no doubt loaded with excited children on their way to meet Santa. *Richard Kirkman*

↓ A 1993 view of No.4 *Loch* arriving at Port Soderick with a southbound five-coach train. While there has long been a platform on the southbound track here, the northbound track now has a platform too. *Richard Kirkman*

↓↓ Probably one of the most photographed stretches of line is at Keristal, where the line runs along high above the Irish Sea coastline. Operating a Santa train to Santon on 15th December 2019 is No.13 *Kissack*. The train is passing the 2¾ milepost, from Douglas. *Barry Edwards*

↘ Manx Electric locomotive No.34 almost matches the colour of the gorse flowers, as it runs along at Keristal with trailer 43 during a test run on 1st May 2010. *Barry Edwards*

1 *Sutherland* was in steam for the Santa weekend on 8th and 9th December; although the 9th was expected to be her last day in steam prior to her boiler being returned to 8 *Fenella*, by then away at RMS Locotec for rebuilding. In the event she remained in service for the 2002 season.

Ballasalla received a full-height platform on the Douglas side to match that on the Port Erin side built in 1985. Bus-style shelters were installed on the Douglas side at Castletown and Ballasalla, and a new wooden one at Port Soderick; these provided an improved ambience for passengers.

When the pipelaying was completed between Meary Veg and Santon station, the track was reinstated using completely new materials and testing completed, this length of line reopened, as planned, on 15th April 2002. The 2002 timetable saw trains between Douglas and Santon, and between Castletown and Port Erin, with a connecting bus service linking the two parts. Two new water towers were constructed to accommodate the timetable, one at Santon and one at Castletown.

A severe storm on the night of 21st October caused major problems on the east coast of the Island and damaged the line between Douglas and Santon; this section did not reopen for the rest of the season.

Ronaldsway Halt received a full height platform in early 2003, and Port Soderick gained its second platform at the same time. A full-scale study into the provision of commuter trains was undertaken but concluded that a service was not viable. It was noted that the majority of those driving to work in Douglas park their car further from their office than the distance to the railway station!

The IRIS work on the section between Santon and Castletown was completed on schedule, including the

installation of automatic crossing barriers at most level crossings. These did cause a few problems in the early weeks of the 2003 timetable. With the northern section completed, the IRIS scheme moved to the southern section. Trains operated between Douglas and Castletown and between Port St. Mary and Port Erin for the 2003 season with a connecting bus service between Castletown and Port St Mary.

Locomotive 8 *Fenella* was re-inaugurated on Friday 5th September 2003 in a short ceremony at Douglas station.

Additional work was completed at Ronaldsway Halt to improve the platform with the installation of a wooden platform edge, while Colby received full-height platforms on

↖Locomotive No.6 *Peveril* leads a sister towards Douglas, past Keristal, where there appears to have been a lineside fire during a 1960's summer. *Barry Edwards Collection*

↑No.8 *Fenella* with a three-coach train that includes the Foxdale coach F39, is about to begin the long descent into Douglas, against the perfect blue sky of 6th June 2013. *Barry Edwards*

←With the afternoon sun providing illumination of the locomotive and train, No.13 *Kissack* heads towards Douglas on 21st October 2021. *Richard Kirkman*

↓No.1 *Sutherland* leads a long train, banked by a sister locomotive past Keristal and onwards towards Port Soderick. The train has just completed the long climb up from Douglas, during the 1993 Year of Railways. *Barry Edwards*

During the late afternoon or evening, the position of the sun allows the Keristal section to be photographed from inside the line, with the coastline and sea as a background. The coastline visible was once the route of the Douglas Head and Marine Drive Tramway. No.4 *Loch* passes with an evening dining train to Port Erin on 15th July 2021. *Barry Edwards*

Fireman Will Bradley keeps a watch on the way ahead, having provided a suitable fire for his driver to make the climb out of Douglas to Keristal, where this view was recorded, on 9th August 2021. No.15 *Caledonia* is in the livery of its original company, the Manx Northern Railway. *Barry Edwards*

During the evening of 28th July 2022, following the launch of No.11 *Maitland*, there was a Pie and Mash dining train, strengthened by two coaches to accommodate non-dining passengers, and double-headed with No.4 *Loch*. The Dalrymple Maitland headboard was carried on the train, seen here during a brief stop at Keristal to allow passengers to take in the view. *Barry Edwards*

both tracks and its former Braddan station building was refurbished and repainted. The IRIS pipeline laying on the southern section went to plan, the new track work arriving on the Island during 2003 and the relaying started at the end of the season.

Several contractors' wagons and a Hunslet 3ft 0in gauge locomotive were used during the relay work. Further automated level crossings were installed, the whole project being completed on time, or almost, for the start of the new season, delayed until Monday 3rd May, a date that marked another milestone in the long history of the railway.

After two years of curtailed running, the steam railway returned to its full length for the 2004 season, with the now standard four-train service operating in each direction and passing again at Ballasalla, not Castletown. Many mourned the loss of the rattle and roll but the new track gave the line a whole new lease of life.

The colour light starter signals at the end of the Douglas

The annual New Year's Eve dining train usually stops at Keristal on the return journey around 23:50, to see in the new year, before continuing to Douglas in the first minutes of the new year. The camera recorded this image as taken on 1st January 2015, although the shutter was pressed in the last seconds of 2014! Light pollution from Douglas is clearly visible. *Barry Edwards*

No.4 *Loch* is still working hard as it approaches the top of the climb and emerges onto the ledge that runs along high above the sea at Keristal. *Barry Edwards*

Nearing the end of the long climb out of Douglas, No.8 *Fenella* brings the 15:50 Douglas to Port Erin out of the top of Oakhill Cutting on 4th September 2020.

platforms were replaced by more authentic semaphore ones at the beginning of the 2005 season. During race periods on the Southern 100 circuit and the suspension of through bus services, a special train was operated from Port Erin to Castletown and back to convey some stranded commuters.

On Monday 25th July 2005 a short ceremony was held at Douglas station to officially name recently acquired Hunslet diesel, numbered 18 in the fleet. The name *Ailsa*, kept secret until the day, was unveiled by Mr Cecil Mitchell, a Ballasalla resident who celebrated his 100th birthday that year. Mr

Mitchell was then photographed alongside locomotives Nos. 10 *GH Wood* and 11 *Maitland* both of which were celebrating their centenaries.

A Samaritans Christmas Child 'Shoebox' campaign special train operated from Port Erin to Douglas on Tuesday 1st November 2005, a couple of days after the end of the season services that had produced 143,736 passengers, up from 140,499 the year before. The line received a top 10 place in the National newspaper 'The Independent' Top 10 best car-free days out, beating the likes of the Orient Express in the process.

During the winter of 2005/06 winter, track was re-laid between Meary Veg and a point just south of Port Soderick station. Various problems with the automatic crossing barriers at the beginning of the season were swiftly attended to. 4 *Loch* returned to service after overhaul at the beginning of the 2006 season. Sadness swept through the entire staff of Isle of Man Transport on 2nd August 2006 with the news of the death of Assistant Engineer Colin Goldsmith; on 10th August, the day of his funeral, the railway's locomotives carried wreaths in his memory. The Shoebox special operated again on 7th November 2006.

Work over the 2006/07 winter included the complete relaying of Port Soderick station, joining up with the earlier relay through Crogga woods to Meary Veg. New tastefully produced enamelled metal signs were installed above the doors in all the rolling stock, warning of the dangers of leaning out.

The same four-train service was in the timetable for 2007. Locomotive 10 *G. H. Wood* was repainted into Ailsa green livery and had the honour of hauling the railway's first commuter train for many years, when during the TT fortnight an 07:45 train operated from Port Erin to Douglas with a 17:30 return. A special commuter ticket was available but regrettably very few people used the service. Congestion on the approaches to Douglas during the rush hour periods led to the call for the two former County Donegal railcars to be completed and operated as a commuter service. The idea stalled but there are still efforts to find a way forward, possibly

using some external funding and/or manpower. The 40th anniversary of the start of the important Ailsa period was marked by a short ceremony at Douglas but sadly No 10 failed and was only able to take part as a static exhibit.

Santon and Ballasalla stations were repainted in the standard red and cream colours over the winter. At Castletown some work was carried out on the former goods shed, including the removal of a large wooden advertising board, thus revealing more of the building's stonework. At Port Erin, two of the level crossing gates were replaced with wooden ones, which look far more in keeping than the old metal ones.

Following the end of the season, the now annual 'Shoebox' train operated on 6th November and the Santa trains over the weekend of 8th and 9th December.

23 years before the previous image, No.12 *Hutchinson* in blue livery is still working as it brings its short three-coach train towards Keristal in the spring of 1997. *Ray Hulock*

←Locomotive No.11 *Maitland* has just passed under Oakhill Bridge that carries the A25 road over the railway. The engine is working hard as it climbs the 1 in 65 gradient, the next station stop will be Port Soderick. *Barry Edwards Collection*

↑Ellenbrook is a location that affords this view of the trains with a backdrop of the mountains, including Snaefell. No.5 *Mona* has emerged onto the open stretch of track, with a good deal of spare steam as it makes its way out of Douglas during 1964. *Barry Edwards Collection*

An image taken just a few hundred yards before the previous image, shows an unidentified locomotive approaching Ellenbrook during 1964. One of the old cooling towers of Pulrose Power Station is just visible over the trees to the right of the train. *Barry Edwards Collection*

On 1st April 2022 the Island awoke to a sprinkling of snow on the high hills, and a sunny morning. No.13 *Kissack* makes a spirited departure from the outskirts of Douglas with the 09:50 to Port Erin. The picture was worth the effort, the snow had pretty much disappeared by the time the 11:50 left Douglas! *Barry Edwards*

↑A 1993 view of No.4 *Loch* climbing hard towards Kewaigue with a short train. *Richard Kirkman*

→Shortly after departing from Douglas the trains cross the Nunnery Bridge over the River Glass. No.11 *Maitland* heads south during a 1960's summer. *Barry Edwards Collection*

↓An image that has been seen many times before but worthy of inclusion here, as we celebrate the 150th anniversary of this very event. Locomotive No.1 is at the head of the official opening train at Douglas on 1st July 1873. Bands played on the Platform ahead of the train departing to Peel. *Manx National Heritage*

Stored locomotives Nos. 5 *Mona* and 6 *Peveril* spent a considerable time in the old carriage shed at Douglas in the 1980s and 1990s. No.6 was cosmetically restored and is now on display in the Port Erin Museum, while No.5 is in the process of receiving the same treatment. Photographed on 20th July 1985. *Barry Edwards*

↑A busy scene at Douglas station taken around the turn of the 20th century. The main station building was constructed in 1891/92 and had a steel and glass canopy added on the platform side in 1909. A range of coach types and indeed various wagons are visible. *Manx National Heritage*

↗Locomotive No.3 *Pender* is now in the Manchester Museum of Science and Industry as a sectionalised exhibit. In happier times it is seen here at Douglas with a short freight train consisting of G17, M48, M43 and a further 'M' wagon. The photograph is dated 1957. *Barry Edwards Collection*

→A selection of rolling stock occupying the yard at Douglas. An 'E' van thought to be E5, well wagon 1, an 'L' wagon, a crane and a line of coaches with one of the Empress vans on the rear. *Barry Edwards Collection*

↓An early 20th century image taken at Douglas shows No.9 *Douglas* awaiting departure with a mixed train, consisting of a 'G' van and three passenger coaches. *Manx National Heritage*

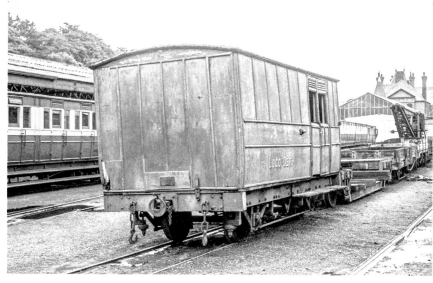

↑Former Manx Northern Railway No.4 *Caledonia*, now Isle of Man Railway No.15 was restored to working order as part of the 1995 International Railway Festival, held in 1995 to celebrate the centenary of the Snaefell Mountain Railway. She is seen here departing from Douglas with the official launch train on 14th April 1995. *Barry Edwards*

→An image from 24 years ago, No.1 *Sutherland* with No.15 *Caledonia* break the banner to celebrate the 125th anniversary of the Port Erin line. Robert Smith, then Director of Public Transport, is to the left of the locomotive. *Barry Edwards*

The TT trains were repeated in 2008, and appeared in the annual timetable leaflet, this time with reduced fares and the availability of Manx12 bus tickets and residents' tickets, resulting in far more commuter passengers being carried.

The beginning of the 2009 season witnessed good passenger loads, necessitating the need for up to six-coach trains on occasions. Shortly before the services started it was announced that the shoulder season service from the end of September until early November, would comprise of one train operating two departures each way daily. A welcome addition was the re-instatement of mileposts along the line, replacing the previous posts lost in the major relay in the early 2000s.

A new Director of Public Transport brought some interesting initiatives. On the eve of the last day of the season a Hop-tu-Naa train ran from Douglas to Castletown, the 240 passengers then enjoying a ghost walk around the town before the journey back to Douglas and a hotpot supper. The Santa trains were such a success that four additional trains ran the following weekend and a 'Blow away the Cobwebs' special on 30th December carried a full load of passengers.

The success of the 'Blow Away the Cobwebs' special in late 2009 led to several special events in subsequent years, including Valentine's Day, Mother's Day, and Father's Day specials. The 2010 season featured a longer operating period – starting on 13th March – but with some non-operational days. Santa trains operated to and from Castletown and, in

↑↑Douglas station seen with its canopies and the concourse canopy during the 1960's, all now sadly demolished. No.10 *G H Wood* has shunted off its train and heading for the shed via the middle release road. *Barry Edwards Collection*

↗During 1967 several coach bodies were removed so that their chassis could be used in an experiment to carry containers on the railway. R3 was converted to have a well allowing a slightly larger container to be accommodated. It is seen here at Douglas in the early 1970s. It survived until 1974 when it was broken up at Ballasalla by Manx Metals Ltd. *Ray Hulock*

↑Making a spectacular departure from Douglas is No.4 *Loch*, the leading coach being F15 that survives in service. The wonderful array of semaphore signals makes for an interesting image, all controlled from the signal box visible to the right of the rear of the train. *Barry Edwards Collection*

→The two County Donegal railcars purchased in 1961 are seen during shunting at Douglas. No.19 is nearest the camera. The signal gantry is attached to the side of the Douglas water tower. *Barry Edwards Collection*

co-operation with Manx National Heritage, Santa was at Castle Rushen. Trains also operated from Port Erin and provided a through service. Unusually severe snow caused the cancellation of all services on 18th and 19th December; additional trains were provided on 20th December.

Many special events begun to revolve around the normal timetable, thereby increasing revenue at minimal extra operating cost. Another timetable innovation was the introduction of a six-train peak service that operated at peak weekends and during school summer holidays.

Ballastrang crossing received a new larger hut and is now the only manned crossing. A new road crossing was installed just north of Colby station to provide access to the new Colby Football Club premises.

Easter 2011 played host to a new idea, 'Rush Hour on the Railways', an event that quickly established itself as the official curtain raiser to the season. Special displays and intensive service days and workshop tours proved very

↑An interesting line up at Douglas during the 1998 Steam 125 celebrations. No.16 *Mannin*, No.4 *Loch* and No.1 *Sutherland*. *Ray Hulock*

↗An undated but superb study of No.3 *Pender* at Douglas. *Barry Edwards Collection*

→A look under the concourse canopy at Douglas in 1964. The Parcels, Left Luggage and Enquiry Office is to the left, whilst a group of passengers are exiting the ticket office. *Barry Edwards*

↓On 4th April 2015, No.13 *Kissack* has arrived at Douglas in the late evening with a special from Port Erin. *Barry Edwards*

←The beautifully laid up tables, await their guests for the New Year Extravaganza. Seven courses will be served, each with a dedicated wine, and then Champagne to see in the New Year. *Barry Edwards*

↓Brown Marshalls 1894 coach F15 is seen in the workshops at Douglas, on 6th October 2019, in the final stages of full refurbishment and return to service. *Barry Edwards*

↓In recent years, a couple of locomotives have been sent off Island for refurbishment. Here the frames and bunker of No.12 *Hutchinson* sit on accommodation trucks in the yard of the Severn Valley Railway at Bridgnorth on 23rd April 2022. *Barry Edwards*

↘In addition to locomotive refurbishment, any new boilers required are manufactured off-Island. This new boiler is under construction at the works of the Severn Valley Railway and is seen on 23rd April 2022. *Barry Edwards*

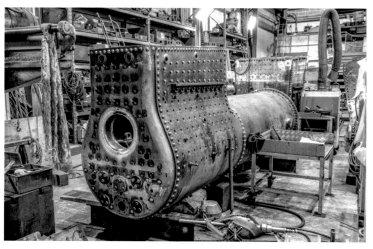

The Christmas dining trains offer the opportunity to capture a departure from Douglas in the dark. Under the lights from the adjacent bus depot, No.4 *Loch* departs with the New Year's Eve train on 31st December 2021, the train arriving back at Douglas in the first few minutes of 2022. *Barry Edwards*

↑Another task that requires specialist equipment is re-tyring of wheels. Here a set of Isle of Man wheels have received their new tyres, a process that requires the tyre to be heated up, the wheel inserted into the tyre, and then as it cools, the tyre grips the wheel. *Barry Edwards*

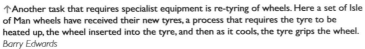

↗The frames of No.10 *G H Wood* is in the workshops of Alan Keef during their 50th anniversary open day, 24th September 2022. *Ian Mylroi*

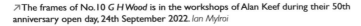

→The railway conveyed considerable numbers to the open-air church service at Braddan on Sunday mornings, before the line to Peel closed in 1968. Here we see railcars 20 and 19, with No.11 *Maitland* at the head of a long train, with another locomotive probably on the other end. The small station building later moved to Colby. *Barry Edwards Collection*

←A special train operated to celebrate the Silver Jubilee of Her Majesty Queen Elizabeth II, seen here departing from Douglas behind No.11 *Maitland*. The railway had only returned to Douglas in 1977, following a period of operating only between Port Erin and Ballasalla or Castletown. *Barry Edwards Collection*

↙On re-opening day, 3rd June 1967, No.8 *Fenella* approaches Union Mills with a train for either Peel or Ramsey. *Gavin Morrison*

↓The 1893-built, Richard Gibbins & Co of Birmingham, eight-ton hand crane is preserved at Union Mills station. It sits on a short section of track adjacent to a section of the platform. Photographed on 27th July 2022. *Les Ward*

popular. The main festival weekend was timed at the end of July to include events involving other vintage transport and the many private lines and museums around the Island.

The increasing success of these events led to the creation of the dining train and the complete rebuild, on a new steel chassis, of full brake F27 into a kitchen car. This vehicle provides kitchen support to the Ticket Hall Restaurant, allowing full meals to be served on the train. Officially launched in late 2013, the dining train has been a huge success, offering superb food in a set of coaches that have been restored and refurbished to a high standard. Corporate charters, Sunday dinner trains, and other events now include the full dining option.

A second steel frame is available to allow the second full brake (F28) to be rebuilt and accommodate disabled access, toilets, and further kitchen facilities.

The line celebrated the 140th anniversary of the opening of the Douglas to Peel line in 2013 and to Port Erin in 2014. As part of the 2013 celebrations, locomotive number 8 *Fenella* was taken by road to Peel and placed on the short length of track alongside the former water tower in Peel. This site is maintained by the Manx Transport Heritage Museum, this group having restored the body of 4-wheeled coach C1 dating from 1873, the two pieces of rolling stock making a fine sight.

There was considerable discussion and debate about the ordering of a new diesel locomotive for the line during 2013.

18 *Viking* was deemed unserviceable, and the specification was for a diesel capable of hauling passenger trains at normal line speeds, with availability for service within a few minutes. After several changes of plan, the new locomotive number 21 arrived on the Island in December 2013, with its first testing taking place during the 2013 Santa train weekends. However, the locomotive has been beset by a series of issues and has not been used as planned.

The dining train provided the ultimate special on New Year's Eve 2014, travelling the whole length of the line, stopping at Keristal on the return trip to welcome in the New Year. The train therefore had the honour of being the last passenger train of 2014 and the first of 2015.

The now established long season timetable operated in 2015, with annual events taking their slots throughout the year. From the start of the season the trains passed at Castletown rather than Ballasalla, allowing the latter to become an unmanned station. In May the Transport Trust visited the line as part of their 2015 AGM weekend, presenting one of the society Red Wheels. Controversial plans to refurbish Douglas station building were put forward during 2015; planning permission was granted, and the work completed over the 2015/16 winter. While there were objections to the plan, the building would likely have closed completely had the work not been completed.

The TT services begun to utilise the dining set, with breakfast being served on the morning train and an evening

This stonework station name at Union Mills survives to this day, despite the station not having seen a train for over 50 years. *Barry Edwards*

St John's was the junction for Peel, Ramsey or Foxdale, and therefore a busy station, particularly on Tynwald day when an open-air service is held on the nearby Tynwald hill. Judging by the crowds, this was one such Tynwald Day, with passengers boarding a Ramsey train, while others wait for one to Peel or Douglas. No.3 *Pender* is at the head of the Ramsey train. *Barry Edwards Collection*

Another view of a busy St John's, showing the footbridge that spanned the tracks at the Peel end of the station. A Douglas-bound train occupies the platform. The hotel, more recently known as the Farmers Arms has been demolished. *Manx National Heritage*

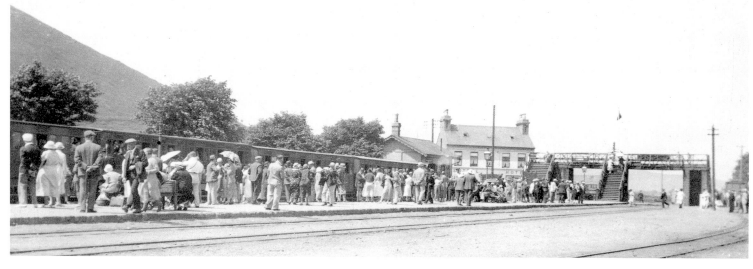

↑A view of St John's taken in April 1975, during the dismantling of the Peel and Ramsey lines. One half of F55, either B2 or C6, lies derelict on the platform. *Ray Hulock*

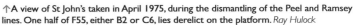

↗A further view of St John's looking towards Tynwald Hill. Coach F39 is behind M50, M13 or 23 and M49, while a 'G' van is in the distance. The Railway Junction Hotel is now used as offices. *Manx National Heritage*

→A good general view of St John's carriage shed and signal box, with No.5 *Mona* arriving from Douglas, with a train for Peel during the 1960's. *Barry Edwards Collection*

↓Former Manx Northern Railway No.3 *Thornhill*, later Isle of Man Railway No.14, is in the Ramsey line platform at St Johns with a mixed train. *E Paget Tomlinson*

↑A look inside the St John's carriage shed in April 1975. *Ray Hulock*

↗The Peel and Ramsey lines left St John's parallel to each other before the Ramsey line climbed away and headed north. Here we see a five-coach train headed by an unidentified locomotive, and being banked, shortly after departing from St John's. The Ramsey line is visible to the left. *Barry Edwards Collection*

→A busy scene at Peel station. The picture says, 'Liverpool Scottish marching to camp'. A selection of bogie and four-wheeled coaches are in the background, including F1 and two 'B' coaches. *Manx National Heritage*

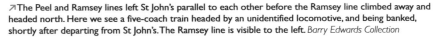

↑A view of Peel station taken from nearby Peel Hill, the home of the Corrin's Hill Tramway, taken in the 1960's. A single locomotive with an eight-coach train is preparing to depart, while two further coaches and a van are also visible. The Brickworks Office is adjacent to the level crossing; this building is now home to the Manx Transport Heritage Museum. The engine shed has been demolished but the water tower survives. The area behind the station has all been redeveloped and the station site itself is now occupied by the House of Manannan. *Barry Edwards Collection*

↑Locomotive No.12 *Hutchinson*, about to cross the Mill Road level crossing with the tower of St Germans Cathedral visible in the distance. *Manx National Heritage*

←During the First World War, an internment camp was created at Knockaloe to the south of Peel. A short line was constructed to get supplies to the camp; this left the main line just to the east of Glenfaba. Here we see three 'H' wagons being unloaded within the camp, having been pushed here by No.15 *Caledonia*. *Manx National Heritage*

During the 2014 Summer Festival, and to celebrate the 140th anniversary of the railway, No.8 *Fenella* made the trip to Peel, and was placed onto a short length of track adjacent to the water tower. The level crossing gates and short platform, that is home to the body of coach C1, add to the atmosphere. Taken on 27th July 2013. *Barry Edwards*

←A general view of the railway entrance to the Knockaloe Camp, the walls of which survive and are still the road entrance to the area. Locomotive No.15 *Caledonia* is seen in the entrance. *Manx National Heritage*

↓A side on view of the spoil being loaded onto the 'M' wagons. M42 and M61 are identifiable in this view. The chap with the shovel has got his work cut out, keeping up with the digger! *Manx National Heritage*

↑The other short branch in the west of the Island was from St John's to Foxdale. No.15 *Caledonia* is in charge of a short rake of 'M' wagons that are being loaded with spoil from the nearby mines. The image is dated mid 20th Century. *Manx National Heritage*

↘The remains of one of the Foxdale line bridges at Slieauwhallian, just to the south of St John's, photographed during 1993. *Richard Kirkman*

↑A section of the former Foxdale Line trackbed on the approach to Foxdale station, seen in 1993. The barbed wire fence makes the trackbed look narrower than it was, the wall being the original boundary. *Richard Kirkman*

→The Foxdale Line official opening train in June 1886, consisting of locomotive No.4, later IMR No.15, *Caledonia* and a Cleminson six-wheeled coach. *Manx National Heritage*

↑During 1992 this short section of old track from the branch, was visible where the line crossed the road between Lower and Higher Foxdale. *Richard Kirkman*

↗Returning to St Johns to continue our Journey to Ramsey, we see No.8 *Fenella* arriving with a train for Peel, while No.10 *G H Wood* is ready to depart for Douglas on 3rd June 1967. *Gavin Morrison*

←Another image showing the diverging lines to the west of St John's in the 1960's. No.6 *Peveril* is climbing away with a train for Ramsey, while a sister engine struggles to keep up, with its train for Peel. *Barry Edwards Collection*

↑Locomotive No.1 *Sutherland* stuck in the snow at Peel Road station in January 1940. *Manx National Heritage*

←The next station stop after Peel Road was St Germain's. Here we see No.5 *Mona* approaching the station with a train for Ramsey, in the 1960's. *Trevor Nall*

↑The town of Peel is in the background as No.11 *Maitland* approaches Ballaquine Bridge with a train for Ramsey, just a few months before the line closed in September 1968. *Barry Edwards Collection*

meal on the late afternoon train. The same format was introduced on a monthly commuter service, operating on the first Friday of each month. The same timetable format operated for both 2016 and 2017.

During 2019 thoughts turned to the 150th anniversary in 2023, and plans were put in place to remove locomotive 16 *Mannin* from Port Erin railway museum and take it to Douglas for assessment.

The first train of the 2020 season operated on 3rd March to convey a coach party from Douglas to Port Erin. The full timetable started on 6th March, with the railway set for a busy season. Sadly, the onset of Covid-19 changed everything and during the late afternoon of 19th March, it was announced that all services had been withdrawn until further notice. There were fears that with the Island borders closed, there may have been no further trains in 2020.

However, as the Island eased out of lockdown, an air

↑Snow obviously caused some issues for the northern line, as this view of Ballaquine Bridge shows. No.15 *Caledonia* is attempting to clear a way through. *Trevor Nall*

↗The line crossed Glen Wyllin on the first of two superb viaducts. This view dated around 1900, shows the viaduct over the pleasure grounds that were developed by the railway in the Glen. *Manx National Heritage*

→A superb picture of the two former County Donegal railcars crossing the Glen Wyllin viaduct in 1964. *Barry Edwards Collection*

↓A 1960s view of the viaduct with a train crossing. The six coaches are in the hands of No.5 *Mona* and another sister but unidentified locomotive. The pillars still exist, a recent plan to construct a new bridge has now been shelved. *Trevor Nall*

↖Kirk Michael station is a short distance north of Glen Wyllin, where we see the two railcars again. The station staff appear to be checking the timetable! The station is now home to the local fire station, the station building acting as the office. *Barry Edwards Collection*

↑A little way north of the station, the line crosses the Bayr Ny Balleira road on this interesting looking bridge. *Barry Edwards*

←Locomotive No.6 *Peveril* passing Rhencullen, having just passed under the bridge that carries the Orrisdale Road. *Trevor Nall*

Departing from Ballaugh with a train for Ramsey during the 1960's. Unusually the guard seems to be in the middle coach. *Barry Edwards Collection*

The elaborate Sulby Glen station is now a private residence. There is a fine selection of enamel advertisements on the station. A Douglas-bound train is approaching from the east. *Manx National Heritage*

The Manx Northern Railway purchased one Beyer Peacock locomotive, as their No.3 *Thornhill*, it became IMR No.14. It is seen here at Ballaugh, the driver checking his locomotive before departing for Ramsey. *Barry Edwards Collection*

Ballaugh station, captured on film in 1966. *Ray Hulock*

corridor operating two or three times a week was created by Aurigny of Guernsey, between the two covid-free jurisdictions. The railway re-opened on 23rd July, initially until 13th September, with a four-train service operating on just five days a week. The air corridor continued, and large numbers of residents made use of the railway as they were unable to travel off-island; services continued until the usual season end at the beginning of November. After a short break, the full Christmas programme of dining trains was operated.

Further lockdowns in early 2021 delayed the start of the season until 27th May, with trains expected to operate until early November. The island begun to open its borders as the year progressed and soon was busy with visiting coach parties. This led to some very busy days on the railway with six- and even seven-coach trains becoming a regular sight. In July it was announced that the Saturday service would be increased to six trains a day to cope with the high passenger numbers.

A short summer transport festival was held at the end of July and a five-day winter festival planned around the last weekend of services at the end of October. The summer festival attracted a good number of visitors, the October event was plagued by bad weather but was again well attended and enjoyed by those that braved the elements to ride on and photograph the railway. The annual Christmas dining train programme operated through December and into January 2022, with over 50 departures from Douglas during that time.

On Thursday 6th January, locomotive 11 *Maitland* returned from a major rebuild at the Stratfold Barn Railway and re-entered service later in the year. It was officially launched at the Summer Transport festival by the Speaker of the House of Keys, The Hon Juan Watterson SHK.

The railway has enjoyed a buoyant season, with trains often having to be lengthened to accommodate intending passengers. Large numbers of visiting coach tours have also contributed to the high numbers.

As the 2022 season draws to a close, the focus has been on 2023 and celebrating the 150th anniversary of the opening of the railway.

↖Ramsey was the northern terminus of the line, where we see No.8 *Fenella* awaiting departure with a short two coach train, during 1964. The building on the left was the carriage shed. *Barry Edwards Collection*

↑A general view of Ramsey station from the buffer stops in 1964. The goods shed is on the right, station building on the left and the carriage shed to the right beyond the goods shed. Sadly, the entire station was demolished to make way for a new Ramsey Bakery building; the bakery closed in May 2022. *Barry Edwards Collection*

↑Beyond Ramsey station, there was a short extension to the quayside to allow loading and unloading ships. Here No.3 *Pender* has a short train of three 'M' wagons including M2, alongside the Quay in 1946. *Manx National Heritage*

→The Manx Northern Railway initially ordered two Sharp Stewart 2-4-0 Tank locomotives. They were numbered 1 *Ramsey* and 2 *Northern*. This picture shows No.1 *Ramsey* departing from Ramsey just prior to the line being taken over by the Isle of Man Railway. Both locomotives were scrapped by 1923. *Manx National Heritage*

Over the weekend of 22nd and 23 May 2022, the Welshpool and Llanfair Railway hosted a Bagnall event. The Isle of Man sent No.8 *Fenella* to Wales to be exhibited. She is seen here among other exhibits in brilliant sunshine. *Antony Christie*

THE GROUDLE GLEN RAILWAY

Like many of the island's glens, Groudle Glen was developed as a tourist pleasure ground by Richard Maltby Broadbent during the late 19th century. A zoo was built at the mouth of the Glen along with a refreshment room, and a further refreshment room was constructed just below the headland. A number of attractions were provided within the glen, including a bandstand, a water mill, walkways, and stalls. The Groudle Glen Railway was conceived to transport visitors from Lhen Coan station, a short walk from the entrance to the Glen near the Manx Electric Railway station, out to the refreshment rooms and the zoo.

The 2ft gauge railway was constructed by local labour during 1895 and the early part of 1896. Spring 1896 saw the arrival of the railway's first locomotive, *Sea Lion*, built by W.G. Bagnall Ltd. of Castle Engine Works, Stafford (works no 1484), and three 4-wheeled coaches, a fourth coach arriving later the same year. The 'line that goes uphill to the sea' opened to the public on 23rd May 1896, with 10,000 passengers being carried in the first two months and over 100,000 in the first three years, with up to 40 return trips being worked each day.

During the winter of 1904/05 a new longer shed was constructed at Lhen Coan station and a run-round loop installed at Headland, in readiness for the arrival in May 1905 of the second steam locomotive from Bagnall's, *Polar Bear* (works no 1781), and four further coaches.

The outbreak of World War I caused the railway to close, but it soon reopened at the end of hostilities and visitors flooded back to the Glen. Sadly, a steep rise in coal prices caused the two steam engines to be stored and replaced by battery electric locomotives. These proved troublesome, one of them becoming derailed and losing a wheel soon after entering service. The electric locomotives were withdrawn after just six years of operation, and the two steam locomotives were overhauled by their builders and returned to service.

The Second World War caused the railway to close once

A general view of Sea Lion Rocks station, with *Annie* having arrived with a train from Lhen Coan on 5th July 2009. A couple of the RAF Fauld wagons are visible in the foreground. In the background are the remains of the Howstrake camp with the Manx Electric Railway running just above. *Barry Edwards*

2431.7 Feeding the Sea Lions, Groudle, I.O.M.

again, and it did not reopen until 1950; services operated as far as the Headland due to a serious rock fall between this point and Sea Lion Rocks. *Polar Bear* was the only serviceable locomotive, with six coaches available for traffic. A small petrol locomotive was tried out on the line as a spare, but soon disappeared as it was too weak for the gradients and uncontrollable on downward sections. The 1950s saw a decline in the number of visitors and an irregular service was operated.

A change of ownership of the glen in 1960 resulted in a revival, with *Polar Bear* and the six coaches operating regular services until the end of the 1962 season. During the 1962/63 winter a good deal of repair work was carried out and attempts were made to purchase a second-hand locomotive, but none could be found. The 1963 season came and went but the railway was unable to operate any trains, due to the failure of *Polar Bear*. The 'old' railway never reopened.

In 1965 the Groudle Glen Railway Preservation Society was formed. At first things looked promising, but in 1967 the owners of the Glen ordered the removal of all railway equipment, with the result that, by June 1968, the locomotives and rolling stock were dispersed all over the British Isles. *Sea Lion* and a few coaches managed to stay on the Island, being exhibited at the Steam Centre in Kirk Michael and these items were left behind when, in the late 1970s, the Steam Centre closed and moved to the newly established Midlands Steam Centre at Loughborough. This little line had surely gone for good.

The Sea Lion Locomotive Association was formed in 1981, eventually moving their locomotive to Loughborough

in October 1981, where it was cosmetically restored.

In January 1982 the Isle of Man Steam Railway Supporters' Association embarked on one of the most impressive narrow gauge railway restoration projects. Structural surveys demonstrated that the railway could be reinstated, providing the original formation was kept. The new owners of the Glen and the Manx Government gave full support, and planning permission was received in May 1982.

Supporters' Association members needed no further encouragement and restoration work started, with clearing the trackbed of fallen trees, gorse and bracken being the first job. A borrowed mechanical digger meant that what would have been months of clearing work was completed in a matter of weeks, while a smaller digger was used to dig trenches for new drains to be installed.

A batch of four-wheeled wagons formerly used at RAF Fauld, Staffordshire were purchased and these arrived on the Island in October 1982. Spring 1983 saw the purchase of the entire Dodington House Railway, situated near Chipping Sodbury, Avon, that had gone into voluntary liquidation. This provided two diesel locomotives, two coaches, plus a spare coach frame, two points and 1,080 yards of track.

Sea Lion was also the subject of negotiations with her owners, and it was agreed that the Association could complete the restoration, on which little progress had been made at Loughborough, and operate the locomotive for as long as they continued to run the railway. The locomotive returned to

↖Historically, the railway took passengers to the zoo at Sea Lion Rocks. The remains of the zoo are still visible today, although much of the structures have disappeared. A popular time to visit was at feeding time, this image shows the sea lions being fed. The keeper will have climbed down the ladder!
Barry Edwards Collection

↑At the beginning of the 2013 season the railway announced a major project to build a replica of *Polar Bear*, the second locomotive delivered to the railway in 1905, and now preserved at the Amberley Chalk Pits Museum in West Sussex. Just six years later the finished locomotive arrived on the railway. It is seen here at Sea Lion Rocks on 18th September 2022.
Barry Edwards

←When the restored railway returned to Sea Lion Rocks in 1992, the track was laid around eight feet inland from the original 1896 track. The remains of the old track remain visible to this day, as does the substantial stone block, installed to prevent trains plunging into the sea lion pool below. This it did to great effect when *Polar Bear* collided with it in 1905. *Barry Edwards*

In 1921 the railway took delivery of two battery electric locomotives from British Electric Vehicles. They took the names of the two steam locomotives, that were put into store. Here we see the electric *Polar Bear* at Sea Lion Rocks. The original café building is on the right, the Zoo is beyond. *Manx National Heritage*

October 1984 bound for Cumbria. Tracklaying was completed as far as Lhen Coan station, to permit a repeat of the Santa trains. A second diesel locomotive was delivered to the line, along with the first coach, built on one of the former Dodington underframes. The two diesels were named *Dolphin* and *Walrus* and the Yuletide running was another outstanding success.

Work continued through 1985, whilst Tynwald passed the Groudle Glen Railway Order, which meant that the railway had to be inspected before any more passengers could be carried. The inspector called in November and issued a pass certificate, opening the way for 1,300 people to visit the line over Christmas.

February 1986 saw the steelwork for the new shed arrive in the Glen and, by the end of March, the 20ft by 50ft steel framework was in place. A second coach was delivered, and the temporary wooden shed was moved underneath the steelwork of the new one. On 25th May 1986, to the delight of the Isle of Man Steam Railway Supporters' Association volunteers and to the sound of Rushen Silver Band, *Dolphin* was driven through a white tape, by Mrs Carolyn Rawson, daughter of the late Dennis Jeavons who had conceived and developed the Groudle Glen holiday village. After 24 years the Groudle Glen Railway was now officially open again, probably in better condition than it had ever been before. Trains ran every Sunday for the rest of the year, with the Santa trains attracting 1,600 people.

Early 1987 was spent completing the new running shed, ready for the season, the highlight of which was the return of *Sea Lion* to the railway on 8th September. Steam was raised for the first time in 25 years on 21st September and an official handing over ceremony took place on 3rd October. The now annual Santa specials were steam hauled for the first time.

the Island in March 1983. Meanwhile, 150 tons of ballast had been delivered in the glen, and track laying was completed from Headland to Lime Kiln Halt.

Towards the end of 1983, the volunteers could wait no longer. They set up a Santa's grotto in the engine shed at Headland and on 18th December 550 people rode between Lime Kiln Halt and the grotto, the first passengers to travel on the line for 21 years. Two of the Fauld wagons were used, hauled by one of the diesel locomotives, specially named *Rudolph* for the day. Boxing Day saw more Santa specials and a further 200 visitors.

Track laying had reached halfway to Lhen Coan by mid-1984 and, as the Apprentice Training Centre at BNFL Sellafield had offered to carry out all remaining restoration work on *Sea Lion*, the locomotive left the Island once again in

During the reconstruction of the railway in the early 1980s, the railway purchased two Hudson Hunslet diesel locomotives, along with other rolling stock and track from the former Doddington House Railway. Built in 1952, the locomotives continue to serve the railway well. No.1 *Dolphin* was given a thorough refurbishment over a few years and was re-launched on 8th May 2022. It is seen here at Sea Lion Rocks on re-launch day. *Barry Edwards*

↑In 2006 a replica BEV locomotive was delivered from Alan Keef. Named *Polar Bear*, it is awaiting departure from Sea Lion Rocks with a train for Lhen Coan on 8th May 2022. *Barry Edwards*

↓The line also has an EE Baguley locomotive dating from 1947. It was completely rebuilt after arrival at the railway and named *Maltby*, after Richard Maltby Broadbent, who built the railway. *Dolphin* is on the right. *Barry Edwards*

Shortly after leaving Sea Lion Rocks, *Sea Lion* is heading for Lhen Coan with a complete rake of four-wheeled coaches, on 18th September 2022. These are all replicas but much of the metalwork was rescued from the derelict coaches in the Glen. *Barry Edwards*

The pointwork into the station loop at Sea Lion Rocks is just visible in this view of *Sea Lion* arriving with just three of the original style four-wheeled coaches, on 5th July 2009. *Barry Edwards*

Restoration work continued between running trains with, in 1988, the completion of run-round facilities at Lhen Coan and thoughts turning to the reinstatement of the line to Sea Lion Rocks. Cosmetic work included a start on the building of a replica station canopy at Lhen Coan.

During late 1990, after much negotiation and the purchase of a strip of land from a local farmer, work started on the extension of the line to its original terminus at Sea Lion Rocks. A mechanical digger shifted tons of soil, moving the railway ledge further inland. Track laying commenced in early 1991, continuing throughout the year and on into 1992. New fences were erected around the cliff edges at Sea Lion Rocks to prevent accidents, the finishing touches being made to the track work during March. Diesel locomotive No.1 *Dolphin* operated a test run over the new track on 29th March, then permission was given by the Railway Inspector for public services to commence.

Test runs in early April brought the return of *Sea Lion* to the terminus for the first time in 53 years, with public services commencing on Easter Sunday, 19th April. The extension was officially reopened on Saturday 23rd May 1992 by Mr James Cain, Speaker of the House of Keys and Chairman of the Manx Heritage Foundation, the 96th anniversary of the railway first opening to the public.

Polar Bear had left the Island in 1967, going to the now closed Brockham Museum in Surrey, where restoration commenced. Following the transfer of much of the equipment from there to the Amberley Chalk Pits Museum in West Sussex, this work was completed, and *Polar Bear* saw occasional operation, alongside many other interesting narrow gauge railway exhibits. A further complete overhaul was completed in July 1993, prior to a visit to the Island.

The replica overall station roof at Lhen Coan was completed in early 1993 and at the request of the Railway Inspector, substantial barriers were erected at Sea Lion Rocks to prevent passengers falling over the steep cliff edges. The visit of *Polar Bear* along with three original style four-wheeled coaches no doubt contributed to the 13,000 passengers carried on the railway in 1993, a 136% increase on the previous year. A third new bogie coach entered service, while electric lighting was installed at Lhen Coan for the sheds and station.

Two visiting locomotives *Rishra* and *Chaloner* operated on the railway for part of the 1995 season, as part of the 'International Railway Festival' celebrating the centenary of the Snaefell Mountain Railway. A new loop was installed at

The current café building at Sea Lion rocks is visible in this image of *Sea Lion* heading towards Lime Kiln Halt and Lhen Coan with two of the 2014-built bogie coaches. The original track is just visible to the right of the train on 27th July 2016. *Barry Edwards*

Former Doddington diesel locomotive, now No.2 *Walrus* is leaving the Headland Loop, while taking two of the new bogie coaches towards Sea Lion rocks on 12th May 2019. The Isle of Man Steam Packet Company fast craft *Manannan* is seen in the distance heading for Liverpool. *Barry Edwards*

0-4-0 Saddle tank locomotive *Otter* was delivered to the railway in early 2019. Kept a secret until immediately before delivery, the locomotive has proved very capable. It is seen at the Headland Loop with a well loaded train for Sea Lion Rocks on 9th June 2019. *Barry Edwards*

Sea Lion was delivered to the railway in 1896, and as part of the restoration of the line, was restored by BNFL apprentices at Sellafield and returned to the railway in late 1987. She is seen heading through the Headland Loop on 22nd May 2016. *Barry Edwards*

The railway's second locomotive, *Polar Bear*, arrived from W G Bagnall in 1905. Now preserved at the Amberley Chalk Pits Museum, it visited the railway in 2016 as part of the 120th Birthday celebrations. She is seen at Headland on 27th July 2016 with the replica four-wheeled coach set. *Barry Edwards*

On 24th August 1962, *Polar Bear* has run round its short train and is preparing to return to Lhen Coan. This was the terminus at that time, due to a serious rock fall beyond the loop. The locomotive and train are painted in what is known as the fairground livery, a bold attempt to try and boost passenger numbers. *Barry Edwards Collection*

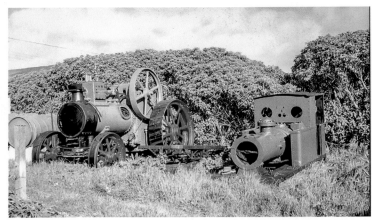

↑A pleasant study of *Polar Bear* in a green livery and looking rather tatty, the locomotive is leaving the Headland Loop and heading for Lhen Coan. The picture is dated in the late 1950s. *Barry Edwards Collection*

↗Following removal from the railway after the initial closure, *Sea Lion* spent some time at the Kirk Michael Steam Centre, before moving to Loughborough. It is seen here looking a little sorry for itself. *Barry Edwards Collection*

→A scene typical of the situation that greeted the restoration team in the early 1980s. The Headland track had been taken over by vegetation. Thankfully, the team were not put off and hence we can all enjoy the wonderful railway that operates today. *Travel Lens Photographic*

Working out on the Headland during the restoration could be testing. On a reasonable day in June 1984, former RAF Fauld wagon No.179 and a spare bogie chassis from Doddington are in use for re-instatement work. *Barry Edwards*

Headland during the 1995/96 winter. *Sea Lion* was moved to the Steam Railway workshops in Douglas on 7th October 1995 for its ten-year overhaul, while plans were in hand for the Groudle's own centenary in 1996 and another visit of *Polar Bear*.

Sea Lion went on a tour on the mainland during May 1997 visiting the Festiniog Railway, Amerton Farm Railway in Staffordshire and the Leighton Buzzard Railway, operating service trains at the latter two. The locomotive returned to service at Groudle on 1st June.

Work on a second replica four-wheeled coach got underway at the workshops of Harold Flavell towards the end of 1997, this along with the first replica and a coach from Lytham St Annes, made up a train of three as originally used on the railway. Also nearing completion was a replica of 1911 W. G. Bagnall locomotive *Annie* and, following testing, she made her first passenger trip on 28th June. Visiting locomotives for the 1998 season were *Jonathan* and *Peter Pan*.

The second Flavell-built replica 1896 style coach entered service on 8th May 1998 and a third was started. After much negotiation, planning consent was received for a building at Sea Lion Rocks on the site of the original 1896 structure. Work on the building started soon after consent was received. Later that month the railway mourned the sudden death of the steam engineer and long-term member Alistair Lamberton.

Sea Lion, having completed 15 years' service was treated to a full overhaul and new boiler at the Ross-on-Wye works of Alan Keef Ltd, at the beginning of the 2002 season. The following winter the locomotive lost its light green livery in favour of a Brunswick green.

The line's motive power fleet enjoyed the addition of a replica of one of the BEV electric locomotives, converted at the works of Alan Keef from a 1990's-built battery electric locomotive from the same manufacturer as the originals. It

↑↑*Annie* was built by one of the railway volunteers in 1998. She is seen arriving at Lime Kiln Halt with a train of two of the 1980's bogie coaches, on 27th May 2012. *Barry Edwards*

↑The Groudle Glen Railway is known as 'the Line that goes uphill to the sea'. *Sea Lion* is making the climb towards Lime Kiln Halt on 18th May 2008 with a shortened train of replica four-wheeled coaches. *Barry Edwards*

←A 1993 view of *Sea Lion* beginning the climb through the Glen with two of the bogie coaches. *Richard Kirkman*

Having run through the Glen, the line emerges on the approach to Lhen Coan. *Sea Lion* is making the approach on 13th July 2016 and has just passed the junction giving access to the main rolling stock shed. *Barry Edwards*

was inaugurated on 8th August 2004 and named *Polar Bear*. Before being transported to the Island the replica was exhibited at the York Railfest from 28th May to 6th June, arriving on the Railway on 7th July. The line played host to visiting locomotive *Taffy* from the collection of Patrick and Alan Keef later the same month.

The station at Lime Kiln received a new shelter over the 2004/05 winter and the whole area was tidied up and enhanced. 2005 marked the 100th birthday of the original Groudle locomotive *Polar Bear*, now at the Amberley Chalk Pits Museum in Sussex. To celebrate the occasion, it was arranged that the Island-based *Sea Lion* should travel to Amberley at the beginning of July, returning on 16th July with *Polar Bear*, the latter spending two weeks at Groudle before returning home to West Sussex. The third replica 4-wheeled

coach arrived at Groudle from the workshops of Harold Flavell on 22nd July 2005.

Relaying and replacement of the former Donnington rail saw the section between Blue Lagoon and Lime Kiln Halt completed during the 2006/07 winter. A new steam outline diesel locomotive arrived on the line in early 2007.

Planning permission was sought for the construction of a new locomotive shed at Lhen Coan in February 2007. Based on the original design the 9m x 4.8m and 4.03m high two track shed would have a concrete floor with pits and a workshop area. Work on the new engine shed started soon after planning permission had been received. The main structure was supplied by Kingsland Stabling of Leominster and was completed and erected by them on site in June 2007. The shed was officially opened later that summer. 2007 marked the 25th anniversary of the beginning of the restoration of the line, and by way of a celebration a special running day was held during August.

The railway adopted a newly designed crest, similar in appearance to that of the Isle of Man Railway and used for the Groudle centenary. Transfers were applied to the sides of most items of stock.

At the end of 2007 Harold Flavell a stalwart of the restoration of the line, finally retired. Sadly just a few months later Harold died at his home aged 80. He was responsible for the construction of all the early sheds and equipment boxes, the booking office, shop, catering unit and many other smaller items for the restored railway. The second and third red bogie coaches came from his workshop as did the three replica four-wheeled coaches, utilising as many original metal parts as possible. He had finished fabricating the parts for a fourth four-wheeler.

Throughout 2008 preparations were made for the

The annual Santa trains at Groudle are very popular with passengers. Two locomotives top and tail the full rake of 2014 bogie coaches. Here *Sea Lion* departs from Lhen Coan with a full complement of children clutching their parcel collected from Father Christmas on 15th December 2019. *Barry Edwards*

installation of a new shop at Lhen Coan, the building arriving on the site in kit form towards the end of the season. Amongst the regular track maintenance during the winter the new building was put together and finished off, providing a walk-in shop as opposed to the kiosk style it replaced.

On 6th March 2009, just as the beginning of the new season was in sight, the news broke of the death of Tony Beard. Tony had for nearly 30 years been the voice of Groudle and was one of the original band of enthusiasts who believed that it could be done. Indeed, it could, and Tony was always there in the thick of it and there is no doubt that he is sadly missed down in the Glen.

The railway celebrated its 125th anniversary on 23rd May 2021. *Sea Lion* and *Brown Bear* posed side by side at Lhen Coan ahead of the formal speeches and as is customary at Groudle, the cake cutting. *Barry Edwards*

A view of the Lhen Coan station building before it was demolished. The image taken in the late 1960s looking towards the head shunt, shows the tracks still in place. *Travel Lens photographic*

The line enjoyed a buoyant season with passenger numbers up on 2008, the new shop was partially opened in July while plans to extend the Sea Lion Rocks building were announced. The summer evening operation was combined with the Manx Electric service and through tickets offered, a combination that worked well.

The usual winter relay programme commenced shortly after the season ended, briefly stopping for the annual Santa trains, while plans for the 2010 timetable include operating on Saturdays in the high summer as well as on Sundays. The fourth four-wheeled replica coach arrived at Groudle from the Laxey Village Workshops on 17th July, entering service shortly afterwards. Following a good season, the 2010 Santa Train were disrupted by severe snow, so at very short notice trains ran on New Year's Day to cater for those who had missed out. A major relay took place at the headland over that winter, the work sufficiently completed in time to operate the 2011 Easter Bunny trains. The work included the installation of a new siding to facilitate moving stock on and off the line.

After a normal season in 2012, the railway launched two major projects in 2013. While the line's other original locomotive, *Polar Bear*, is fully restored and operational at the Amberley Chalk Pits Museum in West Sussex, it is unlikely that it will return to the line full time. That has led the railway to embark on the construction of an identical locomotive, to be named *Brown Bear*. At the same time, replacement of the three coaches dating from the 1980's was becoming necessary. Laxey Village workshops was commissioned to construct three new coaches onto new underframes build by Midcam Engineering, the project getting underway in early 2014. The new coaches were launched by His Excellency the Lieutenant

Polar Bear, the second of the original locomotives, has made several trips back to the railway from its home in West Sussex. She is seen here alongside *Sea Lion* outside the rolling stock shed at Lhen Coan after an evening running session in 1993. *Barry Edwards*

Governor on Saturday 13th September 2014. Featuring disabled and wheelchair accommodation, the three coaches look superb and will no doubt serve the railway for many years to come. The work on *Brown Bear* proceeded well and the frames and wheels were transferred to John Fowler & Sons in Cumbria for the locomotive to be completed.

Brown Bear returned to the Island on the *Ben-my-Chree* on 8th July 2019. The locomotive was steamed immediately after arrival in the glen and made its first trips along the line later the same day.

The battery electric locomotive *Polar Bear* was shipped to John Fowler & Sons on 20th July 2020 for a rebuild, despite the ongoing Covid-19 movement restrictions. A new braking system was fitted, and a full overhaul completed; the locomotive was repainted before returning to the Island.

The 2020 season eventually started in July and trains ran until the end of September. Similar delays at the start of the 2021 season, the 125th anniversary year, caused the cancellation of the Easter Bunny trains due to the Covid-19 restrictions. The railway was able to celebrate its 125th birthday with a huge family fun day and treasure hunt on Sunday 23rd May. The track at Lhen Coan was completely re-laid in the weeks leading to the anniversary event.

The Groudle Glen Railway is now in stronger health than at any time in its history. Services operate on Sundays from May to September, and on Wednesday evenings in the peak season. The popular Easter Bunny and Santa Special trains supplement the summer timetable.

A view inside the rolling stock shed at Lhen Coan on 27th March 2016, following refurbishment in early 2016. Diesel locomotive No.2 *Walrus*, the Steamplex, and *Parracombe*, now *Maltby*, are in the shed. The new floor incorporates an inspection pit, allowing running gear inspections to be undertaken without the need to lift rolling stock. *Barry Edwards*

The 125th Anniversary cake on display at Lhen Coan station on 23rd May 2021. *Barry Edwards*

GREAT LAXEY MINES RAILWAY

On the Isle of Man, the extensive ore mines at Laxey had several small tramways running in the underground tunnels, initially employing horses to move the wagons. The mines were formed on a mineral lode running north-south under Glen Mooar, a tributary of the Laxey valley, with workings eventually stretching to some 2,200 feet underground. The shafts included the Engine shaft, which was kept clear of water by pumps powered by the Lady Isabella, the Welsh shaft, where a man lift was installed in 1881 to allow miners to access the lower parts of the mine, and the Dumbell's shaft, which accessed the deepest part of the mine. Workings and levels extended outwards from these shafts along the lines of the mineral veins. The Adit entered the workings below the Laxey Wheel and reached 1½ miles into the hillside, joining the various shafts and providing an exit route for the mined ores.

Ore mining at Laxey dates to around 1780, but the early years of the mines were not successful. The Kirk Lonan Mining Association was formed to work the mine in 1822 and over 200 people were employed by 1833, when profits were made for the first time. In 1849 the Mining Association was reformed as the Great Laxey Mining Company. The low-level workings were constantly flooded, leading to the construction of a waterwheel, the largest in the world, to power new pumps and solve the problem. The waterwheel was christened the 'Lady Isabella' and set in motion for the first time on 27th September 1854.

In 1862 the company became the Great Laxey Mining Company Ltd. Production peaked in 1875 when 2,400 tons of lead ore and 11,753 tons of zinc ore were mined, the latter being almost half of UK output.

By the mid 1880's the mines were competing with cheaper imported ores, the quality and value of the ore was declining, and equipment was worn out. A gradual decline began, and the company was restructured as Great Laxey Ltd in 1903 but went into liquidation in 1920 despite bringing new capital and machinery. Mining continued until 1929 when the Great Laxey Mine closed for the final time, bringing an end to the Manx mining industry.

The Laxey mine systems were served by two tramways.

The horse powered Glen tramway transferred ore to Laxey harbour for onward shipment and brought materials for the mine back up the valley from the harbour. Construction of the single track 3 ft gauge tramway was completed in 1871, with track laid from the washing floors down the Glen Road to the harbour, with sidings laid in Jack Yard and onto the pier. Eighteen waggons were noted in use on the tramway by 1922, but the line closed shortly thereafter and was lifted in 1924. No traces of the Glen tramway remain, although part of the route is marked in white cobbles in the Valley Gardens.

The Adit level of the Great Laxey mine was worked from the early years of the nineteenth century, through to closure in 1930. The tramway at the 'Cross Cut Adit', the entrance to which is still visible on the riverbank opposite Laxey Fire station, dates to 1823. Human power was used until April 1827, when the mine owners employed their first pony. As the

↓This early image shows one of the two original locomotives and an ore wagon, along with three of the mine workers. The locomotive has no nameplate, while there appears to be some sort of loading device. *Barry Edwards Collection*

→Forming part of the display around the Laxey wheel site, is this ore wagon sitting in one of the tunnels that led into the mine. Hard hats are provided. *Barry Edwards*

mine expanded so did the number of ponies, reaching five by 1846; these were stabled behind the present Mines Tavern. The growing volume of material being handled prompted the building of new washing and dressing floors, and the line was extended to its current terminus in Valley Gardens in 1848. By 1855 the tramway had been taken over by a private concern, who received 7d for each full wagon of ore moved from the mine. The mine company later took the line back under their control.

The tramway continued to expand; 30 new wagons were purchased in 1873 and the number of ponies increased to nine. In the first six months of 1873 some 27,528 wagons of ore were brought out of the mine, equivalent to 177 each day or almost 20 for each horse.

The ponies were replaced by steam traction in 1877. Small fires were lit within the mine to determine the impact of smoke emissions from the locomotives. The experiment was successful, so new locomotives were ordered from Stephen Lewin of Poole, Dorset, to the odd gauge of 19 inches, and much of the track re-laid to accommodate the locomotives' additional weight. The two locomotives arrived together by steamer on 6th April 1877. Named *Ant* and *Bee*, they had works nos. 684 and 685. These tiny machines were just 8′7″ long, 3′0″ wide and 4′9″ high. They had solid 14-inch diameter wheels with wooden brake blocks on the rear set of wheels and drivers standing within the rear frames; the two locomotives entered service in the mine during May 1877.

Several local modifications appeared on the locomotives over the years, probably undertaken by their drivers, but their overall condition deteriorated to the extent that their replacement was actively considered. Quotes were sought in early 1905 and Bagnall's, no doubt keen to access the potential market for locomotives on the Island, even got as far as producing detailed drawings in May 1905. The cost proved prohibitive, so the existing fleet was overhauled with Bagnall receiving the contract to build new boilers. One of the boilers was removed and shipped to the Bagnall workshops as a pattern in mid-1905. The first new boiler arrived at a cost of

One of the many, thought to have been about 200, ore wagons is on display in a garden at Laxey. It is seen here during 2019. *Barry Edwards*

A number of other wagons retrieved from the Mine by enthusiasts are stored by Manx National Heritage. *Barry Edwards*

↑ Taken in May 2006, the replica *Ant* heads into the tunnel with a train load of passengers for the Mines Yard. The driver will need to sit down to go through the very tight tunnel. *Barry Edwards*

→ To mark the Platinum Jubilee of the late Queen Elizabeth II, the roof of coach 1 was painted purple. The coach is seen here on 13th August. *Barry Edwards*

A popular event across all the railways on the Island, is Santa Trains. Here a snow machine is put to very good use, creating a suitably wintery scene at Valley Gardens. 28th November 2021. *Barry Edwards*

£53 and was fitted before the second was removed. The project was a success, and a second boiler was ordered and delivered by February 1906. One of the two locomotives also received a new chimney.

Ore from the mine was transported in chunky four-wheeled wagons, built on a cast-iron underframe; they were unsprung and unbraked and stood just three feet high. The bodies were hinged to the underframe to allow the ore to be tipped out on reaching the washing floors. A fleet of up to 200 wagons were used in the mine at once, most of which were built in the mine's own workshops, although some underframes were bought in. A train usually comprised of six or seven wagons.

The locomotives hauled wagons into the mines and propelled them out to prevent the smoke blinding the driver, with the employee responsible for tipping wagons usually riding in the first or last wagon. An ingenious uncoupling method using a chain across the boiler of the locomotive enabled the driver to uncouple the wagons without leaving his driving position.

Trains operated for 16 hours each day, with crews working eight hours shifts starting at 06:00 and finishing at 22:00 with a changeover at 14:00. The early turn crew were required to prepare the train and load equipment required in the mine in readiness for the first train of the day.

The tramway ran over the top of one of the vertical shafts within the mine, requiring substantial timberwork to support the weight of a full train, although the line went round the top of other shafts.

On leaving the mine, the line ran through a tunnel under the heaps of waste material – the 'deads' – and then passed through another tunnel under the Laxey to Ramsey road and the Manx Electric Railway, before emerging onto the upper level of the washing floors, terminating close to where the line's current carriage shed is situated.

The line operated up to the end of the 1920s but, in early 1930 the diminutive locomotives were locked away in their shed and left. Sadly in 1935 they were both broken up for scrap and the little line closed for good, or so it seemed. Several the original wagons survive and were brought to the surface by the Manx Mines Research Group in the early 1970s. Two are now on display at the Manx Museum and one in the Mines yard at Laxey. Some examples of rails survive in use as fence posts, particularly around the Machine House.

Restoration of the line between the Valley Gardens and the Adit was proposed by actor and one-time Laxey resident Michael Billington during the early 1980s. His project failed following opposition from residents and the Manx Electricity Authority, which had an electrical transformer in the tunnel at the start of the line. Further plans to restore a short length of the line were announced by Laxey and Lonan Heritage Trust in 1999 following the removal of the transformer. A donation from the estate of former Ramsey resident Lt Col Randolph Glen funded much of the infrastructure, allowing a replica engine shed to be completed in 2003, and the construction of working replicas of both the *Ant* and the *Bee* to be commissioned from Great Northern Steam Ltd of Darlington; the replica *Ant* was delivered to the railway in April 2004. Six replica wagons were built by the Laxey blacksmith. Work to build a concrete buttress to support the Manx Electric Railway and main road above the new Great Laxey Mines Railway station were completed, allowing work on the locomotive shed to be completed. The formal opening of the Great Laxey Mines Railway – as the venture was now known – by the Hon Steve Rodan MHK, chairman of the Laxey and Lonan Heritage Trust, took place on 25th

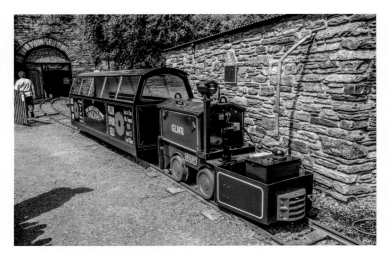

In 2009 the railway purchased this 1973 Clayton battery electric locomotive. Painted into this green livery, it is named *Wasp*, to keep the theme of locomotive names on the line. The locomotive is seen here with coach 1 on 11th July 2020. *Barry Edwards*

Coach 2 is propelled through the glen by *Ant* while working towards Mines Yard on 13th August 2022. The design of the coaches is dictated by the need to be able to evacuate a train inside the tunnel if necessary. *Barry Edwards*

Another popular event is the annual Hop-tu-Naa trains, the very narrow tunnel lending itself to be suitably decorated. Coach 2 propelled by *Ant* heads into the tunnel. Who knows what surprises are in store for the passengers. *Richard Kirkman*

Ant emerges from the tunnel and rounds the tight curve into the Valley Gardens station, with coach 1 on 8th May 2016.
Barry Edwards

The two replicas, *Ant* and *Bee* captured at Valley Gardens station during a busy day on 21st July 2012.
Barry Edwards

Having emerged from the tunnel under the Manx Electric Railway and the main A2, Douglas to Ramsey road, the line runs along the side of the valley. Coach 2 has a full load of passengers on 11th July 2020. *Barry Edwards*

During 2021 the railway launched a project to replace the fleet of ore wagons. An appeal was launched to gain sponsors for the project, and construction started during 2022. The chassis and frames of the first of the wagons is seen here under construction. *Paul Marshall*

September 2004, as part of the Laxey Wheel's 150th anniversary celebrations.

The western end of the line was extended to a new terminus opposite the Laxey fire station for the 2005 season, making the total length of the line just over a quarter of a mile, while a revised track layout at the Glen Gardens end allowed easier shunting of the locomotives.

The first Hop-tu-Naa (Halloween) trains were operated on 22nd October 2005, with the coach decorated with suitable spiders etc. and the tunnel adorned with skeletons and witches painted onto boards attached to the tunnel sides. Special lighting enhanced the spookiness. A siding was added at the outer end of the line before Christmas 2005, adding the flexibility to operate more than one train. Meanwhile plans were drawn up to relay and move the Glen terminus to a site parallel with the main road.

The railway enjoyed a good season in 2006 with growing passenger numbers, the highlight being the official starting of the former Snaefell mine waterwheel in the Valley Gardens on Sunday 20th August when the railway operated trains until 21:00. The Hop-tu-Naa trains were repeated, again attracting considerable numbers of passengers. The performance of *Ant* proved severely disappointing during 2006. An inspection of the locomotive at the end of the season resulted in the locomotive leaving the railway for the Alan Keef works on 13th January 2007. A highly successful appeal raised funds for a second passenger coach, ordered from Alan Keef in February 2007. This was delivered on 8th August 2007; seating nine or ten it had additional glazing behind the passenger seat, running lengthwise inside the coach. The existing coach was repainted over the 2007/08 winter having carried 21,000 passengers over the first three seasons of operation.

Meanwhile work on a new carriage shed and relocation of the Valley Gardens terminus started in October 2006 following planning approval; the two platform tracks and pointwork at the entrance to the tunnel were completed in February 2007, although the joining curve was not finished. The coach moved from its tunnel storage to the shed after track laying on 10th March. An extension to the siding at Mines Yard was also planned. The *Ant* returned to the railway in July 2007, and plans were formulated to send the *Bee* for similar treatment. The railway enjoyed another good season, with several special events bringing large numbers of passengers.

The new Valley Gardens station was operational in time for the 2008 season. In May 2009 the first non-steam locomotive arrived on the line, allowing trains to be operated quickly if demand required. Built by Clayton in 1973, the locomotive was previously owned by a construction company, and refurbished by Alan Keef before arriving on the Island. It was given the name *Wasp*, continuing the railway's locomotive naming theme.

The continuing unsatisfactory performance of the two replica locomotives, led to *Ant* being dismantled for a detailed boiler inspection. This led to the decision to replace both locomotive boilers and an order was placed with Alan Keef. *Ant* was not reassembled, work concentrating on getting *Bee* through its test in readiness for the 2011 season. *Bee* passed its test at the end of the 2010 season and was used for the annual Hop-tu-Naa trains. The two new boilers arrived on the Island on 15th April 2011; *Ant*'s was fitted first, and she re-entered service whilst *Bee* was withdrawn for her boiler to be fitted. The boilers significantly increased the reliability of the two locomotives.

The restored line celebrated its 10th birthday on 27 September 2014, when historian Andrew Scarffe drove the special anniversary train for the volunteers. There was of course a cake!

In 2021, the railway launched a project to replace the six replica ore wagons with six new ones, utilising several parts from the original vehicles. An appeal to sponsor a wagon resulted in sufficient funding being made available for all six wagons, to be built. The project got underway in the latter months of the year with completion of the first wagon expected in 2022 and all six during 2023.

The Great Laxey Mine Railway is now owned, operated,

and maintained by volunteers from the Laxey and Lonan Heritage Trust, a registered Manx Charity, which was formed in 1997 to promote the rich industrial and natural histories of Laxey Village and Lonan Parish. The Railway now operates every Saturday from Easter until the end of September, with Hop Tu Naa ghost trains running on the last two weekends of October. Christmas trains normally run over the last weekend of November to coincide with the Laxey Christmas Market. Passengers can travel from the terminus in the Valley Gardens, close to the site of the Washing Floors, through the island's only railway tunnel, and along the historic route over which the metal ore was once carried. The Laxey Wheel is a short walk from the line's terminus.

Bee poses with coach 1 at Mines Yard station in a brief pause between trips, on 26th September 2020. The footpath to the left of the image leads to the Lady Isabella wheel. *Barry Edwards*

Ant brings coach 1 towards Valley Gardens through the tranquil glen, on 11th May 2019. This would have been a very busy place back in the days of the active mine. *Barry Edwards*

THE CROGGA VALLEY RAILWAY

The Isle of Man's newest passenger-carrying railway is situated in the grounds of Crogga, an extensive Victorian Estate south of Port Soderick station. The 7¼″ gauge railway takes its name from the river that flows through the grounds and the valley in which it sits. The original owner, Nick Dodson, operated a short 7¼″ gauge railway round the garden of his home at Port-e-Vullen in the north of the Island, and this was dismantled when he moved to Crogga. The line was never intended to be open to the public on a regular basis and is currently owned by Chris Beauman.

Construction of the line began in 2001, the first task being to dig out and lay the concrete base for the locomotive shed, workshops and office. The main station and workshop area are adjacent to and visible from the Isle of Man Steam Railway between Port Soderick and Santon. Nick Dodson enlisted the help of Jack Dibnah, son of the late Fred Dibnah to build the railway. Following construction of the buildings, track was laid in the sheds and then outside, the whole station area being completed before track laying began towards the stable block, situated adjacent to the Old Castletown Road.

The line eventually reached the main road at the side of the lake, and plans were made by Chris Beauman to bridge the river and extend into the wooded area on the other side

of the lake. A run round loop was installed at the temporary terminus to allow trains to operate. Most of the point work was built on site by Jack Dibnah, although some was bought in.

Nick Dodson is the owner of several main line passenger coaches including the Pullman car *Pegasus*, now a regular part of the Orient Express train. This vehicle was rebuilt and refurbished before being allowed to operate back on the main line. This rebuilding left many original fittings spare and so the toilet, its panelling, and fittings at Crogga all came from this famous Pullman car.

An extension was planned to take the railway round the end of the lake through a short tunnel and into a new station. Groundwork was soon underway, and the new station area was prepared for track laying. Former Isle of Man Railway sleepers were used to build a retaining wall to hold up the ground for the new station. A decking-style platform was constructed with steps down to a waterside deck and landing point. A small locomotive and storage shed was provided at the new station, with three tracks and a traverser across the end to allow the release of the locomotive. The traverser was built from redundant former mobile office racking.

The track was laid towards the site of the bridge that would cross the river that feeds into the lake adjacent to the

The Crogga Valley Railway began life as a smaller system in a garden in Port e Vullen. Locomotive *Samastipur* runs light engine past the spectacular coastline. *Barry Edwards Collection*

←*Union Pacific 1776* awaits departure from Crogga Heights station with a Christmas event train for Lakeside, on 5th December 2020. *Barry Edwards*

↙The railway owns and operates this Lister petrol locomotive. It is normally used for permanent way duties. *Barry Edwards*

↓*Union Pacific 1776* arrives at Crogga Heights with a well loaded three-coach train on 22nd June 2019. *Barry Edwards*

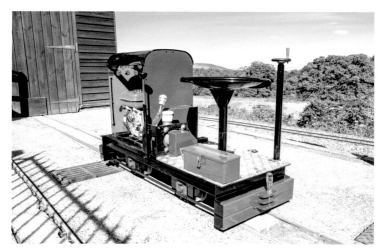

An early undated image of an unusual train formation passing Isle of Man Steam Railway No.8 *Fenella*. The leading locomotive is *Thomas*. *Barry Edwards Collection*

Departing from Lakeside station is *Santa Fe 98* on 22nd June 2019. The locomotive has a steep climb ahead. *Barry Edwards*

The same locomotive as in the opening picture in this section. This time it is climbing steeply past what is now known as Gym Junction. *Barry Edwards Collection*

↑The railway runs round the large lake at the estate. Here *Santa Fe 98* passes Boathouse Halt, the steps on the right lead down to the Boathouse. *Barry Edwards*

↗Captured in almost the same location as the previous image, *Santa Fe 98* has passed Gym Junction on 22nd June 2019. *Barry Edwards*

The line features this short tunnel, shortly before the trains arrive at Lakeside station. Here *Union Pacific 1776* brings its train towards the station on 4th December 2021. *Barry Edwards*

Old Castletown Road. The bridge was constructed over the 2006/07 winter, the first train completing the ¼ mile journey during the summer of 2007; a canopy was also added at the original station during that year. The passing loop below the stable block was then removed and what was a siding higher up the lawns became a passing loop. The steepest parts of the line now have a gradient of 1 in 31.

Some sections of the straight track were re-laid using six-metre lengths rather than the original four-metre lengths. Points are controlled by conventional drop over levers and the line has yet to receive any signalling. All the sleepers and ballast were sourced from supplies on the Island.

A Santa Fe diesel locomotive was delivered new in 2005 from Knightley Light Railway, near Stafford, England and has Works No. 2212. There is also a small Lister locomotive supplied by L. A. Services Ltd of Bramcote, Warwickshire, and several wagons. The line is also home to an impressive Garrett-style locomotive built by Chris Wedgwood. Based on the Tasmanian K1 class the locomotive is an 0-4-0 + 0-4-0 type; the prototype is now preserved on the Ffestiniog Railway, having been built by Beyer Peacock in 1909.

A tunnel was added to the line in 2013, and in mid-2015 a second American style diesel locomotive was added to the fleet. Considerably more powerful than 2212, it handles the steep gradients with ease. The railway plays a major part in the many special events that take place within the grounds of the estate and is operated by a dedicated volunteer crew.

Sections of the main line have now been doubled and turntables installed at both ends of the line, allowing the locomotives to be turned and released from their trains. The traverser in the shed area has been replaced by conventional pointwork.

The railway is only accessible by invitation or prior arrangement, as it is set in private grounds with access strictly by invitation only. All events are organised for charity and local community groups.

Lakeside station is set in woodland as well as being alongside the lake, albeit a bit higher up the embankment. *Union Pacific 1776* is captured between duties in April 2019. *Barry Edwards*

The railway operates an annual Christmas event, usually in early December. Here under the station lights, *Union Pacific 1776* has just arrived with a train from Crogga Heights. *Barry Edwards Collection*

WILDLIFE PARK MINIATURE RAILWAY

The Manx Steam and Model Engineering Club was formed in 1985 by a group of enthusiasts who had built several 5″ or 3½″ gauge live steam locomotives between them. After several seasons travelling around the Island with a portable dual gauge track, the decision was taken to look for a site where a permanent miniature railway could be built. Negotiations with the Government resulted in an agreement to build and operate a three gauge (3½″, 5″ and 7¼″) circular line within the Curraghs Wildlife Park, near Ballaugh.

Construction started in the late summer of 1991, and the 'Orchid Line' railway, so named because of the wild orchids growing in the park, was officially opened by the Chief Minister in May 1992. At first the railway consisted of a single-track circuit with a passing loop and a station. A steaming up area with a turntable was also constructed. The agreement with the Wildlife Park Authority required the railway to be open for the public every fortnight.

After two years of successful operation, the Club approached the Wildlife Park Authority and agreement was reached to extend the railway from its initial 550ft length to around 1,750ft. This was carried out in two stages. The first stage in 1996 created an additional circuit round the outside of the original; the second stage was completed in 1997 by laying a third circuit, south of the original and 1996 extension, creating a figure of eight. At this stage the locomotive stock had increased with the addition of four 7¼″ gauge locomotives.

↑ The Orchid line operates within the Curraghs Wildlife Park near Ballaugh. Visitors to the line will walk across the former route of the Manx Northern Railway as they enter the park. Here diesel locomotive *Maurice* departs from Wagstaffe Central on 30th October 2019. *Barry Edwards*

→ 0-4-0 tender locomotive *Alice* runs through the station area at Wagstaff Central on 19th July 2020, heading towards the Millennium extension of the railway. *Barry Edwards*

In 1999 the Club was given permission for a further extension of the line, bringing the total length to 3,042ft, by laying an extension through the wooded bog area called the Curragh, to the north of the original circle. The construction of this ambitious project was made possible by a grant received from the Mann 2000 Committee and a substantial private donation. The Millennium extension, as it has become known, opened in August 2000.

The railway is controlled by working signals throughout its length, the trains negotiating nine sets of points, two diamond crossings, five steel bridges and four level crossings, each controlled by authentic red flashing lights and buzzers. Each season, before operating commences, the track is inspected by a government-appointed railway inspector. All the trains are fitted with vacuum brakes and carry a guard.

Since the 1992 season passenger numbers have steadily increased passing an annual total of 15,000 during 2003. The railway carried its 100,000th passenger in August 2004, the

honour falling to Mr Robert Cannan of Wakefield who received a certificate and book token.

Just like the other railways on the Island, much of the track maintenance must be carried out during the winter months. One of the bridges across to the bog section had its track and decking removed to allow access to the main steel structure for cleaning and painting during the 2006/07 winter. At the same time additional rolling stock was built to boost the capacity of the line. Winter work for 2007/08 included the re-alignment of a 100-metre-long curve to accommodate six coupled locomotives, two of which arrived on the railway for the 2008 season.

After several years of successful operation, the complete

↖LNER outline 2-6-0 tank 1510 heads out of Wagstaff Central with a full load of excited passengers on 22nd July 2012. *Barry Edwards*

↑Driven by its owner, George B, an 0-4-0ST steam locomotive, runs through the station at Wagstaff Central on 3rd April 2022, while under test following some adjustments. *Barry Edwards*

Modelled on British Railways class 47 D1666, later 47606, *Odin* approaches one of the road crossings on the line before crossing a bridge and entering the millennium extension on 2nd May 2021. *Barry Edwards*

↑↑*Odin* again, this time leaving the Millennium extension and re-joining the original loop of the railway, on 19th May 2020. *Barry Edwards*

↗An early season view, captured on 22nd March 2015, shows *Maurice* leading a well loaded five-coach train. *Barry Edwards*

↑The first extension to the railway was to the south of the original loop, running round what is now the children's area of the park. Here *Maurice* passes under the footbridge on the final part of its journey round the park. *Barry Edwards*

→*Odin* passing the rear of the children's play area on 2nd May 2021. The train will soon pass the workshops for the railway. *Barry Edwards*

On special days the railway offers 'drive a train' experiences. This 0-4-0 battery electric locomotive number 93, *Denys*, is usually used for this. *Barry Edwards*

refurbishment of the station at Wagstaffe Central was undertaken during the 2014/2015 winter. Paving was re-laid with block paviours of varying styles, and all the wooden fencing replaced with vinyl. To celebrate this major refurbishment, His Excellency the Lieutenant Governor of the Isle of Man, Adam Wood, cut a ribbon at the station on 19th July 2015, before enjoying a short trip on the line.

The Railway inaugurated a cleverly designed passenger coach capable of being quickly adapted to convey a wheelchair. The central section of the longitudinal seat lifts off to allow the wheelchair to be loaded. Wooden ramps are provided to allow the chair to gain access. The coach was officially launched by the Minister for Health and Social Care on Sunday 5th August 2018, the first passengers were Charlene Creer and Natasha Moore.

A new carriage shed was commissioned during 2020, despite the restrictions caused by the Covid pandemic, avoiding the need for passenger coaches to be stored in the tunnel when not in use. Much of the trackwork has been re-laid over recent winters with a major project to replace the main pointwork at the departure end of Wagstaffe Halt

station being completed; the $3\frac{1}{2}''$ gauge rail was removed to simplify the new points as part of this project.

The Orchid Line run every Sunday from Easter to October and on Bank Holidays, and frequently runs on Thursdays during the school summer holidays. Trains and the traction engine run on some special events outside scheduled running times. All ticket proceeds go to the club's running costs, and all staff on the trains are volunteers.

←The team at the Orchid Line, keen to make the railway available to wheelchair bound passengers, designed and developed a passenger coach that could very quickly be converted to carry a wheelchair. The coach was officially launched on 5th August 2018 by the Minister for Health and Social Care and is seen here awaiting departure with its first passenger. *Barry Edwards*

←←During the winter of 2019/2020 this new rolling stock shed was built, eliminating the need to store passenger rolling stock in the Millennium extension tunnel. The completed building is seen on 19th July 2020. *Barry Edwards*

←A view inside the new shed, with a collection of rolling stock present, coach 8 nearest the camera. *Barry Edwards*

THE KNOCKALOE BRANCH

The fields at Knockaloe Moar farm near Patrick, just south of Peel, where was an established seasonal army camp when the site was selected as suitable for a detention camp for 'Enemy Aliens' on the outbreak of the First World War; it opened as such on 17th November 1914. The camp eventually grew to accommodate 23,000 internees and 3,000 guards in huts. Supplies initially reached the camp by horse and cart, but the scale of the operation soon made this impractical. The solution was to build a connecting branch line from the Isle of Man Railway to connect the camp with the port of Peel.

Construction of the new railway, which included a crossing of the river Neb, began in Summer 1915; it opened on 1st September 1915. The line left the main Peel to Douglas railway about 200 yards east of Glenfaba Mill, the junction being controlled by a patent Annett's key which locked the point work. The branch curved sharply south over the river Neb climbing at a remarkable 1 in 20 gradient. There was a passing loop on the curve between the junction and the Neb bridge where, for safety reasons, the engine ran around to the back of the train to push it up the gradient. The track continued across the field along the eastern side of the main Patrick road until turning sharply just before Patrick Church, crossing the main road, and entering the camp. It hugged the left-hand side of the main drive to its terminus at the camp headquarters. A second siding and passing loop was provided near Patrick, and there were several sidings within the camp. Two sidings were also laid along the East Quay to the start of the stone pier at Peel.

The only locomotive used on the branch was the 27-ton *Caledonia*, built by Dubs and Co of Glasgow in 1885 for the Manx Northern Railway, and the largest and most powerful locomotive on the Isle of Man. Numbered 4 during her Manx Northern Railway days she was re-numbered 15 upon acquisition by the Isle of Man Railway Company, and wore both numbers for a while.

The line was quickly put to work carrying supplies of fuel, food, general stores, and prison guards to the camp, and removing rubbish for disposal in Peel; prisoners were mad to walk to the camp from Peel station. Some rubbish was retained by the prisoners, large meat bones for instance were carved into figures for sale, many of which still exist and are collectively known as 'Knockaloe Ware'. Use of the railway peaked in 1916/17 when up to 18 trains of six 5-ton wagons were operated daily along the branch.

Some records suggest that it was intended to keep the locomotive in a shed at Knockaloe, but the chimney was too high to enter the shed, so the first two roof joists were sawn off to enable the engine to gain access! However, as the line did not go anywhere near the shed this does not appear to have been the case. Given that the traincrew would have been based in Peel it seems more likely that the *Caledonia* would return to Peel each evening to be stored out in the open, avoiding a long walk.

The railway was officially closed on 14th October 1920; the track was lifted during 1923/24 but in true railway fashion was re-laid on the Isle of Man Railway between Ballahick and Castletown, surviving until the 2002 relaying. The Annett's key was transferred to Poortown to be used for the quarry siding.

The impressive Isle of Man Centre for WW1 Internment, which links human stories and imagery with the camp location in an imaginative and interactive way, opened on 10th May 2019; it has an extensive model of the camp, including the railway. The Centre is in Patrick Old School close to the entrance to the Knockaloe site and is open from the end of May to September.

Manx Northern 4 *Caledonia* was the dedicated locomotive for the Knockaloe branch as she could handle the steep gradients with ease.
Camrose collection

PORT ERIN BREAKWATER RAILWAY

The railway was built to the GWR 'broad gauge' of 7'0¼", commonly used during breakwater construction work around Britain. Here we see locomotive *Henry B Loch* with a single wagon carrying the number N204132 and conveying some substantial lumps of stone. *Manx National Heritage*

Plans to protect the entrance to Port Erin Bay and provide a sheltered harbour were developed in the 1860s. Construction of a new breakwater began in 1863 with the Port Erin Breakwater Railway built to assist with the works. The line had the distinction of being the first steam railway on the Isle of Man and was the only railway on the island to utilise the 7′ 0¼″ broad gauge favoured by Isambard Kingdom Brunel on the Great Western Railway. This gauge was also popular on breakwater construction works around Britain at the time.

The locomotive brought to the island formerly worked on similar breakwater construction at Portland, and was named *Henry Brougham Loch* after the then Lieutenant Governor of the Island. It was an E B Wilson of Leeds-built 0-4-0 inside cylinder saddle tank (works no: 454), the tank only covering the rear third of the boiler. Existing images of the railway only show up to two wagons, one with a number N204132, however extensive research has not identified these vehicles. Substantial quarrying work was undertaken in the headland south of the harbour, and there was eventually over half a mile of sidings for the works. The works were completed in 1876, but the breakwater had a limited life and was destroyed in a storm in 1884.

Some photographs exist of the construction and locomotive; the latter spent a decade on the island, before heading to the ownership of Isaac Watt Boulton at Ashton-under-Lyne where it was converted to a portable or winding engine.

The availability of a sheltered harbour was a factor in the extension of the Isle of Man Railway from Castletown to Port Erin in 1874.

The remains of the breakwater can be seen at low water at the southwestern end of Port Erin bay; the quarried cliffs at this point give an indication of the volume of stone removed to facilitate construction of the breakwater. The line ran from the large workshops which stand on the south side of the Bay to the quarry and breakwater works.

The same locomotive, this time with two wagons, each well loaded with stone, stands on the wooden structure constructed over the new breakwater, from where presumably, the chunks of stone were dropped into position below the railway. The wooden structure does look a little precarious, given the weight being conveyed in the wagons. *Manx National Heritage*

THE CORRINS HILL TRAMWAY

There were several stone quarries on Peel Hill, but the largest and most important was the one on the coast at Contrary Head. Looking down on the site today we can see that a vast amount of stone was removed, most of which was used during the construction of Peel Breakwater. The problem, however, was that Contrary Head was not readily accessible from Peel or by sea, so a system of tramways was constructed. The first tramway started at the quarry at Contrary, this was an incline fed from three spurs at various levels in the quarry, operated by horses. A Horse Gin was built at the top of the incline and is still visible today. This consisted of a pit containing a large wooden drum; at the edge of the pit lay a circular walkway where the horses walked round in a circle, thereby turning the drum, and pulling the stone up the incline in metal trucks running on rails. The incline was around 100ft in length and can still be examined with care.

At the top of the incline was a three-foot tramway heading towards Peel, which became known as the Corrins Hill Tramway. It was first recorded on OS maps in the 1860s but may be much older and was the first surface railway on the Isle of Man; there were earlier systems at Bradda Mines, but these were underground. It is not known whether the Corrins

Hill system ran on metal or wooden rails. It took a level path towards Peel at around the 250ft contour, at times only a mere foot away from a sheer drop down to the sea. The trackbed now forms part of the Coastal Footpath and is well worth the walk, for those with a good head for heights. The track ran for just over half a mile, with two passing loops marked on the 1860 map. Once over the col at the northeast side of the hill a small excavation in the rock marks the site of another incline system down to the road below, just south of the former West Marine Boatyard. The ruins of the timekeeper's office and weighbridge can still be seen just north of the descent point by the road.

This incline was nearly 200ft in length and was 'self-activated', with the weight of the descending wagons pulling the empty wagons back to the top. There was a passing loop halfway down the incline. At the bottom of the incline lay yet another rail system; this was a 3ft gauge system that ran on metal rails leading directly to the workings at Fenella beach and on to the quay.

In 1864 there was great excitement in Peel, when an unidentified ship arrived at the port with a steam locomotive

→Looking up the steep incline from the quarry on Contrary Head to the tramway, showing the different levels in the workings. Horsepower was used to drag wagons up this incline. *Richard Kirkman*

→↗The tramway was cut into a shelf high above the sea as it led from the quarry to a second incline descent to Peel Harbour. This now forms part of the 'Rad-ny-Foillan' (Way of the Gull) coastal path around the Isle of Man. *Richard Kirkman*

→→The route of the 3ft gauge tramway is easily followed, despite being out of use for more than 150 years. *Richard Kirkman*

for use on the quay tramway system. It was not the sort of loco that would be familiar to us today, being a vertical boilered type with strange curved spoked wheels, somewhat resembling a mangle! Once thought to be a de Winton locomotive, it is now believed to be more likely built by Alexander Chaplin of Anderson, Glasgow, as such a machine was advertised for sale on the island in 1869. It was black in colour and soon named *Moddey Dhoo*, after the ghostly black dog said to haunt Peel castle. There is one known magic lantern slide of this locomotive depicting it near the locomotive shed on the quay.

The locomotive was hired to the Manx Northern Railway Company once the works at Peel were completed, to assist with the building of the Foxdale Railway and possibly the Manx Northern route itself. After finishing her work on the Island, *Moddey Dhoo* returned to the mainland for conversion to standard gauge, apparently ending her days back in Scotland.

The rusting remains of a wagon body were still extant at Contrary Head in 1992. The wallet gives an idea of scale. *Richard Kirkman*

The remoteness of Contrary Head quarry is evident in this view from the *Lady of Mann*, during a cruise to Peel. The tramway would have been essential for any substantial movement of stone to Peel, suggesting that the origins of the route date back to the 1840s. *Richard Kirkman*

TRAIE FOGOG MINERAL RAILWAY

Traie Fogog (Manx for Periwinkle Bay) is a small beach at the north end of Peel Bay, which was developed by Robert Archer as a swimming pool and opened in August 1896. A retaining wall allowed the pool to be filled with water at high tide. Archer was a draper who made money by renting towels to potential bathers; he was also responsible for the popular Port Skillion pool in Douglas. The facilities became extremely popular and were a regular venue for swimming galas. The pool was operated by Charlie Cain and Bertie Kelly from 1923, who added wooden changing facilities to replace tents on the beach. However, the site was only accessible by a steep path down from the Headland and this proved to be its downfall when erosion of the cliff face made access unsafe. The pool closed in 1943.

A considerable deposit of high-quality shingle lay to the north of the pool, reputed to be the best quality on the island. Cain and Kelly leased the foreshore and were able to extract the shingle for sale but faced the challenge of hauling the stone to the cliff top. They overcame this by attaching a steel wire to the top of the rock face on the adjacent headland and fixed a 5 cwt bucket to it. A stationary steam engine was housed in a shed on the headland, and the shingle was loaded into the bucket and hauled up to the top. A 2-foot gauge tramway led from here to a point above the end of Peel Promenade; a system of pulleys and wires powered by the steam engine drove three wagons along the short track. The wagons were tipped at the end of the track and the shingle dropped to the road below where it was collected by horse and cart and taken to Peel railway station for distribution.

The business prospered during the 1930s when shingle was used extensively during the alterations to the Queens Promenade in Douglas. But there was a finite amount of shingle on the beach. The volume of extraction was such that very little now remains, with estimates that the beach level was some six feet higher than at present prior to removal of the shingle.

The Isle of Man Railway also benefitted from the shipment of shingle and sand from the beach at White Strand, further north than Traie Fogog; this was much easier to extract and was taken by horse and cart to nearby St Germain's station for onward transportation, one of the few times St Germain's proved to be a useful asset! The traffic waned such that the siding at the station was removed in 1890, but it was restored in 1929 during the island's building boom; the growth in traffic was such the loading bank was extended further in 1931, but the traffic had ceased by the outbreak of the Second World War.

An early twentieth century view of the beach and swimming pool at Traie Fogog illustrates the height to which shingle had to be carried before reaching the tramway. The city of Peel lies in the far distance.
George Goodwin

GLENFABA BRICKWORKS PLATEWAY

Primitive railways existed long before the invention of the steam locomotive, indeed, traces remain from Roman times of flat top stone blocks that chariots ran along, guided by grooves cut into the blocks. In Britain the first evidence of anything like a railway dates back to 1555. Parallel baulks of timber were laid down to enable horses to pull heavy wagons near Barnard Castle in County Durham, and such wooden ways had become relatively common by the 1670s. Wooden baulks were superseded by iron plates around 1700, as these were less prone to wear under the action of the wagon wheels. These plateways became the standard form of tramway for the next 76 years. (The term name 'platelayer' was applied until recently to railway permanent way maintenance staff, originating from the gangers who laid down these early tramways.) The use of flanged wheels, as opposed to flanged 'plates' seems to have originated sometime in the 1730s at the Prior Park tramway, Bath. In 1776 the iron 'plates' were lifted at Sheffield's Nunnery Colliery and replaced by sections of angle iron laid parallel to each other to keep the wagons running truly along the track.

Why a plateway should have been laid at Peel brickworks as late as 1885 is something of a mystery, as it must surely be one of the last such plateways to be laid in Britain. The track was around 3 foot gauge with the flange positioned on the inside, the space between the plates being lined with reject bricks from the brickworks. The system started within the brickworks, and crossed the main Peel to Douglas railway at Mill Cottage through a two right angled sharp bends; bricks were laid on the crossing to assist the horses. The track followed the east bank of the river Neb, with a steep descent to the clay pit after crossing to the west bank. The clay was hand dug 50 to 60 feet down in the pit and was lifted, possibly by steam power, to be loaded for its journey to the brickworks. Trackwork was moved around within the pit as the need arose.

The plateway employed three horse drawn wagons, each with a one-ton bucket mounted on a wooden frame with a 24 inch wheelbase; the wheels measured 20 inches at the door end and 19½ inches at the fixed body end, with the thickness of the wheel tread being 2½ inches. The main plates were 6 ft long with shorter lengths for going round the curves; they were around one inch thick and were bolted down to wooden sleepers, spaced at 3 ft intervals. Each plate had two holes at each end and one in the middle.

Horses were supplied by the Keig family of Crown St, Peel. One of the best known and most loved was one named 'Blossom'. Accidents and derailments were frequent and, sadly, 'Blossom' was in collision with an Isle of Man Railway locomotive at Mill Road crossing on 28th August 1930 and killed instantly. Two similar accidents had occurred during

←The construction of the plateway is evident as an empty wagon leaves the brickworks. The flangeway is on the inside of the plateway and the centre line is filled with redundant bricks for the horse to walk on. *Manx Transport Heritage Museum*

←A plateway wagon complete with chains lies buried in the undergrowth; note the absence of flanges on the wheels. This is now in private preservation on the Isle of Man. *Barry Edwards Collection*

↓An example of 'plates' rescued from the river Neb by members of the Peel Heritage Trust. *Barry Edwards*

A heavily laden truck is hauled at right angles over the Isle of Man Railway line and into the brickworks. The crossing was the location of frequent accidents. *Manx Transport Heritage Museum*

A collar harness from one of the Glenfaba plateway horses, possibly Blossom. Fitted round the front of the leather collar, the harness featured two chains that passed either side of the horse; these were attached to a metal bar behind the horse, with a centre chain to haul the truck. The chains also had leather straps, one over and one under the horse's body around the saddle position. *Barry Edwards*

1926 when other horses were killed, with all three accidents blamed on brickworks employees. The man in charge of the horse for many years was Claude Cannell, who lived in the Gasworks House in Mill Road. Claude was apparently never spotted without a pipe firmly attached to his mouth. The last horse used on the system was called 'Prince' and was led by Fred Cannan.

The 'plates' were lifted after closure in 1945 and it is thought that most were melted down at Gellings Foundry in Douglas. A few were tossed into the river Neb, no doubt great fun for the local kids, and some of these were later rescued and retained. The wagons survived until the mid-1950s, and one truck chassis survives in private ownership on the Island. The route along the river Neb can still be followed, but the claypit is now flooded.

THE WEST BALDWIN RESERVOIR RAILWAY

As the town of Douglas grew rapidly in the latter years of the 19th century, the Corporation sought to safeguard water supplies for the expanding population and tourist industry. A reservoir was opened at Kerrowdhoo in 1893, but there was soon a requirement for more capacity. Plans to build a new reservoir at West Baldwin as the main water supply for Douglas were agreed in July 1899 and work commenced the following year.

The site was remote from existing railways and roads, so it was necessary for a connecting system to be built to bring materials and supplies to enable construction. Work started on a new 3ft gauge railway in October 1900, linking the new construction depot at Sir George's Bridge, Ballaoates, which had good road access to Douglas, with the reservoir construction site. Work was completed rapidly, although the route necessitated the building of nine timber bridges for the repeated crossings of the river Glass along the three-mile route, as the line ascended the West Baldwin valley. The line opened by late January 1901.

The Corporation was able to acquire an Andrew Barclay 0-4-0 saddle tank built in 1892 – used by the Isle of Man Tramway and Electric Power Co Ltd for construction of the Laxey-Ramsey route – for £350, along with 45 ballast wagons, two rail wagons and rails. The locomotive was purchased in October 1900 and named *Injebreck*.

The route was extended at the southern end in July 1901 to Ballacreetch, east of Sir George's Bridge, where there was a convenient supply of Puddle Clay that could be used as an impervious clay inner core to fill the trench then being dug at the reservoir site. The climb to Ballacreetch from Sir George's Bridge was steep, requiring trains to reverse on this new section.

The volume of traffic soon outpaced the capabilities of *Injebreck*, so the 0-6-0 saddle tank *West Baldwin* was purchased new in September 1901 from the Hunslet Engine Co of Leeds, at a cost of £925. A freak storm on 18th October 1901 closed the line for three weeks and put the works seriously behind schedule; several bridges were washed away, and labourers were diverted to reinstating the railway. The new 0-4-0 saddle tank *Ardwhallin* was purchased from the Hunslet Engine Co of Leeds later that month, at a cost of £610. The *Ardwhallin* was largely deployed on works within the reservoir bottom, moving earth to form the cladding around the clay core. By mid 1902 the *West Baldwin* was making up to 18 round trips daily to the worksite.

Resources were further supplemented In February 1903 by

0-6-0 ST *West Baldwin* (HE 758) at Battery Pier Douglas was the second loco acquired by the Corporation as the works reached their peak. She is about to be hauled to the railway by traction engine in September 1901. *Manx National Heritage*

→The diminutive 0-4-0 *Ardwhallin* as built, in an official Hunslet Engine Co photograph. *Hunslet Engine Co*

→→The *West Baldwin* as built (works no: 758), in another official Hunslet Engine Co photograph taken before leaving for the Isle of Man. She was numbered '2' on arrival in the Island. *Hunslet Engine Co*

↘The *Ardwhallin* was sourced in October 1901 to work within the reservoir site after heavy rains washed away the line and put the works behind schedule. She is seen in the sidings at St George's bridge, with the line's primitive passenger coach mounted on wagon chassis. The raised section of the coach was used by foremen and dignitaries. *Manx National Heritage*

↓The line's first loco *Injebreck* stands at the West Baldwin dam face in Douglas Corporation livery; note the wagons have their wheels centred under the chassis. The *Injebreck* was acquired from the Isle of Man Tramway and Electric Power Co Ltd at the start of the work programme after being engaged on tramway construction work. *Manx National Heritage*

→↘An interesting image shows the construction works for the Injebreck Reservoir in progress. One locomotive, *Ardwhallin*, is in the company of no less than 27 four-wheeled wagons. *Barry Edwards Collection*

a second-hand 0-4-0 saddle tank acquired from the Hunslet Engine Co and named *Hannah*. She took over works inside the reservoir assisting *Ardwhallin*, releasing *Injebreck* to help *West Baldwin* haul clay from Ballacreetch.

Supplies of local stone were by now exhausted and a new source was found at Hillberry, to the east of the existing extension. The line from Ballacreetch Clay fields was extended to Hillberry (Cronk Na Mona) Quarry with

another reversal to reach the quarry; the 1¼ mile extension opened in mid-February 1904, making the network now five miles in length.

The works were now nearing completion and rhe reservoir's inauguration ceremony took place on 6th September 1905; the locomotive fleet was gradually disposed of. The railway had been lifted by April 1905 with Hillberry Quarry partly filled in, and Ballacreetch clay field restored for farm use. Little trace now remains of this once intensively operated railway system.

MONORAIL TO PEEL

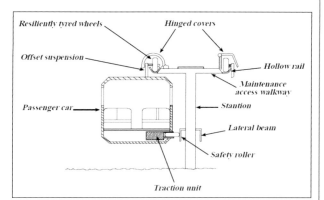

Peel lost its railway in 1968, and is the only sizable town on the Island not to have a rail link to the capital, made even more regrettable by poor road access, particularly when the main direct one is closed for racing purposes.

The relaying of the former Isle of Man Railway route to Douglas has been discussed many times in recent years, but with little progress.

Cyril Cannell, former Managing Director of Peel Engineering, designed and patented a new type of monorail in 2005, patent number GB2401089B, that could be erected quickly to provide a much needed rail link to the west coast. He proposed an elevated monorail – almost certainly the quietest, lowest cost, go anywhere, and quickly erected rail system, that could be mainly constructed by local engineering firms. Traction would have been by rack and pinion, allowing the line to run at ground level to minimise adverse visual impact but able to climb and descend where necessary to cross obstacles or for boarding. The project would have

brought long term and worthwhile benefit to the growing city of Peel, but sadly came to naught.

The monorail vehicle. *Barry Edwards Collection*

The simple mechanism would have enabled many Island firms to participate in construction work. *Barry Edwards Collection*

An impression of the lightweight monorail proposal for the Peel line. *Barry Edwards Collection*

THE MANX ELECTRIC RAILWAY

↓An interesting view of the north end of Douglas Promenade, prior to the construction of King Edward Road with Derby Castle seen in the foreground. It appears to have been taken prior to the construction of the Douglas Bay Horse Tramway, and therefore dates from before 1876. The houses behind which the Horse Tramway stables are now situated are visible. The Castle Mona Hotel building, visible in the distance, looks very lonely!
Manx National Heritage

The first plans for a railway from Douglas to Laxey and Ramsey came in 1882 with the formation of the Douglas, Laxey & Ramsey Railway Co., which proposed a line leaving the Isle of Man Railway Peel route at Quarterbridge, climbing steeply towards Onchan and thence to Laxey. This proposal came to nothing, the same fate as several other projects, including an adventurous plan to tunnel through Bank Hill with a line starting near the Isle of Man Railway terminus in Douglas.

In 1892, Alexander Bruce, Manager of Dumbells Bank in Douglas, and Frederick Saunderson, an engineer who had come from Ireland in 1865 and had connections with the family of Richard Rowe, Captain of the Laxey Mines, sought and were granted powers by Tynwald to develop Howstrake estate, an area to the north of Douglas, as a pleasure gardens. The powers included legal provisions to build an electric tramway to the northern boundary of the estate. The estate was purchased in the name of Mr Saunderson, with backing from Alfred Lusty, a wealthy London merchant who had retired to the Island and lived at Howstrake. Douglas Bay Estates Ltd was registered in September 1892 with a capital of £50,000, and construction of an electric tramway, the first stage of what is now known as the Manx Electric Railway, began quickly.

Electrification was carried out by Mather & Platt of Salford Ironworks, while G.F. Milnes of Birkenhead built the first three tramcars along with six trailers. At the southern end an inlet of the sea was filled in to enable the tramway to pass the site; the name Derby Castle was taken from a private dwelling which was taken over to allow construction of a ballroom and theatre complex. By May 1893 the power station and car sheds were being erected at Derby Castle, and a single track laid.

→Pretty much the only thing in this image that still exists is the tram and trailer. The entrance to the Derby Castle complex made way for the also now demolished Summerland complex, the Manx Electric Railway station awning was removed in the early 1980s. Tram 6, dating from 1894, and its unidentified trailer still operate on the Manx Electric Railway.
Trevor Nall Collection

To mark Her Majesty the Queen's Silver Jubilee, the Manx Electric Railway repainted open toastrack tram 25 with silver end panels and underframe. The tram is seen here at Derby Castle during August 1977. *Manx National Heritage*

An interesting view from above the Derby Castle terminus of the Manx Electric Railway and Douglas Bay Horse Tramway. A winter saloon, 19-22, tram is awaiting departure, while a trailer and van occupy the siding. A horse tram has just arrived from the Sea Terminal. *Manx National Heritage*

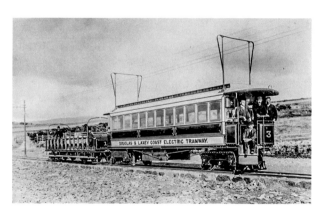

In 1899 the Manx Electric took delivery of three road/rail wagons from the Bonner Wagon Co. Here we see one of the wagons during the transfer from rail to road, using the raised road wheel ramps. *Manx National Heritage*

↑Two Manx Electric tunnel cars, 4-9, along with two trailers share the Derby Castle station area with four horse trams, tram 34 being nearest the camera. The impressive roof over the horse tramway tracks, destroyed as unsafe in the 1980s and the Derby Castle entertainment complex are clearly visible. *Manx National Heritage*

←An early picture of Manx Electric tram 3, taken before the line was doubled, so pre 1894. The tram has its bow collectors, these were removed in 1897. Tram 3 was destroyed in the Laxey shed fire in April 1930. *Manx National Heritage*

↑An image dating from before 1897 shows one of the original three motor trams coupled to 1894 trailer 22. The trailer has canvas side curtains, as delivered. The trailer was renumbered 39 in 1898 and destroyed in the Laxey shed fire in April 1930. *Manx National Heritage*

←An official view of the Derby Castle power station and lower tram shed, dating from 1894. *Barry Edwards Collection*

Steam locomotives were hired from the Isle of Man Railway during the construction of the Manx Electric Railway. This view shows locomotive 2 *Derby*, posed with a group of works just beyond the Princess Motors crossing in Laxey. *Manx National Heritage*

↓The Laxey shed fire of 5th April 1930 consumed eleven trams including power cars 3,4, 8 and 24. This image of Derby Castle includes No. 24 to the right of trailers 57 and 58. It is the only known picture of tram 24. *Late Reverend Bertram J. Kelly*

↘A postcard view of Port Jack with the Douglas Bay Hotel behind. The building was destroyed by fire on 3rd November 1988, the site laying derelict for a number of years before the current modern office complex was built. There are about 100 people visible in this picture, while a tram and trailer approach from Laxey. *Barry Edwards Collection*

The line officially opened to Groudle on 7th September 1893 after some difficulties with current collection from the overhead wire. Some 20,000 passengers were carried by 28th September, when services were suspended to allow construction of an extension to Laxey; this was approved by Tynwald on 17th November 1893. The line was doubled throughout its length, the Groudle viaduct built, and a terminus near the present depot at Laxey constructed, all opening on 27th July 1894.

Six more tramcars were delivered from G.F. Milnes during 1894 to accommodate the increase in traffic expected with the Laxey extension, together with six more trailers. These bore the name Douglas & Laxey Coast Electric Tramway Co. Ltd on their bodysides, as the company had changed during construction of the new line. The company name changed yet again – to Isle of Man Tramways & Electric Power Co.; the new company now also envisaged selling electricity for domestic lighting and commercial use. The Douglas Horse Tramway was added to the portfolio on 30th April 1894 and control of the horse tramway was taken from 1st May. Part of this deal included the requirement to construct a cable tramway to serve the Upper Douglas area, which opened on 15th August 1896.

Construction of the Snaefell Mountain Railway from Laxey to near the summit of the island's highest mountain was undertaken in 1895. It opened on 21st August and, after completion at a cost of around £40,000, the line was bought by the Isle of Man Tramways & Electric Power Co. Ltd for £72,500.

The immediate success of the Douglas to Laxey line prompted the company to petition Tynwald to extend further to Ramsey, as a rival company had engaged George Nobel Fell to survey a route from Laxey to Ramsey. Although consent was not received until 1st November 1897, it seems likely that some land preparation had already started. Steam locomotives were hired from the Isle of Man Railway and the Manx Northern Railway to aid construction. Ballure was

reached by July 1898, after nine months work in which 250,000 tons of spoil had been moved by a workforce of 1,000 men, and Ramsey by July 1899, bringing the total length of the line to 17 miles (28.5 km). The official opening ceremony of the extension was held on 24th July 1899.

The Isle of Man Tramways & Electric Power Co. was paying dividends from capital and had built a line for £500,000 but had raised barely a third of this sum. When Dumbells Bank collapsed in February 1900, with outstanding loans to the Railway of £150,000, the Isle of Man Tramways & Electric Power Co., alongside a considerable number of other local companies, was forced into receivership. A £225,000 offer from the British Electric Traction Co. for the entire undertaking was rejected by the liquidators in 1901. Douglas Corporation offered £50,000 for the horse and cable tramways later that year and this was duly accepted. January 1902 saw an offer of £250,000 from a Manchester-based syndicate, backed by a continental merchant banker, accepted for the electric tramway. the final settlement being made in September 1902. Two months later The Manx Electric Railway Company was incorporated in London and proceeded to purchase the tramway from the Manchester syndicate for £370,000. Amidst the gloom, the railway carried King Edward and Queen Alexandra on 25th August 1902.

The new company had considerable problems in its early days, with unreliable equipment and a backlog of maintenance. The line had been laid quickly on earth and needed 20,000 tons of ballast, new sleepers, and rails. DC current generation was now obsolete, and a 7,000-volt AC supply was taken from a new plant at Laxey power station. Much re-equipping took place both to the rolling stock and permanent way, and by 1906 the line was brought up to date. The Manx Electric soon became a valuable asset for the island's residents, and a visitor attraction with its increasingly elderly rolling stock and beautiful scenery. The company ventured into carrying stone and acquired four wheeled vans for mail traffic but faced increasing competition as bus services were introduced. During the period between 1928 and 1932, a serious accident and three setbacks befell the line.

On 8th August 1928 car No. 1 with trailer No. 39 well laden, stopped in the Fairy Cottage area to collect overhead maintenance staff, when car No.16 with trailer No.56, also well laden, came round the curve and was unable to stop, causing a serious rear end collision that resulted in 32 people being injured. An inquiry mandated the banning of trams stopping on curves.

←In the early 1980s there was a footbridge across King Edward Road as part of the Summerland complex. It afforded this view of the Derby Castle Manx Electric Railway and Horse Tram terminus. There are twelve trams visible in this view, taken on 15th August 1981, with tram 21 running round its trailer 40, while tram 9 awaits departure to Laxey & Ramsey. *Barry Edwards*

↑Winter saloons 21, 20 and 19 line up outside the bottom shed during an evening photographic evening at Derby Castle depot. These trams now operate in three different liveries. *Barry Edwards*

←A view inside the original Derby Castle depot top shed, taken in 1981. Trailers 46 and 49 keep company with open power car 32. *Barry Edwards*

↑The superb restoration of ratchet braked tram 14 is nearing completion in this view taken on 1st April 2018. *Barry Edwards*

↓The conversion of toastrack trailer 56 into a vehicle capable of conveying wheelchairs, is nearing completion in the workshops at Derby Castle in February 1995. *Barry Edwards*

↑The oldest Manx Electric tram 1 sits between winter saloon 22 and former Lisbon tram 360. 360 was built in 1907/08 and purchased in 1996, for possible use on the line. It never entered service and was used as a waiting room at Derby Castle before going into store. It spent some time in a private garden in the south of the Island before being sold to a private buyer in Dublin. *Barry Edwards*

↓The completed wheelchair trailer was launched as part of the International Railway Festival in 1995, to mark the centenary of the Snaefell Mountain Railway. It is seen here at Derby Castle coupled to tram 19, prior to departure to Ramsey on 5th September 2020. *Barry Edwards*

↖The sad sight that greeted workshop staff at Derby Castle on the morning of 1st October 1990, following the fire on tram 22 the previous evening. Remarkably, no other tram was badly damaged other than some scorching of paintwork. The tram was rebuilt and re-entered service during 1992. *Barry Edwards*

↑The replacement tram 22 takes shape in the Derby Castle workshops during 1991. *Barry Edwards*

←Santa trams operated for Christmas 2012, with special decorations added to the trams used. Here winter saloon 21 still has its decoration as it heads towards Derby Castle depot on 22 January 2013. *Trevor Nall*

↑Wickham railcar 22 is seen giving short rides between Derby Castle station and the depot, during the Rush Hour event of 2015. *Barry Edwards*

→Winter saloon 21 with trailer 41 approach Port Jack with a service from Ramsey on 2nd June 2006. The office complex behind replaced the Douglas Bay Hotel building. *Barry Edwards*

↖Tram 26 is seen with trailer 40 as it approaches the Onchan Head stop on King Edward Road with a service to Laxey on 27th July 2007. *Barry Edwards*

↑The warm weather through the summer of 2022 allowed considerable use of the open power cars. Here we see tram 32 sporting nationalised green livery, climbing through the upper Onchan area with the 09:40 Derby Castle to Ramsey on 1st June 2022. *Barry Edwards*

↑The restoration of tram 14 was completed in time for the Manx Electric Railway 125th Anniversary celebration in 2018. Following its official re-launch at Derby Castle on 3rd September 2018, it is seen here climbing through Onchan. *Barry Edwards*

→1899-built winter saloon 21, in the nationalised green livery of 1957, passes Howstrake golf course, with a relief service to Laxey on 29th July 2022. *Barry Edwards*

Winter saloon 19 in Douglas, Laxey & Ramsey Electric Railway livery has just left the residential area of Onchan with an early morning service to Ramsey on 1st June 2022. *Barry Edwards*

↑One of the events of the 2018 celebrations was the operating of a tram and two trailers. Open power car 33 with trailers 60 and 51 approaches Howstrake with a full load of enthusiastic passengers on 4th September 2018. *Barry Edwards*

↓Winter saloon 19 with trailer 40 having just passed Howstrake and beginning the long descent into Derby Castle on 21st September 2008. *Barry Edwards*

The greatest loss to the system occurred on the night of 5th April 1930 when fire broke out in the Laxey car shed, destroying motor cars Nos. 3, 4, 8, and 24, seven trailer cars, all three tower wagons, a mail van, and a considerable amount of other equipment. Only the depot and three trailers were rebuilt. Later in 1930, serious flooding in Laxey after a violent storm was blamed on the Manx Electric's weir, which formed part of the company's generating station. A court ruling ordered the company to clear between 4,000 and 5,000 tons of rubbish from the riverbed and pay all the legal costs. The Manx Electric found it increasingly difficult to pay out debenture interest.

The third disaster occurred on 3rd April 1932, when fire destroyed the hotel and refreshment room at Dhoon Glen, which were never rebuilt.

The Second World War brought unexpected prosperity to the Island, which was used extensively to house prisoners of war. The line was used for the transfer of the lead mine 'deads' from Laxey to Ramsey as construction materials for the development of Jurby airfield. The Manx Electric survived this period of uncertainty and in 1945 was used to film a scene for 'I See a Dark Stranger'.

The immediate post-war period saw the Manx Electric enjoying the benefits of returning tourism but in the early fifties the decline in numbers of visitors and passengers led the company to advise Tynwald that it would be unable to continue trading after 30th September 1956. The entire system was offered for sale for £70,000.

Tynwald, not wanting to lose the Manx Electric as it was still an important tourist attraction – with over 70% of visitors riding the line – and a local lifeline, commissioned report which led to nationalisation of the system on 6th November 1956. The Manx Electric Railway Act was signed on 17th April 1957, creating the Manx Electric Railway Board of Tynwald.

Money was forthcoming for the next few years to enable maintenance and investment in new track and equipment, 200 tons of rail and 3,000 sleepers being delivered. A start was made on repainting the tramcars in a standard livery of green and cream, but objections to this were so severe that it was soon abandoned. The Derby Castle to Laxey section was re-laid completely during this period, whilst the Laxey to Ramsey section was found to be in very good order. This period of relative buoyancy was followed by leaner times, when only essential work was carried out.

On 20th January 1967 part of the retaining wall at Bulgham slipped away followed on 28th January by a further slip causing a section of trackbed to fall into the sea. Perhaps surprisingly, immediate steps were taken to restore the route; temporary crossovers were installed at either side of the breach and passengers transferred from one car to another on foot. Contractors were called in to enact the repairs, and through running resumed on 19th July.

The early 1970s saw a privatisation bid from Rapid Transit Technical Services. With the line in danger of closure, they proposed a complete revision of services, a new workshop at Laxey serving the Snaefell Railway as well as the Manx Electric, new power supplies and marketing initiatives. Nothing came of this offer and, within a short time, Transmark (a division of British Rail) was called in to assess the future of the line. Their broad conclusion was that the line would cease to make a loss only if it was closed. Part, and thankfully only part, of this recommendation was carried out, the Laxey to Ramsey section closing on 30th September 1975 despite considerable public protest.

Transport became a major issue at the general election in 1976, and many of the 'anti-tramway' members were not re-elected. The new Government responded to public pressure and the Laxey to Ramsey line reopened on 25th June 1977, enjoying a buoyant season.

In early 1977 the Manx Electric Railway Board took over the running of the steam railway, the two lines doing reasonably well despite falling visitor numbers. Management of bus services was added in April 1980 and the Board was reformed as the Isle of Man Passenger Transport Board in 1983, becoming part of the Department of Tourism and Transport in 1986.

On 1st December 1987 Robert Smith was appointed Transport Executive, having previously worked for London Transport. Many of the cars received major overhaul over the following years, in an ongoing programme. Disaster returned to the line on the night of 30th September 1990 when car No.22 caught fire in Derby Castle depot and was destroyed

but, once again, Government commitment was shown and a new No. 22 was built on the original chassis, re-entering service in May 1992.

The year 1993 was designated the 'Year of Railways' to

↑↑ Open toastrack power car 32 descends towards Derby Castle during the summer of 1964. *Barry Edwards Collection*

↑ An Easter bunny special approaches Howstrake on 27th March 2016, with decorated tram 19. The recently re-laid track with concrete sleepers is very evident. *Barry Edwards*

← Tram 2 dating from 1893 and still in daily use, approaches the very sharp curve at Howstrake, about eight minutes into its 75 minute trip to Ramsey on 23rd June 2022. The superb condition of these 130 year old trams is a credit to the team at Derby Castle who look after them. *Barry Edwards*

↑Winter saloon 22 with trailer 46 on a southbound working from Laxey, passing the derelict remains of the former Howstrake Camp station on 27th March 2016. *Barry Edwards*

↗Tunnel car 6 dating from 1894 rounds the sharp curve adjacent to Howstrake Camp station. The small building to the right of the tram was an entrance to the holiday camp, situated on the hillside below the road. *Barry Edwards Collection*

→On 30th October 2021, winter saloon 19 slows for the Howstrake curve with Royal saloon 59 in tow. The Sea Lion Rocks terminus of the Groudle Glen railway can be seen immediately to the right of the front of the tram. *Barry Edwards*

→A replica tram 7 was built for the 1995 centenary of the Snaefell Mountain Railway. It was later converted into a diesel electric locomotive for the Manx Electric and re-gauged to 3'0" and renumbered 34. It is seen here during September 2010 just to the north of Groudle. *Trevor Nall*

←A busy scene at Groudle on 7th September 1993 with tram 32 heading north to Laxey while one of the original 1893 trams leads trailer 13 towards Derby Castle. Tram 32 is displaying a destination plate and is in the capable hands of the late Mike Goodwyn. *Barry Edwards*

↓The two surviving 1893 trams 1 and 2 stand at Groudle on centenary day, 7th September 1993. Both trams had worked out from Derby Castle conveying members of the official party, who were enjoying coffee and cakes in the Groudle Hotel. *Barry Edwards*

Shortly after departing from Groudle the line turns through two sharp right hand bends with the Groudle viaduct between them. Coming off the viaduct and on the second of the curves is 1893 tram 2 with trailer 49, with the 11:10 service from Derby Castle on 1st June 2022. *Barry Edwards*

Winter saloon 21 with trailer 41 passes Eskadale between Groudle and Halfway on 10th August 2021, with a service from Derby Castle to Ramsey. *Barry Edwards*

←Tunnel car 7 with Royal trailer 59 in a matching blue livery, cross the Groudle Road as it approaches Halfway on 1st August 2019, with the 10:40 Derby Castle to Ramsey. *Barry Edwards*

↓Tram 7 is seen again, this time on 18th April 2014 between Halfway and Baldrine with matching trailer 48 in tow. *Barry Edwards*

↓In 1895 the Manx Electric took delivery of four further power cars, numbered 10 to 13 in 1895, built in the same year as the Snaefell trams, they were similar in design. Tram 11 is seen here at Garwick, a once busy stop on the line. *William G Cavanagh*

↘Shortly after passing Fairy Cottage station the line crosses the road to Laxey Bay. Winter saloon 21 with an unidentified trailer, is passing tunnel car 7 with trailer 51 on 3rd November 2013. When trams are likely to pass on a road crossing, the first to arrive will stop across the road, until the other is on the crossing. This avoids potential collision, as drivers consider that the tram has gone! *Barry Edwards*

↑A fine study of winter saloon 19 awaits its next turn of duty in the siding to the Derby Castle end of the new Laxey car shed, on 24th October 2021. The new shed provides considerably better accommodation over the one it replaced. *Richard Kirkman*

↗During its holiday on the Manx Electric during 1993, steam locomotive 4 *Loch* was housed inside Laxey car shed. She is seen here in the company of the two closed saloon trailers 57 and 58. *Richard Kirkman*

↖A view inside the old Laxey car shed during 1982 Winter saloon 22 shares space with one of the two original 1893 power cars. The poor condition of the shed is clearly evident in this view. *Barry Edwards*

↑The very warm weather of 2022 allowed the utilisation of the open power cars. Here tram 33 with trailer 47 pass the site of the old Laxey sub-station with a service from Ramsey to Derby Castle on 26th July 2022. *Barry Edwards*

←←The now closed Laxey sub-station sported this wonderful marble switch panel. The unprotected contacts on the switches are clearly visible, something that would simply not be allowed today. *Barry Edwards*

←The sub-station was also home to these magnificent mercury arc rectifiers, each one housed in an individual cage with a wooden bladed cooling fan below. Sadly, these are no longer in use, but a couple have been preserved and it is hoped that they will be connected to a supply in order that the effect can be replicated. *Barry Edwards*

Steam locomotive 4 *Loch* revisited the Manx Electric Railway during the International Railway Festival in 1995. Seen here on the viaduct over Glen Roy on the approach to Laxey station, it has saloon trailers 57 and 58 in tow. *Barry Edwards*

An impressive line up in Laxey station during the 1995 festival. Manx Electric winter saloon 22, keeps company with locomotive 4 *Loch* and Snaefell Mountain Railway trams 1 and 4. *Barry Edwards*

celebrate the centenary of the line. The festivities were officially launched at Derby Castle on Saturday 10th April 1993 by Lieutenant Governor Air Marshal Sir Laurence Jones, who drove car No.1 through a celebration banner. Car 9 was chosen to become the Island's first illuminated tram. It was inaugurated later the same day and was, and still is, often used on the evening services to Groudle. The former Ramsey goods shed was converted into a small museum about the Manx Electric Railway and Snaefell Mountain Railway. Royal trailer No. 59 represented the tram fleet, the rest of the area featuring display boards and a cab mock-up of a Snaefell car.

Loco No.23, with bogies borrowed from car No.17, made a test run on the line on 9th June 1993 and later in the year took part in the celebrations. Car 26 was used extensively during the season for Motorman experience sessions. Isle of Man Railway locomotive 4 *Loch* arrived at Laxey by road and operated several steam trips to Dhoon Quarry, hauling closed trailers Nos. 57 and 58.

Centenary day, Tuesday 7th September 1993, began

with a formal gathering at Derby Castle with invited guests being addressed by the Lieutenant Governor and Minister for Tourism Alan Bell MHK. Following the formalities, the Lieutenant Governor drove car No. 1 hauling trailer 13 to Groudle for a reception in the Groudle Hotel and the unveiling of a centenary plaque at the Laxey end of Groudle station.

Unusually, Santa trams operated on the line in connection with Santa events on the Groudle Glen Railway.

The longest stretch of track relay for many years took place over the 1993/94 winter, from Ballagorry to Dolland, while the section from Howstrake to Groudle had its overhead refurbished.

Trailer 56 was moved to Derby Castle in 1994 for conversion to an accessible vehicle, to allow wheelchair passengers to enjoy a journey on the line. Car Nos.2 and 6 assumed the identity of sister cars 3 and 8 for a short while during the season, both of which had been lost in the Laxey fire.

1995 marked the centenary of the Snaefell Mountain Railway and an 'International Railway Festival' was held. A grand cavalcade took place through Laxey station on Sunday 20th August as part of the celebrations, with virtually all serviceable Manx Electric power and trailer cars taking part, along with various freight and engineering vehicles. During the winter of 1995/96 the crossings at Halfway and Laxey Princess Motors were re-laid. The winter service only operated between Laxey and Ramsey to accommodate these works. Towards the end of 1995 plans were announced for the replacement of the Derby Castle top shed, the one parallel with the running lines. The £600,000 project would replace the original wooden shed that was in a poor state of repair and, by default, used to house most of the priceless rolling stock.

Former Lisbon tram No. 360 arrived on 3rd June 1996. The tram arrived at Ramsey on board the Mezeron Freight Group vessel the *Silver River* and was transported to Douglas by road.

Car No.9 had her illuminated panels changed to promote the Groudle Glen Railway centenary. During the railway events built around the Groudle celebrations, a couple of cars were once again renumbered to take up the guise of sister vehicles destroyed in the Laxey fire; Nos.4 and 24 were played by 6 and 26. A new generator was acquired to allow Manx Electric cars to operate on the steam railway or on their own line in the absence of power. It was mounted on wagon No.8. The old Derby Castle top shed was emptied during September and October, with locomotive No. 23 being the first to leave on 25th September. Some stock went to the steam railway for storage, whilst a long line of trams stretched along the southbound line from Laxey car sheds across the viaduct and nearly into the station; these were covered with tarpaulins. The 1996/97 winter service only operated between Laxey and Ramsey for the second year running, partly due to the rebuilding works at Derby Castle sheds and associated works at the depot entrance.

A policy decision was taken during the 1997 season to keep cars 1 and 2 in different sheds to prevent the loss of both in any disaster. A shortage of available trams led to some passengers being turned away at Derby Castle; a couple of trams

remained resident on the steam railway during the rebuilding of, and issues with the new top shed. Over the winter of 1997/98 maintenance work included renewal of many of the overhead poles between Derby Castle and Groudle. Winter storms caused problems at Garwick and Laxey.

A requirement to turn off the overhead power supply on 24th October 1997 resulted in the most unusual passenger train ever to operate on the line. Car 21 was coupled to wagon 8 and its generator and operated as a diesel electric between Derby Castle and Laxey for the day.

Meanwhile, car 33 emerged from store on the steam railway to make a similar rare working on 2nd December when, with wagon and generator, it made a return trip to Port Erin. This was repeated the following day with invited railway press on board to promote the forthcoming Steam 125 celebrations of 1998. The tram was driven on both days by Cathie Antrobus of Isle of Man Transport.

Car 33 returned to the MER for Ramsey Sprint day, traditionally the busiest day of the year for the line. A new road crossing was installed at Howstrake to allow construction access to a new housing estate at Groudle.

Floods returned on 24th October 1998 when, after a severe storm, Laxey station was flooded and Cornaa was also affected. The storm caused severe damage to the mountain road resulting in its closure, so winter plans to relay the Ballure crossing on the outskirts of Ramsey were postponed due to the increased traffic on the coastal road. Santa trams again operated in conjunction with the Groudle Santa weekend.

Plans were being drawn up to put locomotive No. 23 into operational condition for 1999, the centenary of the completion of the line through to Ramsey. It was also proposed that 23 should form the centrepiece at the 2000 Warley National Model Railway Exhibition at the NEC in Birmingham, but sadly this did not materialise. Much of 1999 was dominated by the continuing problems with the new top shed at Derby Castle, the entire track layout having been re-laid at least once already. The centenary of the line reaching the current Ramsey station and was marked by several events

↑A busy scene at Laxey on 26th July 2013. Snaefell tram 6 is in the company of Manx Electric trailers 59 and 57, tunnel tram 5 and a further unidentified tram. Barry Edwards

↓An image captured ten years ago on 5th August 2012, shows tunnel car 6 with trailer 44, the power car reflected in the large puddle. Its worth comparing this picture with a more recent image. Barry Edwards

↑An 1894 tunnel tram sits in Laxey station with trailer 27, now 60, alongside the large refreshment room that measured 104ft x 40ft. It was destroyed by fire on 24th September 1917. *Barry Edwards Collection*

↗The photogenic winter saloon 19 sits in Laxey station with one of the very last workings of the 2019 season on 2nd November 2019. Snaefell tram 2 is in the background. *Barry Edwards*

→Open power car 27 with a makeshift windscreen, fitted to protect the driver while in departmental use, sits in Laxey station with a tower wagon and tower van. *Barry Edwards*

↓During 2008 trailer 52 was converted to be used as a tower wagon and fitted with a hydraulic lift, in contrast to the previous tower wagons that required the wire team to climb up to the working platform. 52 is seen here at Laxey, during 2013, in the capable hands of winter saloon 21. *Trevor Nall*

↘Taken a year or so after the previous image, trailer 52 is seen with the wiring platform raised and the team busy working on the overhead. Seen at Laxey on 18th April 2014. *Barry Edwards*

↑A winter saloon in wintery conditions. Tram 22 is running down the final part of the long descent from Bulgham and has just passed Minorca station. *Barry Edwards Collection*

↗The leafy approach to Minorca station with tram 22 bathed in sunshine as it works a service from Derby Castle to Ramsey on 29th October 2019. *Barry Edwards*

↖Minorca station is to the north of Laxey on the long climb towards the Bulgham summit. Tram 21 passes with a trailer during centenary year 1993. *Richard Kirkman*

↑Tunnel car 9 passes through Minorca on 3rd November 2013 with Royal trailer 59 behind. Trailer 59 has since been repainted into a blue livery. *Barry Edwards*

←After climbing through Minorca and the outskirts of Laxey, the line emerges into open countryside as it continues to climb. Running wrong line due to engineering works, tram 21 with trailer 46 work a service from Ramsey to Derby Castle on 7th September 2008. *Barry Edwards*

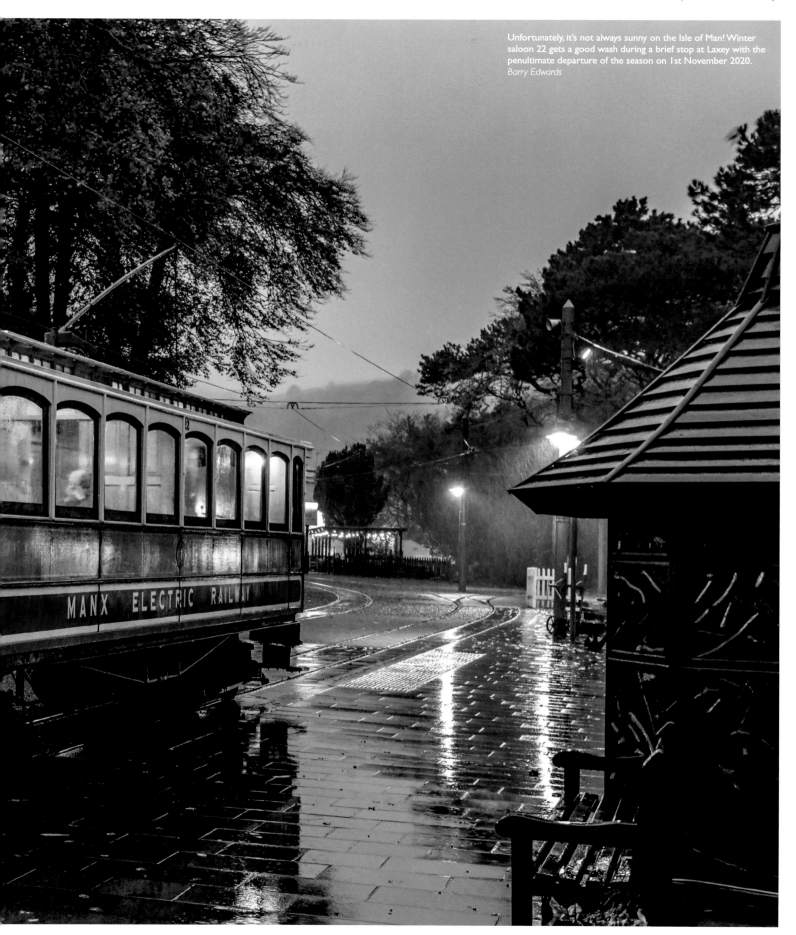

Unfortunately, it's not always sunny on the Isle of Man! Winter saloon 22 gets a good wash during a brief stop at Laxey with the penultimate departure of the season on 1st November 2020.
Barry Edwards

↑A view looking across Laxey Bay towards Clay Head Road, with 1893 power car 2 and trailer 59 heading north to Ramsey on 20th April 2014. *Barry Edwards*

↗Tram 9 with an unidentified trailer have just negotiated the Bulgham curves and begin the descent of the long straight to just above Laxey, on 21st June 2019. Maughold lighthouse is just visible to the right of the picture. This area is well known for the flocks of wild goats that reside either side of the line. *Barry Edwards*

↓Open power car 32 with trailer 43 pass the same point on a bright and sunny 24th August 2020, just about a month after the season had commenced after the initial Covid-19 lockdown. *Barry Edwards*

↘During December 2020 the Little Shed café at Dhoon Glen station, hosted a Christmas event with trams operating from both Laxey and Ramsey. Through services to Derby Castle were not possible due to track work in the Groudle area. Illuminated tram 9 is seen approaching the Bulgham curves, on 23rd December, with a full load of excited passengers. *Barry Edwards*

↑On 20th January 1967 a section of the wall at Bulgham fell into the sea, followed on 28th January by a section of the tramway. Remarkably, the trackbed was replaced and through running returned on 1st May. Here we see the work in progress, with a tram and trailer awaiting departure to Derby Castle, the passengers having arrived on a different tram from Ramsey and walked past the work site. *Barry Edwards Collection*

→1893 tram 1 and trailer 42 approach the summit with a southbound working on 26th July 2022. *Barry Edwards*

↘A view of the line from the Ballaragh Road that runs above the main A2 road. Tram 19 winds round the tight curves with an unidentified trailer on 24th August 2020. *Barry Edwards*

↑A special railtour stopped on the Bulgham section for photographers, on 7th July 2009. Open tram 16 sporting a green livery has trailer 59 behind, while its passengers re-join the tram. *Barry Edwards*

←Having climbed all the way up from Laxey, the trams pass the summit, 588 feet above sea level, and turn left and descend towards Dhoon Glen station. Green-liveried tram 16 with matching trailer, have rounded the curve on a sunny 26th July 2013. *Barry Edwards*

Catching engineering trains on camera is a stroke of luck. Here the photographer was fortunate to capture tram 33 with overhead wiring trailer 52 approaching Bulgham summit, heading for Laxey sheds on 3rd August 2017. *Barry Edwards*

With the summit of South Barrule just covered in cloud, tram 33 is captured at the same point, this time with two trailers 51 and 60, a special working as part of the Manx Electric 125th anniversary celebrations on 4th September 2018. *Barry Edwards*

As mentioned earlier, the open trams saw considerable service during the warm summer of 2022. Dhoon Glen station is the location for this view of tram 32 and trailer 40, on 7th June 2022, with many enjoying the refreshments available from the station café. *Barry Edwards*

115

↑The Christmas event held at Dhoon Glen station were repeated in 2021, although only with trams from Laxey. With a snow machine creating a suitable atmosphere, decorated tram 22 waits in the station. 5th December 2021. *Barry Edwards*

↓Between Dhoon Glen and Dhoon Quarry stations, this view of the trams is possible. With the hills of Cumbria just visible in the background, tram 1 and trailer 60 work south with a well loaded service on 26th July 2022. *Barry Edwards*

↙A 1956 view of tram 32 crossing from the down line to the up with a tour special from Derby Castle on 20th May. The track layout has changed here since this view was taken and the cottage has been demolished. *R J S Wiseman*

↓Steam locomotive 4 *Loch* at Dhoon Quarry during the 1993 steam specials from Laxey. Manx Electric closed trailers 58 and 57 are in the background. *Richard Kirkman*

staged in and around Ramsey station.

In August 1999 a planning application was made to refurbish the Laxey car shed, with doors at the Douglas end only, effectively reducing the shed from four tracks to three.

In an encouraging move the winter service for 1999/2000 was augmented by additional weekend services, the first Saturday winter services since 1975, the first Sundays for considerably longer. Fares were halved in line with the bus service and tickets were interchangeable between the two. The road crossing at Ballabeg was re-laid over the winter, single line operation being maintained throughout.

To mark the beginning of the new millennium and the Manx Electric Railway passing into its third century, a special tram operated on Wednesday 5th January 2000. Car No. 1

departed from Derby Castle at 09:00 for Groudle, the first tram of the new century. It returned to Derby Castle as the 09:20 service car and on arrival at Derby Castle was swapped with car 20 for the rest of the day's operation.

A new café opened inside the station building at Laxey and in an arrangement with the Department of Agriculture, Fisheries & Forestry, the Dhoon Glen station café also reopened. The former Lisbon tram became the waiting room at Derby Castle on 4th May 2000, replacing Leyland National Bus 26. Car 5 emerged from Derby Castle towards

↑Another view of Dhoon Quarry on 20th May 1956, this time with tram 2 and trailer 59, during run round shunting. Bogie open wagons 24 and 25 along with a number of four-wheeled wagons occupy the siding. *Manx National Heritage*

↗During 2006 this small 0-6-0 diesel shunting locomotive was used by contractors during track renewal. Owned at the time by RMS Locotec, it is seen here on the main line at Dhoon Quarry with one of the steam railway ballast wagons, on 10th April 2006. *Barry Edwards*

→Beautifully restored ratchet tram 14 passes Dhoon Quarry with a special working on 29th July 2022. *Barry Edwards*

↑Local contractor Auldyn Construction make use of two former Bord na Mona locomotives LM344 and LM350, now named *Pig* and *Otter*. Photographed on 8th August 2009. *Barry Edwards*

↗Manx Electric wagon 21, fitted with ballast hoppers and distributors sits in the siding at Dhoon Quarry on 31st October 2007. The hoppers have now been removed and just the flat chassis remains in store. *Barry Edwards*

↑Shortly after leaving Dhoon Quarry heading north, the tramway crosses the Glen Mona Loop Road. Having just crossed the junction tram 9 with trailer 49 work south on 1st August 2019. *Barry Edwards*

↗A northbound service operated by tram 22 and trailer 41 have just crossed the Loop Road and head past a good display of spring daffodils on 10th April 2019. *Barry Edwards*

↖The summit of North Barrule looks inviting to climbers as tunnel car 9 with trailer 48 operate a southbound service on 26th July 2022. The village of Glen Mona is visible just to the left of the trailer. *Barry Edwards*

↗Passengers on the left side of tram 20 will have a good view of Ramsey Bay and the hills towards Maughold Head as they travel towards Laxey and eventually Derby Castle on 24th August 2020. *Barry Edwards*

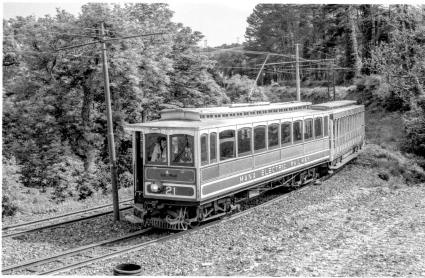

↑In January 2005 a particularly wild storm caused considerable damage to the overhead power lines of the railway, to the north of Dhoon Quarry. Here, on 16th January, we look north at a pile of broken overhead equipment and branches. *Barry Edwards*

→Glen Mona will be the next station for tram 21 and trailer 41. This picture is taken just a few hundred yards along from the devastation shown in the previous image, but just over a year later on 15th June 2006. *Barry Edwards*

An unusual sight on the Manx Electric on 30th July 2018. Auldyn Construction's locomotive *Pig* pushes a loaded ballast wagon a few hundred yards to the work site, where track relaying has taken place. *Barry Edwards*

the end of the 2000 season with its titling in Manx. The 2000/01 winter service was four return trips each way Monday to Saturday and three on Sunday. A full colour winter timetable was produced that also gave details of the forthcoming summer service dates.

In January 2001 several items from Laxey car shed were moved to Derby Castle and then by road to the former Homefield bus depot, following the move of the bus operation to the new facility at Banks Circus adjacent to the steam railway workshops. Derby Castle yard was re-laid again in February 2001 to further improve the situation, whilst the government allocated £600,000 to fund track relaying over

What is now the only bridge over the Manx Electric is situated just north of Glen Mona station and houses a sub station for the railway. Tram 6 heads south on 28th July 2013, with an unidentified trailer and sporting a special tram number panel below the driver's windscreen. *Barry Edwards*

the coming winter, with a further £12 million over the next nine years.

Plans to refurbish Laxey car shed had lapsed and were replaced with more ambitious plans to demolish the existing shed, itself a replacement in 1931, and build a new structure. A further £1.1 million worth of track relaying was carried out over the 2001/02 winter and several overhead poles repainted. New tram stop signs were erected along the line in the same style as bus stops but with a tram instead of bus image. Port-e-Vullen received a new shelter following the demolition of the original decayed structure.

The Manx Electric Railway Society, deeply concerned about the future fate of some rolling stock and buildings, agreed a conservation policy with the then Minister of Tourism and Leisure.

The winter service operated with four return trips through the 2001/02 and 2002/03 winters, with colour timetable leaflets being produced. Car 21 appeared in service with Isle of Man Transport stickers below the cab windows on each end. The body of Lisbon car 360 was removed from its home at Derby Castle station on 19th April 2002 and replaced by an elongated bus-style shelter repositioned across the end of the tracks, the new shelter becoming operational in June.

Flood damage returned to the line once again on 21st October 2002, when a severe storm affected much of the island. The engineers' shed at Derby Castle was damaged from the cliff behind and ballast washed away in a couple of places, with debris being dumped across the track by the

Ballaglass station has no road access and sits in a leafy surround. Tram 6 ambles through the station on 14th September 2020, having slowed for the double curve just beyond as the railway crosses the river, Glass. There is just another 20 minutes left of the journey to Ramsey. *Barry Edwards*

excess water. It took until Friday 25th to reopen the line throughout, even with some single line working. The massive relay programme continued through the 2002/03 winter, whilst in a break with tradition, three trams were repainted at Ramsey car shed by local contractor Brian O'Hare.

The Derby Castle booking office received a repaint during April 2003. The depot wall was enhanced with a series of paintings by London Artist Cian Quayle. Ballagawne received a new shelter while Dhoon Quarry finally lost its shelter, Ballajora was repaired and painted during May/June 2003.

The northern mountains form a backdrop to tram 19 running solo on 29th October 2019. The tram has just passed the Ballaskeig crossover, used for when single line working if required during engineering works. *Barry Edwards*

↑Tram 2 dating from the opening of the line in 1893 is passing Rome's Crossing, with trailer 49 on 26th July 2022. The southern Scottish hills are visible in the distance. *Barry Edwards*

↗Tunnel car 5 with trailer 41 approach Ballajora station on 12th August 2019, just 12 minutes into its 75 minute journey to Derby Castle. *Barry Edwards*

→Tram 9 with trailer, has just passed a southbound service on the approach to Lewaigue station on 10th August 2021. The southbound driver will have handed the single line token to the driver of tram 9 allowing him to continue on the single line to Ramsey, while the up track is closed for engineering works. *Barry Edwards*

←The original tram 22 is passing Dreemskerry station with an unidentified trailer during the summer of 1981. In the distance was the area of the Dreemskerry quarry where there was a crossover and siding. *Barry Edwards*

↙Following the construction of a new housing estate on the outskirts of Ramsey, a new station opened at Queens Valley. On 31st July 2019 tram 6 approaches the new station with a service from Derby Castle to Ramsey. *Barry Edwards*

↓On 21st May 1956 tram 20 with a single van in tow, runs along the side of Walpole Avenue in Ramsey, at the beginning of its journey to Derby Castle. Nowadays there would be a continuous line of cars parked here. *Barry Edwards Collection*

Cornaa shelter had a completely new front and repaint. The Laxey car shed saga continued with the removal of the roof for safety reasons, at the same time as the former Ramsey goods shed was converted into a youth centre. Named 'The Shed' the new facility was officially opened on 16th November 2003.

The 2003/04 winter service was operated with just two return trips daily and although standing passengers were carried on the first day, the numbers soon trailed off. Considerable relaying was due over the 2003/04 winter although there was no work planned for the following winter. Laxey goods shed was used to store overhead wire equipment. A further batch of trams, Nos. 1, 2, 33 and trailer 61 were repainted over the winter at Ramsey.

The evening services, except the Groudle trips, were not included in the 2004 summer timetable. The following winter service announcement was delayed as plans to demolish the former Summerland complex under discussion.

Storms returned to the Island and the Manx Electric on 7th/8th January 2005, with winds over 100mph being recorded. The overhead line was brought down in several places, in most cases by falling trees and debris from trees and buildings blocked the line. The line closed and the winter service was suspended, reopening just in time for the summer season on 21st March. The Dhoon Glen café was closed for the first part of the 2005 season while a new tenant was found and Ballabeg, Cornaa and Dreemskerry station buildings were refurbished and repainted.

Demolition of Summerland went ahead over the winter of 2005/06, requiring track to be lifted from Derby Castle depot to the station. As there was no access for trams the winter service was cancelled, and the opportunity was taken to relay a further 1.25 miles of track. The overhead line at Port Jack was refurbished and several new poles installed. The crossing just north of Laxey station where the two Manx Electric tracks and one Snaefell track cross the main road through the

Tram 9 with an unidentified trailer runs wrong line past Walpole Drive as it approaches the end of its 75 minute journey from Derby Castle. The overhead poles at this location were from the former Douglas Head & Marine Drive Tramway.
Barry Edwards

Winter saloon 20 crosses Ballure Viaduct during the early 20th century. The completion of the viaduct allowed the final stretch of the line into the centre of Ramsey to open. Before the viaduct was completed in 1899, the line terminated behind the photographer.
Manx National Heritage

↑↑During the winter 2014/15 the Ballure viaduct was refurbished. Looking south this view taken on 11th February 2015 shows the viaduct deck in the process of painting after being sandblasted and suitably primed. *Barry Edwards*

↑The now-demolished Ramsey car shed was situated just to the south of the station, almost adjacent to the current temporary station. Once the home of a small museum, it was demolished as unsafe over the winter 2015/16. *Barry Edwards*

village was re-laid at the same time. The finished product greatly enhanced the whole area and incorporated footpaths for pedestrians crossing to Ham and Egg Terrace. A Ruston Hornsby diesel shunter was used to assist the relaying during the winter. Named *Bertie*, the loco dated from 1949. Meanwhile a new wiring wagon was constructed using the chassis of original wagon No. 8.

The demolition works delayed the start of the 2006 operating season, the first trams running on 15th May. Relaying works between the depot entrance and Derby Castle station could not begin until the demolition was almost complete. Residents tidied up the Ballabeg station area, provided planters and plenty of summer bedding plants to give an enhanced look. Meanwhile, the overall state and outside storage of car No. 7 in the roofless Laxey car shed was the subject of a Tynwald debate on 21st March 2006.

The winter 2006/07 service only operated at weekends and the Baldrine and Groudle road crossings were both re-laid. Isle of Man Transport branding was dropped in early 2007, and the system returned to the previous identity of Isle of Man Railways. The winter service ended on 1st April 2007, possibly the end of winter services on the line for the

foreseeable future. The issue of car No. 7 was raised in Tynwald again, with the result that the car was moved to Derby Castle for restoration. Services were disrupted on 3rd August following a road traffic accident in the Onchan area. Car 5 was damaged in a collision with a hedge trimmer during September and remained out of service awaiting winter repairs.

Station buildings at Baldrine, Fairy Cottage, South Cape and Minorca all received attention over winter 2006/07. Following an appeal to local organisations and individuals to 'look after' shelters, Laxey School volunteered to keep Minorca clean and tidy. The former Ballaglass Power Station building, now converted into a private dwelling, was on the market for £2.85 million in early 2007. Recent residential development in Ramsey led to the sighting of a new request stop at Queens Valley Road, the new stop becoming available in June 2007. Passenger figures for the 2007 season showed that 78,665 were carried on the line, a 9.9% increase on the 2006 numbers.

RMS Locotec carried out around three miles of track replacement over the 2007/08 winter at a cost of £1.6 million. Inspection of the line early in 2008 revealed several safety issues on sections of track yet to be replaced. The result was an announcement in Tynwald on 20th February that the Manx Electric would not open between Laxey and Ramsey for the 2008 season. As might be expected, uproar ensued and by 12th March Tynwald had agreed emergency funding to allow the issues on the landside track to be addressed immediately, with a view to single line operation over the northern section by the mid-summer. The northern section opened to traffic on Saturday 19th July with a passing loop installed to allow an improved timetable over that envisaged in March. A short ceremony was held at Laxey on 18th July prior to the departure of a special tram through to Ramsey, the line opening to the public the following day. The single line operation worked well, with virtually a normal service operating until 14th September when the line closed to allow track renewal work to restart.

Meanwhile the old Laxey car shed was demolished at the end of the 2008 season, the site was cleared and by the middle of January 2009, construction of the replacement shed was well under way. The 2009 season began on 6th April, with trams using both tracks on the northern section and in line with the steam railway, the service level was reduced from the end of September through to the end of season in early November. The Laxey car shed was completed in time for the opening of the line, although not actually connected. Trackwork continued and the shed was fully operational by the middle of the season. As soon as the tram operating season finished, the section of track between the entrance to Derby Castle depot and the approach to Onchan Head station was re-laid. The need to empty the former Homefield bus garage in upper Douglas prompted the return of several items of rolling stock that had been absent since the rebuilding of Derby Castle top shed.

In common with the steam railway the 2010 season dates were announced early, something that has now become normal. 'Ultimate Driving Experience' sessions were advertised allowing participants to drive trams between Laxey and Ramsey. Severe snow in March 2010 caused disruption to services, trams only operating as far as Laxey for a few days. Meanwhile the rebuilt body of car No.7 emerged from Laxey Village workshop. The body went to Derby Castle to re-enter service in the blue and cream livery in which the trams were delivered from Milnes in 1899.

The policy of infrastructure upgrade and refurbishment continued and during 2010 the government was asked to approve a plan costing £725,000 to relay Laxey station, move the crossovers out of the station area, re-surface the area and repairs to the viaduct over Church Hill.

The floor in the lower shed at Derby Castle was completely re-laid, resulting in a few trams being stored outside covered with tarpaulins for a short period. In line with the increased operation of specials on the steam railway, a special tram operated between Douglas and Ramsey for the northern fireworks display. Trailer 48 was repainted into blue livery to compliment the rebuilt car No. 7. A pleasing change was the increased use of trailers 57, 58, and 59 in service. These closed trailers spent many years hidden away in the sheds, only venturing out occasionally. Several freight vehicles were moved from storage locations to the yard adjacent to the village blacksmith in Laxey, where the Laxey and Lonan Heritage Trust began work on restoration. Fears that some of the privately owned stock might leave the Island proved unfounded, despite locomotive 23 and freight trailer 26 being mounted onto accommodation bogies and made available to the owner,

neither moved, and both were returned to secure storage.

The Manx Electric Railway played host to the Olympic Flame on 2nd June 2012 when it was carried from Derby Castle to Laxey on-board car No. 1, the tram itself built three years before the first Olympic Games were held in 1896.

2013 was the 120th anniversary of the opening of the Manx Electric, several trams were specially decorated for the season with cast metal plaques.

The Laxey project was completed for the 2014 season and upgraded during the 2014/15 winter as part of the Laxey regeneration project. A new substation was also constructed at Laxey and that at Derby Castle was upgraded. The closure of the original Laxey sub-station ended the use of the impressive mercury arc rectifiers. Trailer 58 became derailed at Laxey in July 2015 and toppled onto its side during an

←A 1979 view inside the Ramsey car shed, then in use as a museum. Manx Electric locomotive 23 keeps company with former 1895 power car 10, now freight car 26. The end of Royal trailer 59 is just visible to the left of the picture. *Barry Edwards*

↓Another view taken nearly 30 years later on 28th November 2008 shows open power car 30 stored in the shed. *Barry Edwards*

One of the busiest days in a normal season is Ramsey Sprint day, held annually as part of the Tourist Trophy, or TT Festival. On 3rd June 2007, the TT centenary year, trams 21 and 33 await their compliment of passengers returning to Derby Castle. *Barry Edwards*

early shunting operation. The tram was recovered later that evening, the line through to Ramsey re-opening around the middle of the following day.

The railway celebrated its 125th anniversary in style in 2018, culminating in a special week of events in early September, including the actual anniversary day. At least one major event took place each day, and in general the weather behaved. Several hundred visitors made the trip to the Island for the week.

The line opened as usual at the beginning of the 2020

season but, in line with the steam railway, all services were suspended from the end of services on 19th March, because of Covid-19 restrictions. The Manx Electric re-opened on 23rd July, initially for just a few weeks but, with the high passenger numbers and continuing air corridor flights from Guernsey, remained open until early November. Following a new tenancy at the Dhoon Glen café, now known as the 'Little Shed', the railway operated trams in December as part of a Christmas event at the station. The event was well attended, the trams specially decorated for the services.

The 2021 season started late again due to the Covid situation but with the island borders gradually opening, visitor numbers increased rapidly, partly due to the high number of visiting coaches. Two events in the summer and at the end of the season attracted good visitor numbers and the Christmas events at Dhoon were repeated, again with high numbers attending.

Sporting Manx language titling, tram 5 awaits departure from Ramsey on 3rd September 2008. The condition of the track across Parsonage Road has meant that the trams currently stop short of the official station. *Barry Edwards*

The former Ramsey Pier Planet locomotive and coach were exhibits in the small museum at Ramsey car shed. During the 1989 season, the locomotive made a few passenger trips as far as Queen's Road. It is seen here re-entering the shed at the end of the day. *Barry Edwards*

THE SNAEFELL MOUNTAIN RAILWAY

The idea of a railway to the summit of the Island's highest mountain first surfaced in 1888, when Tynwald was asked to approve a plan submitted by the Douglas, Laxey & Snaefell Railway to build a steam-operated line. Mr J.B. Fell, the inventor of the 'Fell Incline Railway System', was behind the project but nothing came of it.

The arrival in Laxey of the Manx Electric Railway in 1894 renewed interest in Mr Fell's ideas and, on 4th January 1895, The Snaefell Mountain Railway Association met in Douglas for the first time and announced its intention to build a line from Laxey to near the summit of Snaefell. The syndicate included several members of the Isle of Man Tramways & Electric Power Co., including Mr Bruce of Dumbells Bank and Mr Fell. Discussions were held about motive power and the Association decided on an electric tramway. The route of the line was nearly all on Crown property, which avoided the need for an Act of Tynwald before construction could begin. The line was constructed to 3ft 6in gauge, six inches wider than the Island's standard, to accommodate the 'Fell System' between the wheels and provide greater stability in crosswinds. Manx Northern Railway locomotive 4 *Caledonia* was borrowed to assist with construction trains, necessitating the laying of a temporary 3ft 0in gauge rail.

Construction started in January 1895, bad weather during February delaying the project by about a month, but by early August completion was near. Six trams were delivered by G.F. Milnes of Birkenhead, whilst Mather & Platt supplied the overhead equipment; this was erected along the entire

length of the line in just ten days, the wire being 16 feet above rail level.

The 4-mile 53 chain line was completed in record time, the Fell rail being laid midway between the running rails. However, during construction, it was proved elsewhere that an electric tramcar could climb a 1 in 9 gradient without assistance and so the Fell equipment was never fitted to the cars. The third rail was therefore only used for friction braking in the event of a runaway.

Testing was carried out in mid-August and the line was officially opened from the first Laxey station, situated alongside the current car sheds, to the Summit station 1,990ft above sea level, on 20th August 1895, with the first public services the following day. An average of 900 passengers a day were carried that summer, with the six cars operating a ten-minute service. Cars took the right-hand track in the direction of travel on the 1 in 12 gradient. A power station was built below the Bungalow station, as the DC generating system

Station staff await the next arrival at the original Snaefell summit station at the turn of the twentieth century. The first Summit Hotel was located a short distance below this building. *Barry Edwards Collection*

The semi-castellated hotel at the Summit quickly replaced the original facilities and was built in just four months, opening in August 1905. The flat roof was originally intended as a viewing area. The building was destroyed by fire on 6th August 1982. *Barry Edwards Collection*

Snaefell Mountain freight – a wagon of computer equipment for NATS is propelled to the Summit by Tram 5 boasting Manx Gaelic bodyside wording and sliding wooden windows, 10th May 2006. *Barry Edwards*

Trams 4 and 2 pass near the Summit on 21st September 2019; the down line is blocked by engineering works, necessitating some slick track manoeuvres. *Barry Edwards*

required the supply to be halfway along the route. This necessitated the delivery of all the equipment and coal supplies, with water pumped from the Sulby river.

In December 1895 the Association sold the railway to the Isle of Man Tramways & Electric Power Co. for £72,500, which was £32,500 more than it had cost to build.

The cars, which were delivered unglazed, like the Manx Electric Nos.10 to 13 series, received sliding glazed windows in 1896. The lack of ventilation on hot days led to clerestory roofs being fitted during the winter of 1896/97.

The original Summit Hotel, located a little to the south of the terminus, was extended in 1896 and a new hotel was built at Halfway, now known as Bungalow.

The Isle of Man Tramways & Electric Power Co. considered the distance between their coastal line station and the Snaefell station in Laxey to be too great. The Snaefell terminus was therefore moved to the end of Dumbells Row in 1897, and in 1898 a further move brought it alongside the coastal line station, as it remains today.

The Snaefell line was sold to the Manx Electric Railway Co. in 1902, following the collapse of Dumbells Bank. In common with the coastal line, much re-equipping was needed, and changes were made to the generation and distribution of electricity.

A serious incident occurred on 14th September 1905, as three cars descended the mountain in convoy. The first stalled, the second stopped without difficulty but the third failed to stop, colliding with the second and pushing it forward into the first. All three cars were damaged, and several passengers were injured.

The line continued to be a considerable success and the hotel at the summit proved inadequate to cope with the vast numbers of passengers. An elaborate new hotel was built alongside the railway terminus to overcome this, opening in 1906.

A note in Isle of Man Tramways & Electric Power Co. company documents of 1897 considered the possibility of a line from Bungalow to Tholt-y-Will but this was not progressed. In 1907 however, following the construction of a

Centenary day of 21st August 1995 saw all six cars together at the Summit, each sporting a headboard to mark the occasion. The trams descended to Bungalow, with three cars evenly spaced on each track. *Barry Edwards*

hotel and refreshment room at Tholt-y-Will, the Manx Electric Railway Co. started a motor charabanc service over the route, generally regarded as the first motor bus service on the Island. Both the charabanc and mountain railway services ceased at the outbreak of the First World War.

The inauguration of the TT Races in 1907 led to the laying of crossovers and a siding at Bungalow station to enable the services to operate in two halves when the main road was being utilised for races.

Following the end of hostilities and the clearing of maintenance arrears, the line reopened on 10th June 1919. The Tholt-y-Will service also restarted but with different vehicles, as the charabancs had been sold. Two Ford Model T's took over in 1926 and these later gave way to Bedford coaches in 1939.

All rail and road services were stopped on 20th September 1939 after the outbreak of the Second World War. The Snaefell line did see some traffic during the hostilities, carrying peat down from the Bungalow area to Laxey to assist with fuel shortages. This traffic was handled by freight car No. 7, nicknamed Maria, with bogies borrowed from passenger car No. 5.

The relatively short-lived post-war boom in the tourist industry on the Island provided the line with plenty of

passengers and frequent services were operated. Visitor numbers began to fall in the early 1950s but a decision by the Air Ministry (later the Civil Aviation Authority) to construct a radar station at the summit provided work for the line during the winter of 1950/51. It was customary to remove the overhead wire from the upper section of the line in winter to avoid it becoming damaged. A Wickham railcar fitted with Fell brakes was purchased by the Air Ministry in 1951 to provide year-round availability, and a second followed in 1957. These railcars were housed in a small shed on the Snaefell depot site, as are their modern replacements.

Passenger numbers continued to fall and in 1953 the coach service to Tholt-y-Will was withdrawn. Towards the end of the 1955 season the Manx Electric Railway Co. advised the Isle of Man Government that it would be unable to operate the railway after the end of the following year. Luckily, a nationalisation agreement was reached, and the

↙Isle of Man Railway loco No 15 *Caledonia* propelling MER trailer 57 and an SMR car in spring 1995. An additional rail had to be fitted between Bungalow and Summit to allow the 3ft gauge locomotive to operate, and *Caledonia* was specially equipped with a Fell brake. *Ray Hulock*

↓No 15 *Caledonia* is lost in steam as she makes a spirited departure from Bungalow for the summit with MER car 57 during the centenary celebrations in 1995. *Ray Hulock*

The quality of trackwork is evident as tram 4 nears the end of her climb on 18th July 2021, with good views of Ramsey, Maughold Head and North Barrule in the centre of the picture. *Barry Edwards*

Tram 4 approaches Bungalow on 18th April 2022, sporting a green livery resembling the nationalised green and white livery introduced in 1957, during its descent from the Summit. *Barry Edwards*

Mid-winter on the Snaefell Mountain Railway. Wickham Railcar 4, which sports a hydraulic crane in its goods compartment, services the NATS radio station at the summit. It is seen here just above Bungalow on 9th January 2016. *Barry Edwards*

new Manx Electric Railway Board took control of the line on 1st June 1957.

The Tholt-y-Will coach service was reinstated but with little patronage, then extended to Sulby the following year and soon abandoned altogether. The Summit Hotel was redecorated in 1958, whilst the Bungalow Hotel was closed and demolished. Cars 2 and 4 were repainted into a new livery of green and cream but this was soon abandoned. No. 4 took the honour of being the last car of both the mountain and coastal lines so treated. The line showed considerable signs of age and corrosion by the mid-1960s, the Fell rail being of particular concern. Whilst the track was receiving attention, the cars themselves were becoming in desperate need of mechanical and electrical overhaul and, between 1958 and 1975, several options were considered and rejected.

Disaster struck on 16th August 1970 when, shortly after arrival at the Summit station on a particularly windy day, car No.5 caught fire and was almost destroyed. It was later discovered that a high-tension cable had rubbed on the chassis and worn through. Interestingly, the wind direction meant that some of the paint on the Laxey end of the car was not even scorched. Despite offers of a modern design of car body for the original chassis, the Manx Electric Railway Board elected to rebuild the car in its original form, although aluminium bus-style windows replaced the sliding wooden type of the original body. H.D. Kinnan of Ramsey built the new body and the car re-entered service on 8th July 1971.

The mechanical and electrical equipment on the cars

I.O.M. BUNGALOW HOTEL SNAEFELL.

continued to give serious cause for concern. In a bid to sort out the issues, the Manx Electric Railway Board called in London Transport in the mid 1970s, to look at overhauling the cars' electrical equipment. They recommended that the equipment be replaced, possibly from second-hand trams if a suitable supply could be found. In May 1976 a batch of suitable donors was located in Aachen, Germany.

Six former Aachen trams, Nos.1003/04/05/08/09/11, were shipped to the London Transport Lots Road Power Station works and the seventh, number 1010, made the journey to Douglas, laden with a good stock of spare parts.

Tram 6 pauses alongside the Bungalow Hotel, built in 1896. It was closed and demolished in 1958. *Barry Edwards Collection*

Road racing bisects the Snaefell Mountain Railway at the Bungalow and requires the line to operate in two halves. Tram 4 prepares to shuttle to the summit on 3rd June 2019. *Barry Edwards*

Tram 4 on emergency wire work just below Bungalow station on 29th July 2020. Although the line was not operating, a road vehicle had torn the wires down at Bungalow, necessitating the attention of the wiring team. The modern tower wagon was built on an original 1895 bogie. *Barry Edwards*

↖The exterior of Snaefell Power Station as Tram 3 descends towards Laxey in the early 20th century. The 60ft high chimney was fed by a flue under the tracks. *Manx National Heritage*

↑Four of the five Mather & Platt 120hp engines inside the generating station near the Bungalow. Four boilers were used to supply steam to these engines, with water pumped from the Sulby river; one of these boilers is on display alongside the former generating station site. *Barry Edwards Collection*

←The high quality of the permanent way is shown to good effect in this telephoto shot of Tram 4 descending past the original power station from the Bungalow on 21 June 2019, although the overhead line masts shown signs of age. *Barry Edwards*

Tram 5 crosses over from down to up line at the new crossover at Lhergy Veg on 10th April 2019. This tram differs from the rest of the fleet in not having a clerestory roof as the original tram was destroyed by fire on 16th August 1970. *Barry Edwards*

←Repairs following a landslip near the Snaefell Mine workings in 2015 led to single line working over the down line between Laxey and the Bungalow during the 2016 season. The track was slewed at Lhergy Veg, with a facing turnout later installed on the down line to limit the length of the single line. Tram 2 descends from the Summit on 10th April 2016. *Barry Edwards*

↓A Snaefell Mountain Railway car stands outside of Laxey station in the early years of operation. The wooden accumulator house that contained 250 chloride cells can be seen behind Dumbell's Terrace. *Barry Edwards Collection*

↓The unusual pointwork complete with Fell rail leading from the down line to Snaefell shed which required the efforts of two men to change direction. This has been replaced by a more conventional lead. *Barry Edwards*

↑The fitment of track brake equipment was mandated following an incident to Tram 2 in 2017; four of these fail-safe magnetic brakes were installed on each of Trams 1,2,4, and 5 for the 2019 season. *Barry Edwards*

←Tram 2 stands outside Snaefell shed on 19th March 2022. The roof mounted resistances and bow current collectors can clearly be seen. *Barry Edwards*

This four-wheel open wagon, seen on 22nd Aug 1965, was built by Hurst Nelson of Motherwell in 1895 to carry supplies to the Summit Hotel. The vehicle disintegrated whilst being propelled up the mountain in 1982. *Trevor Nall*

The tramway did not operate during 2020, its 125th anniversary, as a result of the Covid19 situation. On the actual anniversary day, the depot staff at Laxey, lined up trams 1, 2 and 5 outside the shed. *Barry Edwards*

The trams were stripped of the required components and the six in London were then broken up. No. 1010 remained in use as a store until 1985, when it too was broken up.

London Transport suggested that the Snaefell line gauge be changed to one metre to enable the Aachen bogies to be used as purchased. In the event, London Transport built twelve new bogies to the original Snaefell design, using only the Fell gear from the old bogies: the wheels, motors etc. coming from the Aachen trams. The first pair of new bogies arrived at Laxey in April 1977, to be united with car No. 1 which began tests in May 1977 and entered service in June. The other five cars were similarly rebuilt over the next two years.

Several modifications were later enacted, including new wheels for all six cars, after it was found that the finer profile of the Aachen wheels caused problems on the Snaefell track.

Fire returned to the summit on the night of 5th/6th August 1982, and despite the efforts of the local Fire Brigade, who managed to get a small six-wheeler appliance to the summit, the hotel was gutted by the fire. The clearing-up operation resulting in the line being closed until 9th August. To assist with the reconstruction, a crossover was installed just short of the station to enable the cars to terminate without having to go alongside the building. Two old 1895 bogie frames were fitted with small wagon bodies to assist in the conveyance of building materials to the hotel, which reopened for the 1984 season.

As the 1980s ended, plans were announced to rebuild the car sheds at Laxey, to enable all maintenance work to be carried out there, without the need to haul the cars to Derby Castle. The old shed was demolished at the end of the 1994 season, the cars being housed in a temporary structure within the station area. The new shed was completed in early 1995. The level crossing at Bungalow was rebuilt following the end of summer services in 1997.

The outbreak of Foot and Mouth disease on the Mainland, during 2001, led to many restrictions and closed footpaths on the Island, including the short path from the Summit station to the actual summit of Snaefell.

The upgrading of the facilities for staff and passengers at

A cluttered scene inside the original two-road Snaefell car shed during 1981. Several Mather & Platt type 5A motors from 1895 have been stored in the inspection pit. *Barry Edwards*

Bungalow was the subject of a planning application in 2002. Construction of a new building to include a new substation, waiting area, toilets, and staff quarters, commenced over the winter of 2002/03.

The long-term refurbishment of car 5 was completed in time for the 2003 season, the most notable and welcome change being the replacement of the bus-style windows with wooden sliding ones and the addition of Manx lettering on the sides of the tram.

A replica of the withdrawn No.7 Maria was hauled to Derby Castle in June 2003 where conversion to a 3ft 0in gauge works car was to take place. The locomotive emerged from the works with a centrally mounted generator, numbered 34 and painted yellow, with diagonal black lines on the ends.

Services on the line were suspended for a few days just after the start of the 2005 season, after a road vehicle damaged the overhead at Bungalow on 26th April, the line reopening on 29th April. Track was damaged and ballast washed away during a downpour in October 2005 but, no services were disrupted as the line was closed for the winter.

The Laxey road crossing was re-laid along with that of the Manx Electric over the winter of 2005/06, and the opportunity was taken to relay some of the Laxey station track. The dual gauge siding was retained. Bad weather brought down the wires on the upper section in the early part of April 2006 and the line only operated as far as Bungalow on opening day, 24th April; the first car to the Summit station operated on 6th May. A long-term overhaul of car 3 continued throughout the 2006 season. Some 10km of new Fell rail was rolled in China and delivered to the Island during the early months of 2007.

A severe thunderstorm on 22nd June 2007 caused services to be suspended as the risk of a lightning strike was considered too high to continue. The footpath to the summit from the hotel was closed for a short while from 3rd August following a further outbreak of Foot and Mouth on the mainland, whilst the hotel building received new rendering and a fresh coat of paint during the operating season; this work was completed during the summer months due to the difficulties of working on the summit in winter.

Track relay and Fell rail replacement took place over the winter of 2007/08 in several areas, some by contractors and other sections by local staff. The line had good seasons in

↑The original Snaefell car shed at Laxey with its distinctive curved roof in 1981. The building was demolished, and replaced, in 1995; the doors were a later addition. The shed made way for a new facility incorporating a maintenance workshop. A tower car and a Wickham trolley occupies the storage siding. *Barry Edwards*

↗Air Ministry Wickham Railcar No 1 of 1951 is stored in the open on the siding alongside the 1895 Snaefell car shed after ownership was transferred to Isle of Man Railways in 1977; it was sold into preservation in 2007. The vehicle could carry four passengers and a driver and was fitted with a Fell brake at the Snaefell end. Photographed on 18th August 1981. *Barry Edwards*

↑Tram 2 stands at the new Mines Road terminus in 1897, where a single blade point connects the up and down lines. The ornate station building stands in front of a mountain of waste material from the mines. *Manx National Heritage*

↗Tram 2 descends towards the 1897 Laxey station as Tram 3 loads with passengers for the next ascent. The walkway behind the tracks led up to the Vicarage. The 'Hayman' lift used to lift wagons of waste for disposal on the 'Deads' is almost buried by material, towering high above Dumbell's Terrace. *Manx National Heritage*

→Tram 5 begins another ascent of the mountain on 11th May 2019, having left the single line section from the station. 'Right-hand running' is the norm, to keep descending cars away from the steep drops on the northern side of the line below the Bungalow. *Barry Edwards*

2008 and 2009, helped no doubt by the high standards set in the Summit Café by the tenant. The final day of the 2009 season was one of the best days of the year, the early mist over the mountain soon clearing and resulting in high numbers of passengers turning up for a last trip. Further fell rail replacement and re-sleepering was carried out through the winter, while in the workshops car No.3 was completed and returned to service for the 2010 season after its extended overhaul. Car No.1 was next for overhaul.

The 2010 season started in April, and in line with the other railways, new ideas to attract visitors and local passengers were introduced. Wednesday evening services operated in conjunction with the Summit Hotel where full dining was available. All six cars were pressed into service on 22nd August 2010 to cope with large numbers of passengers arriving on a cruise ship, the situation repeating in September as part of a Railway Festival weekend.

Major refurbishment of the Summit Hotel resulted in an unusual operation from the Bungalow up, for the first few weeks of the 2011 season. While both tracks were in use, the terminus was closed to facilitate access for contractors, the cars stopping short of the actual hotel.

Car No.1 was in the workshops for refurbishment throughout 2012, emerging on 19th February 2013 for testing, and sporting a smart blue and cream livery, as applied to Manx Electric car No.7. The car re-entered service at the start of the season, making a welcome variation of livery on the mountain.

The Laxey station relay and refurbishment works

described in the Manx Electric section, were completed in early 2015.

The 2016 Snaefell season started as planned on 24th March. However, car No. 3 ran away from just short of the summit station on 30th March, eventually leaving the rails above Bungalow station and rolling over; the car was destroyed. Fortunately, there were no crew or passengers on the tram at the time.

A further incident occurred on Friday 4th August 2017, when a short break in overhead power resulted in the failure of the rheostatic brake on car No. 2 as it approached Bungalow. The car ran through Bungalow station and crossed over the Mountain Road before beginning the descent towards Laxey. There is no Fell rail in the section through the station and across the road, and so once over Fell rail again, the crew used the Fell brake to bring the tram to a stop. No crew or passengers were injured.

There were several days following the incident, when a very limited service operated as the fleet needed a full inspection. Investigations into the cause of the incident continued and the line closed for the remainder of the season on Monday 25th September, to allow resource to be put into the investigation and inspections.

Services resumed on Friday 30th March 2018, a day later that originally advertised as the Summit hotel needed to be commissioned for the season. Car No. 4 became the first in the fleet to be fitted with new magnetic anti-runaway brakes towards the end of the 2018 season. Fitted within the existing bogie frame, an electromagnet is situated between the wheels

Tram 5 was repainted in the original 1895 livery of teak and ivory to mark the line's 125th anniversary in 2020. It is seen on the single-track section into Laxey station on 26th July 2022. MER services to Laxey utilise the adjacent 3ft gauge tracks. *Barry Edwards*

→Special evening runs up the mountain to celebrate the line's centenary in 1995 proved immensely popular, with tramcars operating beyond midnight. A large crowd awaits the next departure from Laxey, as Tram 6 loads up and all remaining trams are called into service. *Barry Edwards*

→A temporary shed was constructed at Laxey station whilst the Snaefell tramcar shed was demolished to allow the new structure to be built on the same site. MER car 22, John Fowler traction engine No. 15117 of 1920, Wickham Railcar No 4, and Tram 2 line up on 8th February 1995, as part of the Isle of Man Post Office Snaefell 100 stamp launch. *Barry Edwards*

↓A line up of identically liveried trams at Laxey station during 1979. Trams carried a wooden 'Isle of Man Railways' board bolted to the underframes for a brief period to reflect new branding after nationalisation of Isle of Man Railways in 1978. Fortunately, the trams retained their hand-painted signwriting. *Barry Edwards*

→Local builder John Mylroie looks on as a group of railwaymen pose for the camera in front of Tram 3 after the extension of the line into the new Laxey Station in 1899. *Manx National Heritage*

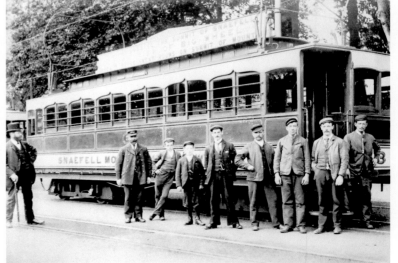

on each side of both bogies. In the event of a loss of power or brakes, the motorman presses a button that activates the magnet and brings the car to a rapid stop.

The 2019 season witnessed some very busy days with just four trams available for service. The bodywork of No. 6 was dismantled at the beginning of the year for reconstruction. A new steel body frame was delivered to the sheds on 20th February 2020, just as the Covid pandemic was taking hold across the world. 2020 was the 125th anniversary year for the line but sadly the pandemic meant that no services were operated that year.

The railway staff, not wishing the anniversary day to go unnoticed, lined up cars 1, 2 & 5 outside the shed on 21st August for a quick photo shoot. This was repeated a bit later in the day for one of the authors of this book and a friend. Having taken a good selection of images, the visitors were treated to a very short ride in car No. 5, within the confines of the depot area, thus making them two of the very few passengers carried in 2020.

The work on the replica car No. 6 continued, and as we approach the end of the 2022 season, the tram is nearing completion. With the easing of border restrictions for the Island in 2021, passenger numbers grew considerably, despite the late start to the season.

Once car 6 is completed, it is hoped that a replacement for the destroyed car 3 will be next in the workshops.

One wonders if the engineers who built the Snaefell Mountain Railway over 127 years ago, would have ever imagined that it would still be operating, largely in its original form in the 21st Century?

A line up of three cars await their custom for the summit at Laxey station in the early 1960s. *Trevor Nall*

The Transport Trust recognised the importance of the Snaefell Mountain Railway with a commemorative plaque on the Booking Office at Laxey station. *Barry Edwards*

THE DOUGLAS BAY HORSE TRAMWAY

→ This fascinating image shows the area to the north of the Derby Castle entertainment complex, sometime between 1886 and 1893. The area in the bottom right of the picture is now the site of the Manx Electric Railway Derby Castle depot, the filling in still to be completed. The King Edward Road and the Manx Electric railway construction is in progress. In the distance is Strathallan Crescent, and just beyond on the seaward side, the Horse Tramway station, and sheds built in 1886. The houses of Summerhill and the quarry behind are also clearly visible. *Manx National Heritage*

The Douglas Bay Horse Tramway was first conceived in 1875 by Thomas Lightfoot, a retired civil engineer from Sheffield, who had been involved in the construction of the original Woodhead Tunnel; later that year he lodged a proposal at the Rolls Office in Douglas. Spring 1876 saw an Act of Tynwald and the granting of Royal Assent for a tramway from Victoria Pier, part of the present sea terminal, to Summer Hill at the northern end of Douglas Bay. The Act specified that only animal power could be used.

A single track 3ft gauge line with passing loops was built with 35 lb/yd rail, the centre walkway for the horses being laid with small stones and tar. The Public Highway Surveyor inspected the line and it opened, without ceremony, between Summer Hill and the Iron Pier, situated opposite the bottom of Broadway, on 7th August 1876. The Starbuck Car & Wagon Co. Ltd, later G.F. Milnes & Co. delivered two double-deck tramcars, only one of which operated on the opening day, hauled by two horses.

The second section from the Iron Pier southwards to Victoria Pier opened in January 1877. After experiments with

Building a tramway in 1876, not a single piece of heras fencing or an orange flashing light in sight! The horse tramway is being laid on the stretch past the Queens Hotel, while the Promenade, lawns and walkway take shape. *Barry Edwards Collection*

just one horse, public opinion obliged the operators to continue to use two horses on the double-deck tramcars. Later that year a stable building was purchased to house the expanding stud of horses. This is still in use today. In 1882 the horse tramway was sold to Isle of Man Tramway Ltd, which added two more passing loops in 1883, to enable an increase in service intervals to every 20 minutes. This still proved insufficient, and in 1884 a further passing loop was added and the tram fleet increased to eight vehicles.

Over 350,000 passengers enjoyed a ride on the line in 1885 and two more single-deck trams were added. Summer Hill terminus was rebuilt and renamed Derby Castle in 1886, permission being granted in the same year to double the track from Falcon Cliff to Derby Castle. Seventeen tramcars were now in the fleet, and they all took part in a ceremony to mark the opening of the double-track section in 1887. In 1888 over half a million passengers were carried and 79,278 tram miles covered.

Twenty-six tramcars were in service by 1891 and all but a short stretch of line had been doubled. Thomas Lightfoot died on 10th January 1893, just eight months before The Douglas & Laxey Coast Electric Tramway Co. opened the first stage of what is now the Manx Electric Railway, from Derby Castle to Groudle. The electric tramway terminus at Derby Castle, just 15ft away from the horse tram terminus, brought even more passengers to the Horse Tramway.

The Isle of Man Tramways & Electric Power Co. purchased the Horse Tramway for £38,000 in April 1894 in a deal that required them to construct a cable tramway to upper Douglas. In 1895 work commenced on the new horse tram depot at Derby Castle, the site of which is still in use today. Offices were added above the depot in 1935 and for a long time were home to what is now Isle of Man Transport. A cast-iron awning over the horse tramway terminal, sadly demolished as unsafe in 1980, was also built at this time.

Electrification of the tramway was considered by the tramway company in 1897 when, following completion of the last piece of double track, over one and a half million passengers were carried,

The Isle of Man Tramways & Electric Power Co. relied on Dumbell's Bank to finance construction of the tramway and the Upper Douglas cable car system; the collapse of the Bank in 1900 forced the Tramway company into liquidation. In September 1901 the Manx Chancery accepted a £50,000 offer from Douglas Corporation for the horse tramway and cable car system. Thirty-six cars now operated on the horse tramway, 13 double-deckers, three single-deck saloons, 14 open toastracks and six roofed toastracks, motive power being

The 1895-built tram shed at Derby Castle, complete with the offices added by 1936, seen here in 1981. Horse Tram shop, tram 22 and open toastrack tram 12 are visible outside the shed. The building was demolished as life expired in late 2018 and replaced with a replica of the original single-storey shed.
Barry Edwards

During the reconstruction of the Derby Castle shed, this temporary structure was provided just beyond the end of the tramway tracks at the terminus. An interesting visitor was Manx Electric diesel electric locomotive No.34, seen here on 22nd May 2019.
Barry Edwards

↖The colourful tram shop, in modified tram 22 is seen outside at Derby Castle in 1993. The various travel ticket prices make interesting reading, although the current equivalent offers superb value for money. *Richard Kirkman*

↑Tram 34 meets Tram 44 at the entrance to Derby castle station during 1993. The horse seems to be getting bored, while waiting for the two crew members to finish their conversation. *Richard Kirkman*

←A wonderful image showing a line up outside the shed in 1993. From left to right they are 18, 27, 44 and 29. The tram numbered 14 is not the real 14, its identity is unknown. *Richard Kirkman*

↓A view inside the new shed taken shortly after the trams were moved in. Double deck tram 18 shares the shed with 36 and 38 among others, on 28th July 2020. *Barry Edwards*

The standard of refurbishment work completed on the trams is superb. Here we see tram 32 part way through its restoration. The tram is sitting over the inspection pit on 17th March 2022. *Barry Edwards*

→Shortly after being taken over by Isle of Man Railways, the tramway was re-branded to Douglas Bay Horse Tramway. Here tram 1 sits outside the old shed proudly displaying its new titles, on 7th August 2016. *Barry Edwards*

↓This was the scene on 23rd May 2019 with the steel frame of the new building taking shape. *Barry Edwards*

↘The work to refurbish the Promenade was due to start at the end of the 2014 season. There was serious concern about the future of the tramway and Douglas Corporation made something of what could have been the very last day. Horse *Mark* is seen leaving Derby Castle, with the Mayor and Mayoress on board tram 18, for the final run of the season, on 14th September 2014. Thankfully as we now know, the tramway survives. *Barry Edwards*

Please do
not enter

27

Following restoration, tram 27 was returned to service in a very smart blue livery, as seen here on 18th April 2022. *Barry Edwards*

Horse *Philip* enjoys a treat from his driver during turnround at Derby Castle on 13th August 2019. The new shed construction site is on the left, while the temporary shed is visible to the left. *Barry Edwards*

provided by 68 horses. The electric tramway was sold in 1902 to a syndicate based in Manchester and later that year to the Manx Electric Railway Company.

In 1906 the Manx Electric Railway Company approached the Corporation with a scheme to electrify the horse tramway and provide a through service from Ramsey to Victoria Pier, but this was again rejected, as was a further approach in 1908. Two more tramcars were delivered in 1907 and in 1909 it was ruled that a maximum of eight return journeys were to be operated by each horse in the course of a day.

A winter schedule operated during the First World War, as the holiday industry slumped. However, by 1920 business was picking up again, with 44 cars available for traffic.

Motor buses were introduced along the Promenade for the first time in 1926 and it was proposed that they would eventually take over from the tramway. In 1927, after almost 50 years unbroken service, the tramway began closing for the winter. Serious threats of closure were hanging over the line by 1933 but the Corporation embarked on a major track relaying programme, using 65 lb/yd rail which would last 40 years, thus assuring the future of the tramway. Indeed, the horse tramway made a profit of £8,000 in 1933 compared with a loss of £4,280 on the bus services, a pattern that continued for several decades. Three more tramcars were

added in 1935 and roller bearings were fitted to the existing fleet; by now, the number of horses had reached 135.

The Second World War caused the tramway to close. All the horses were sold, the tramcars put into store, barbed wire erected between the tracks and many seafront hotels requisitioned as camps to house internees.

In April 1946, 42 horses arrived from Ireland, the tramcars emerged from store and a re-opening ceremony was performed on 22nd May by Sir Geoffrey Bromet, the Lieutenant-Governor of the Island. A reduced service was operated but a profit still resulted. Holidaymakers poured back to the Island in 1947, track laying restarted, and all looked good for the future until 1949, when it was suggested that open-top buses should replace the trams but fortunately the Corporation took no action. All but one of the double-deck cars had by now disappeared and in 1955 the sole survivor (No.14) left the Island for preservation in the Museum of British Transport at Clapham.

An anniversary parade was held in 1956 to mark 80 years of service, the horses and cars assembling at Victoria Pier before returning to Derby Castle in convoy.

Holiday traffic declined towards the end of the 1950s and threats of closure were again rumoured but denied officially. Tynwald granted permission in 1961 for a fare increase, as the tramway was now regarded as a speciality ride. The Fleetwood steamer services ceased after the summer of 1961, resulting in a reduction in the number of day trippers to the Island from 1962.

Tynwald Day 1964 saw Her Majesty Queen Elizabeth, the Queen Mother, ride on specially prepared tram No.44 from Summer Hill to the Villa Marina. The stud of horses was 56 at the beginning of the year being reduced to 43 by the winter. Fifteen new horses were purchased at the beginning of 1965, a year that saw another Royal visit, this time by HRH Princess Margaret and Lord Snowdon.

A flat fare system was introduced in 1966 and the number of passengers showed an increase, which was to continue over the next few years.

HRH the Duke of Edinburgh visited the line in 1970, returning in 1972 with Her Majesty the Queen, HRH Princess Anne and Admiral of the Fleet, Earl Mountbatten of Burma. The Royal party rode from the new terminus at Victoria Pier to the Sefton Hotel in cars 44 and 36, both specially painted and decked out with flowers. The Promenade was crowded with a high percentage of Islanders.

During the early 1970s the Isle of Man Tourist Board actively sought to increase the number of visitors through extensive advertising, which increased the number of passengers on the horse tramway, and by 1973 the numbers were heading back up towards those of the early 1920s. In 1974 over one and a half million passengers were carried. The price of horses rose sharply during 1974/75 resulting in the Corporation deciding to start a breeding programme, new foals not working on the tramway until they were at least three years old.

The centenary fell on 7th August 1976 but as this was a Saturday the celebrations were held on the following Monday, by chance during the author's first visit to the Island. The Science Museum in London, by now the home of double-decker No.14, was persuaded to allow it to return to the Island, be repainted and take part in the celebrations. Three other cars were also repainted including No.44 that was only returned to the depot the evening before. Stable staff worked through the night grooming the 50 horses, all brass work was meticulously polished and nameboards provided for each horse.

At 10:00 the horses were led along the Promenade towards Victoria Pier where the trams were waiting, having been hauled there five at a time by a double-decker bus. Then at 11:15 the double-deck tram left Victoria Pier at the head of the procession that included the newly restored Upper Douglas cable car. Every serviceable tram followed; their passengers being issued with special centenary tickets. It was estimated that 30,000 people lined the Promenade from end to end.

The year 1979 was the millennium of Tynwald and after much promotion the number of visitors to the Island was higher than in previous years and the tramway carried just over 860,000 passengers during the season.

The line made a loss in 1980 for the first time in its history, with passenger numbers down to 742,000, the beginning of what was to be a poor decade with numbers falling, such that by 1989 passengers were down to 264,000 and by 1991 to just

short of 180,000. Car No.46 spent the summer of 1987 on display in Nobles Park, Douglas before being shipped to the mainland, fully restored, for display at the Woodside Ferry terminal, Birkenhead.

The 1993 season started earlier, at Easter, as part of the 'Year of Railways' celebrations. Fares for the year were £1.10 single or runabout, the ticket being valid for the whole day. Stored cars 11, 47 and 49 were moved from Ramsey MER car sheds to Douglas and placed behind the new steam

Following completion of track relaying, the tramway re-opened to the public on 29th July 2022. Ahead of re-opening, there was several weeks of training and re-familiarisation for both the horses and tram crews. On 13th July, *William* is seen here receiving a good deal of attention ahead of a trip to Broadway. *Barry Edwards*

A scene that would have been commonplace in the early years of the tramway. Tram 18 was restored to double deck in 1988/89 while tram 14 was on the Island on loan from the Science Museum. 14 is now a permanent exhibit in the Manx Museum in Douglas. *Barry Edwards Collection*

↑A view inside the old shed in 2006, shows trams 18 and 27 in the company of restored Upper Douglas Cable Tram 72/73. The restoration had been completed in 1976 ahead of the horse tram centenary. The tram now resides at the Jurby Transport Museum. *Barry Edwards*

↗A couple of weeks after re-opening, on 12th August 2022, *Nelson* prepares to depart from Derby Castle with tram 36, still with its decorations from opening day. *Barry Edwards*

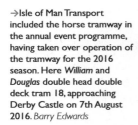

→Isle of Man Transport included the horse tramway in the annual event programme, having taken over operation of the tramway for the 2016 season. Here *William* and *Douglas* double head double deck tram 18, approaching Derby Castle on 7th August 2016. *Barry Edwards*

↓One of the 45-47 batch of trams approaches Derby Castle on 23rd August 1965, while tram 43 departs towards the Sea Terminal. *Trevor Nall*

↘The new track being laid on Queens Promenade as part of the Promenade regeneration project. The rails are being attached to the new concrete slab on 12th April 2019. *Barry Edwards*

The very first public trip on the re-opened tramway, is seen leaving Derby Castle and heading for Broadway on 29th July 2022. Horse *Torrin* is doing the honours at the front. *Barry Edwards*

↑During 2019 the tramway did operate over a short distance, just on the seaward track. Here *Torrin* has tram 45 in tow as the driver slows to cross the traffic and approach Derby Castle. 2nd November 2019. *Barry Edwards*

↗Digging up the old track and concrete base on 17th January 2019. *Barry Edwards*

→Winter saloon tram 29 with *Rocky* operate towards Derby Castle on 24th May 2019. The ongoing works on the promenade are clearly evident in this picture. *Barry Edwards*

Rocky heads along Queens Promenade with tram 36 on 25th June 2016. The Queen's Hotel is in the background. *Barry Edwards*

Horse *Steve* on Central Promenade with tram 43 on 30th July 2016. The Manx electric depot and illuminated sign are visible on the left of the image. *Barry Edwards*

and/or moving it onto the Promenade walkway. These suggestions all formed part of a new Douglas 2000 project, looking at Douglas as it moved towards the 21st Century.

Car No.45 was returned to service in 1994 after a few years stored, the operating season reverting to early May through to 1st October. A safety drive by new management prevented conductors from riding on the front of the car, thus returning them to the rear platform from where they could observe any issues that arose with the passengers.

Cars 21 and 30 had their Douglas 2000 livery removed at the end of the 1995 season. During the 1995/96 winter the track at the Sea Terminal end of the line was lifted to allow work on the Island-wide IRIS sewage project to be undertaken. The track was back in place in good time for the commencement of the 1996 season. This marked the 120th birthday of the Horse Tramway and the centenary of Douglas Corporation; two trams, 36 and 43, appeared carrying illuminations celebrating the birthday.

Despite good loads in the early and mid-evenings the overall Horse Tramway passenger numbers for the 1996 season were disappointing. The evening service proved very worthwhile and was complemented in the mid-summer by the illuminated Manx Electric car working to Groudle in conjunction with the Groudle Glen Railway, enabling travel by horse, electric and steam all in one evening! The general appearance of the entire horse tram fleet was deemed to have improved under the new management.

Toastrack car No.40 was extensively rebuilt during the

railway carriage shed in June 1993. Cars 21 and 38 were repainted into a special blue and gold Douglas 2000 livery. Wilson Gibb retired as General Manager of the horse tramway on 18th August 1993 and Peter Cannan, who had worked on the tramway for 15 years, was appointed Tramway Supervisor. The year's celebrations for the Manx Electric brought large numbers of enthusiast visitors and delivered passenger figures of 205,061.

Many suggestions regarding the future of the Horse Tramway were forthcoming, including making it single track

1996/1997 winter and re-entered service on 23rd July 1997. The all-day ticket for the 1997 season was £1.40 and a four-tram service was operated during the TT festival fortnight.

The oldest surviving car, No 11, returned to Derby Castle in late 1998 with a plan for restoration to service condition. On Friday 17th September, car 35 struck the counterweight of a lorry-mounted crane outside the new Tower Shopping Centre on Loch Promenade, whilst travelling towards Derby Castle. Several passengers were injured, two requiring hospital treatment and the tram was badly damaged, the impact collapsing the roof onto the top of the seats.

Work to rebuild car 35 took place over the winter of 1999/2000, whilst new red on white tram stop signs were installed along the route. During the first half of 2000 the stables received a much-needed upgrade. The traditional bays have been replaced with boxes, giving the horses room to lie down between shifts if they wish.

The 125th anniversary of the Horse Tramway was celebrated in 2001, each tram used in service that year receiving a special 125th logo sticker. On the anniversary evening, 7th August, there was a parade with the Promenade closed to traffic to accommodate the large crowd. Unlike previous parades the start this time was at Derby Castle where the

↖A 1964 view of tram 50, one of the 'Tomato Box' trams on Queens Promenade. The buildings behind have since been replaced with a modern apartment block. The tram was one of three able to be converted from open to closed as required. *Barry Edwards Collection*

↑With the track and road incomplete towards the Sea Terminal, the trams only ran as far as Switzerland Road. Nicknamed as 'T Shirt Terminus' by the tram crews, *Philip* is with tram 29, on 4th July 2019. *Barry Edwards*

←Royal tram 44 with *Charles* at the front is on Queens Promenade on 7th August 2016. It has just passed tram 18 heading towards Derby Castle. *Barry Edwards*

Just a little further along Queens Promenade, tram 1 is decorated for the festive season, and taking lots of excited children to see Santa on 19th December 2009. *Barry Edwards*

→The first of the Tomato Box trams, 48 is seen passing the entrance to the Palace complex as it heads towards the Sea Terminal, probably in the late 1940s or early 1950s. *Manx National Heritage*

↘Tram 24, seen here heading for Derby Castle was built in 1891 by G F Milnes & Co. Ltd. It is passing the Palace Ballroom in the late 19th Century. *Manx National Heritage*

→↘Passing the modern day Palace Hotel, at the time known as Stakis Hotel, is *Alec* with tram No. 1. The Stakis names was short lived, lasting for only a couple of years from September 1994. *Barry Edwards*

↓On Queens Promenade in the 1960's we see tram 46 heading north towards Derby Castle with a full complement of passengers. *Barry Edwards Collection*

↑*Charles* and tram 45 are heading towards Derby Castle and passing the area of the current temporary terminus of the line, on 25th June 2016. The Villa Marina is in the background. *Barry Edwards*

←*William* approaches the temporary terminus of the tramway, with tram 36 in tow, on 12th August 2022. *Barry Edwards*

↑The first terminus of the tramway at the southern end was at the Iron Pier, situated opposite the bottom of Broadway. The pier has been demolished. Here tram 3 and a further unidentified tram pose at the stop, on the opening day of the tramway, 7th August 1876. *Manx National Heritage*

→On the 140th anniversary of the opening of the tramway, *William* and *Douglas* pass the Villa Marina with double deck tram 18. 7th August 2016. *Barry Edwards*

At about the same point of the previous image, *Torrin* brings tram 36 off the temporary terminus and crosses the southbound carriageway of the Promenade on 29th July 2022. *Barry Edwards*

→ The Villa Marina arcade walkway used to offer this elevated view of the tramway. Following the refurbishment of the Promenade, the line is on the seaward side of the road at this point. *Nicola* heads towards the Sea Terminal on 28th June 2006, with tram 37. *Barry Edwards*

↓ Horse *Una* has tram 44 in tow and both the driver and conductor are female. This was believed to be the first time this had occurred on the tramway. The tram is passing the Villa Marina on 2nd May 2016. *Barry Edwards*

Mayor, Councillor Stephen Pitts, made his speech alongside the still-to-be-restored car No.11. Double-deck car 18 led the cavalcade conveying the Lieutenant Governor Air Marshall Ian Macfadyen together with the visiting Governors of Jersey and Guernsey. Car 43 conveyed a party of visiting schoolchildren from the former Soviet Republic. On return to Derby Castle

the party transferred to Summerland for a reception.

The 2003 season was shortened as the growing costs of the tramway threatened its future, the tramway only operating from May to the end of September. The tramway was promoted with a number of banners being placed at prominent roadside locations around the town at the start of

the 2004 season. The Lieutenant Governor and his family visited the horse stables during the year to see the horse *Mark*, adopted by his family during the 2001 adopt-a-horse scheme. Douglas Corporation examined running illuminated cars for the run up to Christmas 2004 but sadly the idea never got off the ground.

Only 76,478 passengers travelled on the tramway in 2005, the trams covering around 20,000 miles. This represents a drop of over 100,000 on the 1995 figure with the mileage covered being less than a third of that of 1995. Despite some cosmetic attention in April and the car moving into the tram depot in May, car No.11 was moved to Homefield on 21st September 2005 for undercover storage, as no time had been available for its full restoration and return to service.

After the success of the local Commonwealth Games team in Australia, Douglas Corporation provided double-deck horse tram No.18 to convey the athletes and officials along the Promenade from the Sea Terminal to the Villa Marina for a reception on 20th April 2006.

Fares for the 2006 season were reduced to £1.00 single and the all-day tickets were withdrawn, a move intended to encourage more use of the tramway. It was suggested that a spare Horse Tramway car should be put on static display on the short length of cable tramway track laid at the bottom of Victoria Street but potential damage to the car by late night revellers resulted in the idea being shelved.

A further threat to the future of the Horse Tramway came when the Corporation announced that it needed to cut overall expenses by £180,000. However, the tramway survived the cuts and the 2007 season produced little change

to the service, although car 36 did return to traffic after several years absence.

However, since the end of the 2007 season, the tramway has been the subject of much discussion. The hidden cost of clearing up after the horses was raised at a Corporation meeting and the possibility of the horses' wearing nappies was considered!

In January 2008 it was announced that the tramway had lost £270,000 the previous year and that the 2008 season would be shortened by four weeks, operating from mid-May to mid-September. The operating deficit was reduced by £20,000 despite a further reduction in passenger numbers.

For the 2009 season trams started later in the morning at 11:00 and continued until 20:00. The double deck tram was in service daily, but the biggest break came towards the end of the year with the announcement that Santa trams would run for six days in the week running up to Christmas. Tramway staff decorated tram No.1 with lights inside and out and provided some appropriate horse names. The operation was a resounding success with trams fully booked in advance and the weather obliged with sunshine on all three days. Soon after the operation, the idea of corporate charters was actively considered.

In early 2010, two of the trams were moved from Derby Castle shed to the new Jurby Transport Museum. Car 22, the former tram shop, saw further use as a shop at Jurby, while the former Upper Douglas Cable Car was to be an exhibit at the new museum. A short while later cars 11, 47, and 49 also went to Jurby from the former Homefield bus depot, that was being emptied in preparation for sale of the building. The

Amby is seen getting a good speed past the Villa Marina on 31st August 2014, with tram 43 and a good load of passengers. The photographer is making use of the narrow pavement that separated the north and southbound carriageways, all now changed. *Barry Edwards*

2010 season started on 10th May and an innovation saw the introduction of Experience days. The days included the opportunity to visit the stables, assist with the horses, a visit to the tram sheds and a trip along the line. The Santa Trams were repeated on eight days of operation with the Derby Castle Manx Electric Railway station ticket office becoming Santa's Grotto.

The Corporation approved the movement of car No.35 to the Home of Rest for Old Horses on Richmond Hill to be displayed within a fenced area on a short length of track. The 2011 season was extended to accommodate the holding of the Commonwealth Youth games on the Island. An attractive four-page timetable and information leaflet was produced for the first time and has appeared annually since.

A towable poop scooper was purchased in 2011 to assist in keeping the Promenade clear of horse droppings. Towards the end of that year, the state of the Promenade and its upgrading was back on the agenda. Previous discussions had come to nothing but, the position of the horse tramway and whether it should be retained prompted many opinions to be expressed. Over the next few years, the discussions continued, with the repositioning of the tramway onto the Promenade walkway being one suggestion or moving it to the seaward side of the roadway being another.

During 2013 a section of the Promenade and Peveril Square were refurbished utilising modern stonework and a resurface of the road. This work included a new island alongside the current tramway terminus. The intention was to continue with this work from Autumn 2014 onwards but there was still no firm decision about the tramway. In anticipation that 2014 would be the last season that the tramway would run along the centre of the promenade, and many believing that it would be the last season ever, Douglas Corporation organised a special final weekend, culminating in a final trip using the double deck tram hauled by *Mark*, the Mayor and Mayoress overseeing the proceedings. There were some tearful eyes as tram No.18 was pushed into the shed after completion of the final trip. As it turned out, the plans were shelved.

The tramway re-opened at the beginning of the 2015 as usual. On 6th May 2015, revised plans were published, with the tramway on the walkway from around halfway, a plan that met with severe objections, and a major campaign was begun to keep the tramway off the walkway. This resulted in a public enquiry towards the end of 2015. Santa trams operated again for Christmas 2015 and in early January the timetable plans for the 2016 season were announced, including a note that there would be some special events to mark the 140th anniversary of the tramway.

However, on 21st January 2016 Douglas Borough Council voted to terminate the service and the government announced plans to reconstruct the Promenade without including the tramway tracks. Negotiations and discussions between various heritage groups, Isle of Man Railways and Manx National Heritage, were immediately instigated. This resulted in an agreement that Isle of Man Railways would

A special movement took place on the final day of services in 2014, when two trams ran in parallel alongside the Villa Marina. With the Islands' war memorial on the background, trams 18 and 44 run side by side with *Ian* and *Teddy* doing the work at the front on 14th September 2014. *Barry Edwards*

Whatever happens with the re-instatement of the tramway along Loch Promenade, trams will never again run along the middle of the road on this section. *Robert* has open toastrack 21 in tow as he approaches the end of the line on 7th July 2012. *Barry Edwards*

operate the line for the next three seasons, as part of the heritage railway portfolio.

The tramway was rebranded as 'The Douglas Bay Horse Tramway' the fleet was tidied up, GO cards were introduced, and a full timetable leaflet published. Trams operated from 30th April through until 30th October, the longest operating season for many years. The 140th anniversary was celebrated on Sunday 7th August with a series of events. Passenger numbers for the season were up by over 40% from 49,000 in 2015 to over 69,500 in 2016.

In July 2017, plans for a £20.7 million scheme to redevelop Douglas Promenade from Peveril Square to Strathallan Crescent, were approved by Tynwald. The first of a series of refurbished trams, No. 36, was in service on the last day of the 2017 season, looking every bit the part, as it made its way along the Promenade.

The 2018 season began on Thursday 29 March, the second refurbished tram, No. 45 entering service soon after, followed in very late May by Number 42. As the season got underway, plans were announced to demolish the existing tram depot and offices at Strathallan and replace them with a single storey building with a replica original front. The tramway purchased the stables for £600,000, considerably less than the original asking price. The new shed and offices were completed in early 2020.

The Promenade upgrade works proved troublesome. In early 2021 the Department of Infrastructure put a hold on completing the track between Broadway and the Sea Terminal to speed up the completion of the project. This led to several questions in the House of Keys, with suggestions that the Department were hiding the true cost of the promenade by cutting out elements that have already been

Horse *Keith* knows a treat awaits as he makes good speed along the final stretch of Loch Promenade with Royal tram 44, on the final day of service of the season, 14th September 2014. *Barry Edwards*

Christmas-decorated closed winter saloon No.1 has just left the Sea Terminal on 19th December 2009 and is running along Loch Promenade on its way to Derby Castle. *Barry Edwards*

Horse *Rocky* gathers speed as he departs from the Sea Terminal with tram 21 and a full complement of passengers on 13th September 2015. *Barry Edwards*

approved. The Promenade works were completed with a truncated tramway running from Derby Castle to the Villa Marina opening on 30th July 2022.

The tramway has enjoyed good patronage through the 2022 season and took part in the Winter Transport festival at the end of October. On certain days, the various different types of tram operated, providing a good variety of trams on the promenade.

It had been hoped that the re-instatement of the section between Broadway and the Sea Terminal would have been completed over the coming winter but, sadly this is unlikely to be the case. It seems that the current Minister is still under the impression that he needs to seek funding for this work, despite it being approved in 2017.

A tramway style traffic light system was installed just to the north of the temporary terminus, with the white horizontal and vertical lights for the trams. The horses soon learnt what these different lines of lights meant!

The tramway can now look forward to its 150th anniversary in 2026, hopefully operating along the full length of the Promenade by then.

Many visitors to the Island enquire about the welfare of the motive power, the horses. The truth is that they are extremely well looked after, spending the winter months, and at least a day a week during the operating season, grazing in fields specially reserved for them. During the operating season they are stabled near the Derby Castle terminus and only work two, sometimes three return trips each, in any one day. They are cared for by a team of dedicated professionals.

↑A superb 1964 view of the terminus area at the Sea Terminal end of the line. Most of these buildings remain, although the names have all changed. The tram is one of the 45 to 47 series. *Barry Edwards Collection*

←A view of Victoria Pier and the old Sea Terminal building sadly now demolished. The approaching steamer is obviously well loaded, there are no less than six horse trams and numerous other vehicles awaiting its arrival. The postcard was posted on 23rd June 1919, so the image pre-dates this. *Barry Edwards Collection*

Another view of the Sea Terminal end of the tramway, this time with tram 47, now preserved in Birkenhead. Wilkins the jewellers, later moved into the main shopping street but has recently closed. *Manx National Heritage*

UPPER DOUGLAS CABLE TRAMWAY

At a public meeting on 19th January 1894, the residents of upper Douglas pressed for a tram service as they felt that their shops and boarding houses were at a disadvantage compared to those on the Promenade. The Upper Douglas Tramway Committee was formed and met for the first time on 9th April 1894; a later meeting of the Commissioners (now Corporation) Improvement Committee resolved that it would be desirable to construct a tramway to the Upper Douglas area.

The proposed route was from the bottom of Victoria Street in a circuit to the bottom of Broadway near its junction with the Promenade. The cost of an electric line was estimated to be around £19,000, whilst a cable tramway would cost around £25,000.

Little progress was made, so a further public meeting on 21st January 1895 attempted to push the project forward. At the same time, negotiations were continuing between the Commissioners and the Isle of Man Tramways & Electric Power Co. (IOMT&EP Co) over the future of the Horse Tramway, and the Tramway company offered to build the new line as part of the deal. A formal offer was made on 30th May 1895. The Commissioners agreed to accept this proposal and promoted a bill to Tynwald, this becoming the Upper Douglas Tramway Act of 1895. Standing Orders were suspended in the house on 10th July to allow a special committee to debate the application urgently.

The Act was passed on 3rd August 1895, specifying a tramway operated by wire, ropes, cable, or chains, with a fixed engine, starting at the junction of Victoria Street and the Promenade, travelling up Victoria Street, Prospect Hill, Bucks Road, Woodbourne Road, York Road, and Ballaquayle Road, before terminating at the bottom of Broadway adjacent to its junction with the Promenades, thus connecting with the Horse Tramway at both ends of the route. The track gauge was specified as 3′0″. The car sheds and winding equipment were to be installed in a new building on York Road, between Laureston Avenue and Waverley Road, from where a continuous cable some three miles in length would drive the tramway, with individual cars gripping on to it when they needed to move (as in the San Francisco system).

Dick, Kerr & Co Ltd began construction of the line, despite some concerns from local traders about the proximity of moving trams to their property. Further problems brought construction to a halt in February 1896, but the issues were soon resolved. Twelve tramcars were ordered from G F Milnes of Birkenhead, which comprised of Nos 71-78 'open' cars, and 79-82 'closed' cars.

The cable was threaded on 6th and 7th August 1896 using two traction engines, and the first tramcar ventured out onto the line late on Friday 7th August. Following testing and

The substantial car shed, winding house, and power station of the Upper Douglas line at the foot of the future York Road. The 80ft brick chimney was fed from two hand-fired Galloway boilers. *Manx National Heritage*

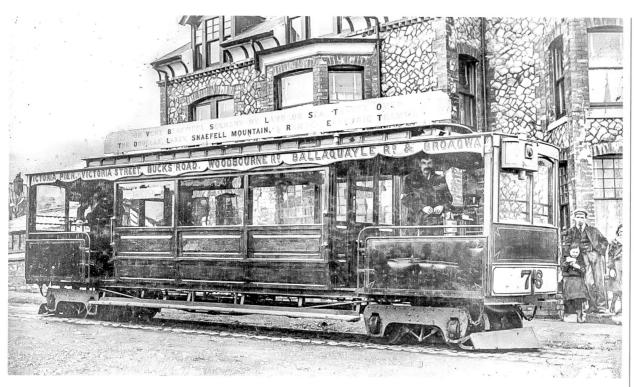

The camera is the centre of attraction as car 78 stands outside Corner House in Palatine Road around 1900. Visitors are implored to travel on the Douglas, Laxey, Snaefell Mountain & Laxey Electric Tramway. *Manx National Heritage*

inspections the tramway opened to the public on Saturday 15th August 1896, with three cars providing a ten-minute interval service. The line carried 193,645 passengers between opening and the end of the year.

The collapse of Dumbell's Bank collapsed in February 1900 led to the demise of many companies including the IOMT&EP Co. After many reports and inspections, the Corporation, as they were now known, offered £40,000 to purchase both the Horse and Cable tramways. This was rejected but an improved offer of £50,000 was accepted on 25th September 1901.

The line was shortened at the Broadway end in 1902 to terminate just below the depot on Ballaquayle Road. In 1905 connecting tracks were installed for a shuttle horse tram connection from Victoria Street to the Pier. Traffic levels encouraged the purchase of further tramcars; 69 and 70 were

Car 73 is seen at Avondale in the very early days of operation around August 1896; the crossover, with the pointsman's hut visible in the background, allowed cars to turn back here. *Richard Kirkman collection*

Inset: Construction work under way in Victoria Street, Douglas in 1898. The central wire conduit is clearly visible between the tracks. *Richard Kirkman Collection*

provided by the United Electric Car Co in 1907, and cars 67 (1911) and 68 (1909) were purchased from Milnes.

The tramway continued to operate with strong passenger numbers, including throughout the First World War, when a reduced service was provided. But after the War the Corporation became increasingly concerned about the condition of the tramway and the cost of necessary repairs and ordered five Tilling Stevens petrol electric buses in 1920; these took over the tramway route for the 1921/22 winter service. The tramway only operated during the summer season thereafter, each year for a shorter period than the last, until eventually it ran only for just a few weeks in 1929.

Sadly, the end had come, and the last cars ran on Monday 19th August 1929, the press reporting Douglas to be 'strangely quiet on the Tuesday', without the clanking noise of the trams. The cable was soon removed, and the removal of trackwork started. The York Road depot was converted to a bus garage for the Corporation, surviving into National Transport days; the site is now a sheltered housing complex.

The tramcar fleet was sold to a local businessman who

intended to sell them on as holiday bungalows; two did find their way for use as a dwelling at Crawyn, Ballaugh, in the north of the Island, whilst the rest were eventually broken up.

The two survivors were rescued by the Douglas Cable Car Group and moved to space loaned to the Group in the former depot in York Road, where over an eight-year period the two vehicles were combined into one, and a fully restored car took part in the centenary celebration cavalcade for the Horse Tramway in August 1976. The car was then displayed in the Horse Tramway depot at Derby Castle, moving to the new Jurby Transport Museum in 2009.

The tramway returned to the news in January 2000, when excavations in connection with the Island-wide IRIS scheme unearthed two of the original cable wheels at the bottom of Victoria Street. Local enthusiasts and the engineering firm employed on the contract worked together to enable one of these wheels to be retrieved intact. This was stored at several locations before being put on permanent public display at the entrance to the Bottleneck car park on Douglas Promenade, close to the junction with Victoria Street.

A quiet moment inside the car shed as cars 74 and 76 await their next duties. The 235ft car shed had four roads linked by the traverser. *Barry Edwards Collection*

DOUGLAS HEAD AND MARINE DRIVE TRAMWAY

By the 1880s Douglas Head was becoming an increasingly popular tourist spot with a wide range of attractions, despite being situated some distance from the town's hotels. Several schemes were contemplated to improve access, including a tunnel under the harbour with a spiral staircase climbing to the Head, a suspension bridge providing access over the harbour and even a tramway up from South Quay. Steam ferries provided a popular means of crossing the harbour.

Construction of a scenic Marine Drive along the coast from Douglas Head to Port Soderick began in December 1890. The road opened to Wallberry on 23rd July 1891, but various financial and building difficulties, including receivership, slowed further progress. A new syndicate took over in 1892 and by 7th August 1893 the road had reached Little Ness, prompting a 'Grand Re-opening' function at which it was announced that the Douglas Head Marine Drive Limited would take up a concession to construct an electric tramway along the route. The Marine Drive from Douglas Head to the Castletown Road was completed in 1894. Douglas Southern Electric Tramways Ltd was incorporated on 21st October 1895 to build and own a new tramway from Douglas Head to Little Ness with a later extension to Port Soderick and a possible branch to join up with the Old Castletown Road near Oakhill.

Construction of the tramway on the landward side of the Marine Drive started at the beginning of 1896 and progress was rapid; the trackbed was almost completed by late February, and the track had arrived. Rolling stock was stored in a four-road car shed, complete with traverser, built in an isolated location at Little Ness, whilst a substantial steam power station was erected at Pigeon Stream, the only point on the line with a supply of fresh water. Building the original road involved several timber bridges, and these were replaced by steel structures designed to accommodate the tramway. Unlike all the other railways on the Island, the tramway was built to the British standard gauge of 4' 8½".

Six single truck motor cars and six identical trailers were ordered from Brush Electrical Engineering Co of Loughborough. These were double deck vehicles with 36 crossbench seats on the lower deck and transverse seating for 39 on the upper deck. The cars were subjected to an 8mph speed limit.

An opening ceremony was held on Thursday 16th July 1896, to mark completion of the tramway as far as Keristal (No 1 Loop). Three special cars conveyed invited guests along the completed section despite the absence of any formal inspections. The line opened to the public as far as The Whing on 7th August after inspectors visited and mandated a series of improvements. The season ended on 26th September with an impressive 53,536 passengers travelling on the trams over the course of the inaugural summer. Two of the trailer cars were quickly converted to power operation.

Construction of the remainder of the tramway was undertaken over the following winter and the complete three-mile line to Port Soderick with eleven passing loops opened to the public on the first day of the 1897 season, 1st April.

A journey along the line, high above the sea and with the cliff face climbing high above the tram on the landward side and some warm sunshine, must have been a memorable experience. The route started close to Douglas Head and passed through a rock cutting and under the inland arch at the entrance to the Marine Drive. There was a lengthy loop here to store trailers required to strengthen trams at busy periods. The route then followed the inland side of the drive, cut into the rockface. A three-span bridge crossed Pigeon Stream, where a tearoom was supplied with hot water from the line's power station. A twin spanned 256ft long lattice girder steel bridge at Wallberry provided memorable views of the cliff side and the sea far below, and this was followed by a similar 120ft span single girder bridge at Horse Leap. The isolated depot at Little Ness was situated on the only flat ground on the route. Earthworks were need to cross Keristal gorge, but completion of the line gave access to the attractive destination of Port Soderick, albeit 180ft below the terminus. Access to Port Soderick was improved by the opening of a cliff lift on 11th July 1898, and a funicular was added in 1900 to link the terminus at Douglas Head with the Harbour.

At peak times a 7½ minute interval service was provided, and a simple system was employed to prevent accidents. Numbers were painted on the overhead poles at each passing

The spectacular Walberry viaduct lay some 200ft above sea level on a gradient of 1 in 17. The two-span 256ft girder structure replaced the original wooden bridge provided on construction of the Marine Drive roadway. *Tony Wilson Collection*

The line has been lifted at Pigeon Stream and the imposing power station is showing signs of decay prior to demolition. This site is now unrecognisable, with the present roadway carried on an embankment. *Tony Wilson Collection*

→The tollgates at the entrance to the Marine Drive; pedestrians passed through the doorway on the left. The tracks beyond this point were used to store trams on busy days. *Barry Edwards Collection*

→In the days before 'health and safety' car No 1 heads through the toll gates for Port Soderick. With live wires just above the heads of upper deck passengers, the warning notice is very relevant. *Manx National Heritage*

→→Little Ness depot was remote, over a mile from the nearest property. Cars were stored here after the line closed, fortunately allowing No 1 to be preserved at the National Tramway Museum, Crich. Enthusiasts gather at Little Ness to begin her rescue in 1951. *Barry Edwards Collection*

loop, representing the number of cars in service. If a seven-car service was operating, then cars should pass at loops marked with a seven, five car services passed at loops marked five, and so on. Each car sported a 'car disk', as a reminder of the number of vehicles in operation.

Douglas Head Marine Drive Limited went into receivership in 1899, but the tramway proved profitable; a record 231,664 passengers were carried in the 1907 season. Services were curtailed at the outbreak of war in August 1914 and for around four years the line was silent, although the Marine Drive remained open. In early 1919 preparations begun for a reopening of the line and 1920 provided one of the best operating seasons ever, as passengers rose to 267,671. Passenger numbers declined through the 1920s as the attractiveness of Douglas Head waned, and the tramway made a loss of £94 in 1929 despite carrying 101,600 passengers.

Like other railways on the Island the line was increasingly having to compete with motor bus services and excursions, and itself tried to get consent to operate a charabanc service

from the town centre up to Douglas Head to boost traffic on the tramway, but this application was unsuccessful. Fares were reduced for the 1936 season and electric headlights fitted to the cars to allow late evening special excursion trips in a bid to increase passenger numbers. In the event, nothing seemed to bring passengers in sufficient numbers and the line struggled on until the end of the 1939 season on Wednesday 15th September, when the line closed for the duration of the Second World War.

The line did not re-open after the War; the cost of repairs to the viaducts at Pigeon Stream and Horse Leap, coupled with the dereliction of Port Soderick, left the tramcar fleet isolated at Little Ness. The Douglas Head Marine Drive Limited and the Tramway were purchased by the Highways Board, who began a protracted scheme to rebuild the Drive which was not completed until 1963. Trackwork and the overhead line were removed in 1946/47 but the depot and its contents remained untouched, until in 1951 a group led by Keith Pearson acquired and removed car No.1 from Little Ness shed, hauled it along the narrow Marine Drive and into preservation. It was intended to return and claim a second car, but this proved impossible. The remainder of the cars and the shed were demolished over the winter of 1951/52. Trackwork at Little Ness remained in situ until 1960 when it was removed by volunteers for re-use at Crich Tramway Museum in Derbyshire, where the restored Car No 1 is now preserved.

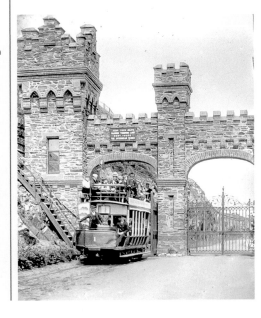

DOUGLAS HEAD INCLINE RAILWAY

When the Douglas Southern Electric Tramway opened in 1896, access to Douglas Head from the harbour area involved a steep climb, deterring visitors from reaching the tramway terminus and the many attractions which evolved to include a camera obscura, the short-lived 200ft Warwick Observation Tower (1899-1900), a waxworks pavilion, switchback railway, and pierrot concerts. The solution came in the form of a 450ft-long (137m) 4ft gauge railway. An agreement of 21st April 1898 between Sir John Goldie-Taubman and Richard Maltby Broadbent, allowed for a single or double-track mechanical tramway, lift or railway and lift, from a point near Battery Pier to a point seaward of the Douglas Southern Electric Tramway terminus on Douglas Head. Broadbent had been instrumental in establishing the attractions and railway at Groudle Glen, and he formed Douglas Head Incline Railway Company Ltd with his wife and private capital of £10,000.

The line was built in 1900 and consisted of a double-track funicular railway climbing at a gradient of 1 in 4.5. The lower station was behind the Douglas Head Lighthouse near Port Skillion and the Battery Pier, whilst the upper end had a combined station and an oil engine house not far from the Douglas Southern Electric Tramway terminus. Unusually, there was a curve about one-third of the way up from the bottom and the track was laid with 70lb flat bottom rail. Two cars with stepped seating were delivered by Hurst Nelson & Co. of Motherwell in July 1900 (drawing numbers 5072 & 5025) and the line opened towards the end of that summer.

After a satisfactory inspection by Mr Neville, engineer to the Isle of Man Harbour Commissioners in April 1901, the line opened to visitors in time for the Whit holiday. It soon proved popular; crowds of around 10,000 visitors would gather for Sunday afternoon open air services. The line was closed during the First World War, and the entire undertaking sold to Douglas Head Incline Railway Ltd on 7th July 1922,

the new company having its offices at the upper station. A Nunnery estate deed of 30th June 1926 required the line to operate from the Friday before Whitsun Monday until 30th September each year. War again intervened at the end of the 1939 season and the closed line was sold in 1940 to the Morley family of Beckenham, Kent. They in turn sold it in 1947 to Mrs Bolton and others of Onchan.

The service restarted in 1949; a connecting bus service was provided to the bottom terminus of the funicular on South Quay the following year. These buses were diverted to Douglas Head in 1951, spelling the end for the ferry service across the harbour and, at the end of the 1953 season, the incline railway.

The line was liquidated at the start of 1954 and the Douglas Head Incline Railway Ltd dissolved on 15th October 1956. The track had already been dismantled in October and November 1955 with several lengths of rail reused on the MER at Lewaigue Flat on the outskirts of Ramsey.

The route of the incline railway can still be followed on Douglas Head; the Camera Obscura is the sole remaining visitor attraction from this once popular destination.

Two lightly loaded toast rack cars of the Douglas Head Incline Railway cross alongside the parallel footpath. The harbour crane is visible on the quay, and the white livery of the Isle of Man Steam Packet Company vessel dates the image to the 1930s. *Manx National Heritage*

A crowd gathers on the footpath whilst passengers queue to buy tickets from the lower terminus kiosk. Note the unusual significant curvature in the track one third of the way up the incline. *Manx National Heritage*

A busy day beckons at Douglas Head as a fresh carload of well-dressed visitors heads for the summit in this pre-First World War view. There is a distinct absence of barriers to prevent passengers leaning out of the cars. *Barry Edwards Collection*

THE PORT SODERICK FUNICULAR

⬐An early 20th century view looking up the funicular. The steeper gradient of this line necessitated the construction of new passenger cars when the railway was transferred from Falcon Cliff. William G Cavanagh: Manx National Heritage

→⬐The old cars were recycled as kiosks on the promenade at Port Soderick and can be seen at the foot of the funicular. The new cars were larger, in anticipation of the crowds to be attracted to the wide range of amusements on offer. Manx National Heritage

↓The Forresters created a pleasure resort at Port Soderick and built a hotel. The incline railway eased the steep drop down to the facilities; the walkway from the funicular to the Douglas Marine Drive Tramway can be seen above the upper terminus. Tony Wilson Collection

During the last years of the 19th century, the attractive Bay at Port Soderick was developed by the Maurice and Thomas Forrester to become a major tourist attraction. Facilities grew to include a short promenade, hotel, restaurant, camera obscura and children's playground. The arrival of the Douglas Southern Electric Tramway at the top of the cliff to the north of the bay in 1897 brought opportunities for a substantial increase in visitors, but the new southern terminus was 180ft above sea level, and there were 150 steps between the tramway and the bay.

Fortuitously, the 1887-built Falcon Cliff Lift in Douglas had ceased operating and was purchased by the Forresters in 1896 in anticipation of the arrival of the tramway. They bought the complete structure and arranged for it to be moved to Port Soderick. At 218ft, the reconstructed line was longer than at Falcon Cliff, so some new sections had to be built but the basic structure of twin 4ft gauge tracks of flat bottom rail was retained. Driven by an oil engine housed in a corrugated iron building at the top station, the cables were of 3½″ circumference. The lower sections of the line, essentially a wooden structure, were raised on stone pillars that are still visible today. The promenade station was provided with a pagoda hut for ticket sales.

Two new larger passenger cars were acquired, each with stepped seating, as the line's gradient of 1:2.2 differed from the Falcon Cliff installation; the original cars were retained and survived for many years as kiosks on the promenade at Port Soderick.

Construction occupied the whole of 1897 and the line was inspected six times before finally being approved in a letter from the Governor's secretary dated 11th July 1898. The line

opened shortly thereafter. Port Soderick proved an attractive destination, with circular tours by the Douglas Southern Electric Tramway, Cliff Lift, and the Isle of Man Railway from Port Soderick back to Douglas, heavily promoted. The Forresters also brought visitors from Douglas by their steam launch *Karina*.

It is not clear how long the line survived; it seems likely however that it closed around the same time as the Marine Drive tramway with the outbreak of the Second World War in the 1939 season. The complex at Port Soderick was sold in 1947, when the lift had ceased operating. It was dismantled by 1949, the cars surviving as hen houses until several cattle were poisoned by chewing the lead paint on the roofs.

The original footpath from the former terminus of the Douglas Southern Electric Tramway down to the beach still survives and some fencing and the stone pillars that supported the wooden viaduct have been exposed by recent demolition work. There is now little evidence to suggest that Port Soderick was once a thriving tourist destination; all buildings have been demolished and only the wide promenade survives.

THE FALCON CLIFF LIFT

The First Lift (1887-1896)

The Falcon Cliff Hotel was built in the 1840s for John Stanway Jackson, then the manager of the Bank of Mona. As the attractiveness of the resort of Douglas grew, so the prominent position of the property, which commanded superb views over Douglas Bay from high above the promenade, encouraged its conversion into a hotel and entertainment complex in 1877, coinciding with the liquidation of the Bank of Mona in 1876. Rivalling the Derby Castle site, attractions included a skating rink, cycling and athletics track, a bowling green and, from 1887, a glass dance pavilion to the south. The site's position necessitated a steep climb from the foreshore, so plans were developed to provide a cliff lift to encourage visitors.

T Cain was engaged to build a 'Patent Tram' lift; sadly, his son was killed during the construction works. The lift was first tested on 26th May 1887. It was 218ft long and rose to a point 110ft above the base station at a gradient of 1:1.98. It was a double track 4′0″ gauge line with flat bottom rail fastened to 12″ square timbers that formed the top of a viaduct-like construction up the cliff side. A castellated entrance was built for the lift on the foreshore, matching the style of the complex above.

The lift was inspected by the Harbour Commissioners in July and the line started operating on 6th August 1887. It is not clear whether this lift was powered by steam, oil or gas. The journey time was 1 min 25 seconds.

Competition between attractions at Douglas was intense, and the Falcon Cliff attractions found it hard to compete despite the operation of the lift. The dance pavilion was taken out of use and demolished in 1896, and the lift closed. This provided the opportunity for the Forrester brothers to purchase and dismantle the redundant lift and re-install it at Port Soderick in 1898.

The Second Lift (1927-1990)

This was not the end of lift services to Falcon Cliff. Access to the promenade remained an issue for hotel guests and visitors, and in 1927, 31 years after the closure of the first lift, a new single-track line was installed at a new site to the south of the original route. William Wadsworth & Sons Ltd of Bolton were the engineers, the new line being of 5′0″ gauge running in channel section rails set at a gradient of 1:1.15 on a 129 ft-long track – thereby making it the steepest cliff railway in the British Isles. The single car carried six passengers plus an attendant. A balance weight (set at the weight of the car plus a half load of three passengers) ran up and down in its own guides under the car.

The new line was operated by a 400-volt DC electric motor driving twin 1″ diameter cables. The lift was rebuilt in 1932 and the hotel and lift was sold to Okell & Sons Ltd in 1945. A rectifier was installed on the site in 1950 when DC supply ceased in Douglas, and electricity was delivered at 415 volts in three phase alternating current. Overhead wires supplied the rectified current to the motor and operate the safety gates at each terminus.

Initially the line operated all year round but in later years it operated seasonally from June to September, finally running only on Friday evenings.

Declining tourist visitors led to the hotel becoming a non-residential public house in the 1980s led to the closure of the hotel complex and the lift at the end of the 1990 season. The site was sold and developed as private office and, although still in situ, the lift has not operated in service since then.

Plans were considered to move the lift to Groudle Glen to improve access to the Groudle Glen Railway, or even be relocated at Douglas Head, but these came to naught, and the track and surrounding area has become so overgrown that it is impossible to discern the route of the lift, although the promenade level entrance in Palace View Terrace is still visible.

↑↑The original Falcon Cliff lift, built in 1887, was double track. Sadly it was out of use by 1896 and sold to the Forrester family and moved to Port Soderick. This view shows the original elaborate promenade station. The upper station was much closer to the actual hotel than the replacement opened in 1927. *Manx National Heritage*

↑In a sight now thoroughly overgrown, the second Falcon Cliff lift of 1927 lies disused in 1991, although advertising still tries to attract visitors to the closed Hotel. The single car is stranded at the upper terminus. *Richard Kirkman*

←A close-up image of the 1927 car at the upper terminus, with the lift long closed. The overhead electric wires are still in situ. *Tony Wilson Collection*

THE CUNNINGHAM CAMP ESCALATOR

Joseph Cunningham and his wife organised an annual summer camp for the Florence Working Lads' Institute in Liverpool; in 1892 and 1893 they brought the group to Laxey, camping in tents alongside the river. Encouraged by the success of this venture, the Cunningham's moved to the island and opened the all-male Howstrake Camp on the MER in 1894; a decade later they moved to Victoria Road, Douglas and built Cunningham's Young Men's Holiday Camp with a large dining pavilion and 1,500 tents sleeping up to eight persons each. Cunningham died in 1924 but the camp continued to flourish with an average annual attendance during the 1930s of 36,000 campers. The camp was later renamed Douglas Holiday Camp and eventually became the Isle of Man Holiday Centre.

On 24th August 1908 Archibald Laidlaw Baird of 5 and 6 Clements Inn, London WC2, provisionally applied for a patent, with the actual application following on 4th March 1909. The application had been communicated from Joseph O. Boufard of 108 Dearborn Street, Chicago, USA, and noted: 'This invention relates to improvements in escalators or inclined elevators of that type in which seats are fitted at intervals to an endless driving chain.' The patent was accepted on 3rd June 1909 and given UK Patent number 17757.

Cunningham's Camp was located high above the promenade, necessitating a steep climb up Switzerland Road. Attention turned to making improvements for campers, with planning applications outlining ideas for an escalator from before the First World War. A substantial castellated entrance to the camp was built in Switzerland Road in 1914. There was a stone gravel path up to the camp from this entrance,

The lower level of the escalator and the ticket office was located just inside the imposing castellated entrance to what became the Douglas Holiday Camp. This is clearly no longer an all-male establishment! *Barry Edwards Collection*

but this may be afterthought, when it became clear that the escalator could not be completed before the end of hostilities.

Plans for an escalator were submitted on 13th January 1923 and soon approved. Drawings produced by Geo Kay & Sons were traced from the engineering company, but their authorship remains a mystery. Construction was quick, and the escalator opened late that summer.

The chairs were driven electrically, the motor running continuously with a clutch at the top that could be used to stop the escalator if necessary. The motor installations for both sets were housed in a concrete building under the top platform of the structure. There are indications that the escalator ran on 110 volts until early 1964 when the voltage was increased but the newer motor shows three phase 415 volts. There is evidence of an electrical intake at the lower station, but this may have been for lighting. There was bell communication between the attendants at the top and bottom of the installation, a start lever at the bottom, and a safety bar at the top that stopped the seats moving if a passenger failed to get off at the top. There would have been a continuous clicking sound as the chairs travelled up, created by wooden safety wedges that stopped chairs sliding back down in the event of a failure.

Recent research, during the dismantling of the structure in February 2013, revealed that the brick and concrete upper and lower stations were constructed by J T Skillicorn, as were the retaining walls that supported the wooden structure up the cliffside. High quality virgin timber, supplied by Douglas Steam Sawmills, would have been 50 to 60 years old when cut. Although the structure's roof had suffered badly, much of the escalator areas were as solid as when constructed.

Each chair was made up of seven pieces of wood, screwed together and braced with iron for additional strength. The upper side of the chairs had an extended base to prevent passengers putting their hands onto the chain. The chairs had a wrought iron chassis, the four wheels individually attached with bolts; during the dismantling, many of the chair bolts came undone with a spanner, the grease still in situ. Many of the wheels still turned, despite the escalator not having moved since 1968.

The whole structure was nearly lost in 1933 when a nearby bush fire was said to be licking the roof, but the local Fire Brigade saved it from destruction.

The escalator was a considerable success and in July 1937 an application was lodged to extend the building to allow a second set of seats to be installed to the right of the existing set when looking from the bottom. Work on the extension started on 15th November 1937 and was completed by 27th June. The architect this time was J. E. Teare and J. Skillicorn were the builders of at least the wooden structure.

Each individual set of seats comprised of 100 chairs, 48 of which are visible, with the remaining 52 making their way back to the bottom underneath and upside down. Adjacent to each set of seats was a 170-step staircase. Only the original set continued in service to the end; the newer set did not operate after the 1964 season.

Campers originally rode on the escalator free of charge, but other members of the public were charged 1d. This charge did rise very slowly over the years and by the time the escalator closed in 1968 it had reached 3d! The escalator ran throughout the season from May to September from early morning to late evening. Actual times vary from source to source but appear to be from 06:00 or 06:30 until 23:30 or 23:45. Campers returning after midnight who were caught had to walk up and were fined 1 shilling. The first passenger on the escalator is believed to have been a Mr Tinker from Middleton in Manchester.

From 1938 onwards there was a small ticket office on the right-hand side of the entrance at the bottom.

Previous research into the history of the Cunningham's installation indicated a link with a similar machine in Southend-on-Sea. It is possible that several parts, including motors and gearboxes, were sold to Cunningham although the installation type was completely different. The Southend installation was installed inside a long wooden shed and opened on 3rd September 1901. It was a moving walkway consisting of an endless wooden-slatted conveyor on a chain angled at 20 to 25 degrees (1 in 5) and was found to be uncomfortable for passengers to stand on. It was powered by a 35hp electric motor and could carry 3,000 passengers per hour.

Complaints about the noise and frequent mechanical breakdowns, led to closure in 1912, and later the whole thing being dismantled and stored. This coincides with Cunningham's entrance construction in 1914 and it is possible that Cunningham acquired the Southend equipment and stored it on the island until 1923.

Cunningham's Escalator was built at a time when such technology was advancing rapidly and names such as Otis were beginning to appear on the scene. Jessie Reno whose name appears on many early patents, produced the early versions of what was installed at Cunningham's. No evidence of any similar structure or mechanism has been uncovered, and it seems probable that the Douglas escalator was unique and will remain so. The camp represented the beginnings of the holiday camp business, ancestor to such establishments as Butlins, and had within its boundary a fabulous example of early escalator technology, the forerunner to another piece of everyday life today.

↑ Passengers sat sideways on the simple chairs on the 1938 escalator, facing those choosing to walk up to the camp. The driving chain is just visible below the chairs. The original 1923 escalator lay to the left of the wall. *Barry Edwards Collection*

← A sad sight of dereliction as the escalator is demolished. A small length of driving chain has yet to be removed from the 1938-installation on the right-hand-side of the structure. *Barry Edwards*

THE BROWSIDE TRAMWAY

The Lady Isabella Water Wheel proved a popular tourist destination in Laxey, especially after the opening of the Manx Electric Railway. Visitors passed a succession of refreshment rooms and fairground attractions as they walked from the village but were faced with a modest climb to reach the wheel itself. The Browside Tramway, was built by Great Laxey Mine manager Captain Francis Reddicliffe, Company clerk John Callow, and John Corlett, Captain of the North Laxey Mine, to overcome this final hurdle.

The tramway opened on 16th August 1890 and was a short funicular railway, 130 yards long, with a track gauge of 6′ 0″, the two tracks being about a foot apart. Two cars seated around 50 passengers on eight completely open toastrack-style seats. The lower set of wheels on each car was of larger diameter than the upper set to counteract the gradient and keep the cars level.

The line was worked by water sourced from inside the wheel case of the Laxey wheel. The two cars sat atop water tanks, the car at the top having its tank filled whilst the one at the bottom was emptied. When the brake was released the extra weight of the upper car was sufficient to move both cars. The process was reversed on completion of the journey. The line employed a bung boy at the lower station whose role was to empty the tank of the car that had just completed the descent. The tramway paid the Mining Company £25 per year for the water. An average of 45,000 passengers used the tramway annually in its early years of operation.

↗A rare view showing the twin tracks of the Browside Tramway and its proximity to the Lady Isabella. Substantial structures are provided at each end of the incline, with a fairground shooting range adjacent to the lower station. Barry Edwards Collection

↓Looking down the incline from the upper station, the varied wheel diameters that maintain a horizontal carriage, and the simple passenger seating, are evident. The heavy wire linking the two carriages passes behind the photographer and descends on rollers to the lower level. Barry Edwards Collection

A small accident occurred in 1893 when the brake was not applied properly and the cars ran away, one slamming into the bottom station: the other into the top and jamming itself. No injuries were suffered by passengers but Mr Callow, who happened to be at the top station, received minor injuries after being hit by the ascending car.

The fare charged seemed to vary, some sources state a 1d return, some a 1d each way and indeed one suggestion is 1d up and ½d down, with Ladies travelling down free of charge!

Restructuring of the Mining Company in 1903 led to a deterioration of relationships with the tramway management. The 1904 rent had not been paid by January 1905 and negotiations led to a reduction to £15 for the forthcoming season. The owners offered the Mining Company a share in the line, but this was rejected.

At the beginning of 1906, the Mining Company increased the rent to £50 for the approaching season, eventually an agreement was reached for a payment of £25. The year of 1906 is thought to have been the last season of operation. The line and adjacent land was sold to Robert Kelly of Douglas, and he received a letter from the Mining Company in 1907 saying that they could no longer supply water to operate the tramway because they did not have enough. This appeared to be a convenient excuse to force closure.

The line was dismantled by 1910 but there is no record of the fate of the trams; the remains of the upper station eventually disappeared under the new car park at the wheel. Mention was made by Laxey Village Commissioners of restoring the line in the mid-1970s, but nothing came of the idea.

RAMSEY QUEEN'S PIER TRAMWAY

The 2,160 ft (658.4m) long Ramsey Pier was designed by Sir John Coode and built by Messrs. Head, Wrighton & Sons of Stockton-on-Tees at a cost of £40,752. Construction began in 1882 and the iron pier was opened by the Lord Bishop of Sodor and Man on 22nd July 1886. Timbers were installed to support a tramway for the movement of materials during construction, but the tramway was not added until a decade later. The rails were ordered in 1895, the tramway opening around 1896. The original rolling stock comprised of seven luggage trucks and one low flat truck all dating from either 1886 or 1899. Initially used to carry passengers' baggage to pleasure steamers and ferry services to Ardrossan, Belfast, and Whitehaven, a passenger-carrying hand-propelled vehicle with upholstered seats for

around six was added when the landing stage was extended in 1899.

The single track 3-foot gauge tramway laid with 45lb tramway type grooved rail was 2,080ft (634.0m) long with a central passing loop, a short siding at both ends and, at the shore end, two divided spurs stretched off the pier onto the road. These were removed in 1955/56.

Modernisation came in 1937 with the addition of a Planet locomotive and a 15-seat bogie passenger coach, both from F. C. Hibberd & Co. of Park Royal, London, the 8hp locomotive having works number 2037 and the coach number 2038. In 1950 a Wickham railcar, works No.5763, with Ford V8 engine and seating for eleven passengers arrived. Two members of the Royal Family have travelled on the line,

The restored Planet locomotive in new steam outline guise re-joins her trailer on the first stage of the restored Queens Pier in 2021. The train was loaned to the Queens Pier restoration Trust for the official re-opening of the first three restored bays, by the Jurby Transport Museum. *Barry Edwards*

Edward VII and Queen Elizabeth the Queen Mother on 4th July 1963, the Planet locomotive and coach doing the honours on this occasion.

Steamer services were withdrawn at the end of the 1970 season, but the tramway operated until 9th September 1981, when it closed following the discovery that the wooden track bearers needed replacement. In its final season the line carried 7,000 passengers and completed 900 operational miles. The pier closed to the public in June 1991.

The Planet locomotive and the Wickham railcar were used in the dismantling of the former Manx Northern Railway from St. John's to Ramsey. The Wickham was dismantled in 1983, the Planet and coach were initially preserved by the Isle of Man Railway & Tramway Preservation Society and displayed in the former car shed museum at Ramsey MER station. The pair moved to storage at the former Homefield bus depot in Douglas, before moving again in 2009 to the new Jurby Transport Museum.

After many years of uncertainty, the Queens Pier Restoration Trust (QPRT) was formed and registered on 8 March 2017. The QPRT begun the long and complex process of restoration of the first three pier bays, raising funds as they went along. Many local companies pledged support and pier planks were sold to boost the coffers. After some four years of hard work, the team were ready to open the first three bays, and a ceremony was arranged for 22nd July 2021, the 135th anniversary of the opening of the pier. The re-opening was performed by the Lieutenant Governor Sir Richard Gozney.

The team at Jurby Transport Museum decided that the official re-opening would not be complete without the Planet locomotive and coach being present. Arrangements were made with a local carrier, and the train was repainted at Jurby before being moved to the pier on 19th July 2021, the first time in 40 years that it had been on the pier.

↑↑ The Planet locomotive lies ready to propel the trailer car from the pier entrance during 1964; shutters are down to protect passengers from a southerly wind. Baggage trolleys and wagons await their next duties alongside the old passenger van, in use as a store. *Barry Edwards Collection*

↑ One of the original baggage cars, fully restored and used to carry materials during the pier restoration project, is seen on the Pier on 18th April 2022. *Barry Edwards*

BALLAJORA QUARRY (DREEMSKERRY)

The MER had extensive interests in quarrying and opened sites at Dhoon, Dhoon West and Ballajora (Dreemskerry). The quarries supplied the MER with ballast, as well as providing material for roads and other building projects. There was also a considerable export trade up until the First World War, when this dried up.

Ballajora Quarry, opened in 1900, provided good building stone and was last worked around 1932, although stocks of stone were still being removed after the Second World War, with the site finally closing to rail traffic in the late 1940s.

The quarry was located on the west side of the line on the southerly approach to Dreemskerry station. A retaining wall hides where the headshunt for the quarry was situated. There was a crossover on the MER to allow departing trains from the headshunt to cross to the southbound track. The headshunt was steep and passed under a tippler fed by a short 2′0″ gauge line from the quarry worked by two small four-wheeled hand-propelled tubs, one of which survives at the Laxey Mines Railway.

The quarry had a section of mixed gauge 2ft and 3ft track heading to the north, and a second 2ft gauge line heading south, laid with lightweight jubilee style track. The headshunt was eventually lifted in 1989 and the crossover removed by 2008. The official stop for Ballajora Quarry is at Pole 777, and a short section of 2ft gauge track, including the loading gantry, remains in position to this day.

↑ The remains of what appears to be winding gear, or a conveyor pulley, lies in the undergrowth to the east of the Manx Electric Railway. *Barry Edwards*

← The two-foot gauge line running over the top of the former three-foot gauge Manx Electric Railway siding is still in situ. The cutting that contained the siding has become overgrown. The two rails are simply bent upwards to prevent the wagons running off the end. Photographed in January 2022. *Barry Edwards*

DHOON QUARRY TRAMWAY AND AERIAL ROPEWAY

↓A general recent view of the Dhoon Quarry station site. The ropeway down to the quarry below was on the right of the picture, while the narrow-gauge railway that served the quarry off to the left of the picture went under the road close to where the white van is parked. Today the station is used as a permanent way depot and access point. *Barry Edwards*

↓↓The well protected entrance to the former quarry, that was down below the Manx Electric Railway on the right of the previous picture. *Barry Edwards*

Dhoon Quarry station on the MER, now a rural request stop, was once served by two other transport systems. One was a railway, the other an aerial ropeway included here for completeness.

Dhoon and Dhoon West quarries were leased by Alexander Bruce in October 1895, the year after the tramway reached Laxey, and formed part of the motivation for the planned 1897 extension to Ramsey harbour to facilitate development of a profitable business; exports of granite setts had begun before the tramway was built. Dhoon setts were later used to pave the route of the Upper Douglas cable tramway. Sidings were laid to accommodate the traffic when the tramway opened, and two 12-ton stone wagons (Nos 19 and 20), known as Dreadnoughts, were built in 1912 on old 1893/4 motor bogies to handle the traffic.

The 53-acre Dhoon West quarry, situated on the western side of the railway, closed in 1900 following the collapse of Dumbell's Bank, but was purchased by the MER in 1903. Initially served by horse and cart, these primitive arrangements were quickly superseded by a 2ft gauge railway. This headed west on a level crossing over the public road, then into a narrow tunnel underneath the A2 Ramsey Road to connect into the quarry. The traffic was handled in its own MER siding complete with a stone crushing unit and weighbridge built by H Pooley and Son, works No.10293. This was added during the construction of the exchange sidings in 1900 and weighed all the quarry operations. Stone traffic by rail declined in the 1920s and ceased in the following decade. Eventually taken over by the Highways Board, the quarry survived until 1972 under lease to Pochins contractors.

The Dhoon Quarry exchange sidings also serviced the MER's wood and corrugated iron-built sawmill, and sleeper depot, which lay between the weighbridge and Creosote Cottage, where the wood was creosoted. The sawmill processed timber sourced from the MER-owned glens to be utilised for fencing, buildings, and sleepers; it remained in use until the 1950s. The depot was demolished during 1973 (an ex-MER 10-13 series Car, 25hp traction motor used to power it being salvaged for further use). The stone-built Creosote Cottage is still visible from passing trams and remains in use for permanent way duties; other items often of interest here include stockpiles of replacement sleepers, rails, and associated fixings.

The aerial ropeway to Dhoon Quarry was 225m long, and located on the eastern side of the MER. The small buckets operated from inside the Highways Board Quarry, located below railway level, to a loading platform located on a siding running parallel with the adjacent road alongside the line, each bucket capable of loading one wagon. Quarrying ceased on this site in the mid-1930's.

Dhoon Quarry sidings enjoyed a brief return to prominence in 1993, when they became the terminus for 'Steam on the MER' services from Laxey operated by IoMR locomotive No 4 Loch, forming the showpiece of the Year of Railways celebrations to mark the centenary of the opening of the MER from Derby Castle to Groudle.

POORTOWN QUARRY TRAMWAY

Peel Road station (originally Poortown until 1885) on the Manx Northern Railway route, which opened in 1883, was the site of a two-foot gauge tramway laid by the Manx Northern in 1885/6 to serve the Isle of Man Highway Board's stone quarry located at Poortown. Operated by gravity and horsepower there were two sets of three tipper wagons, each hopper capable of holding one ton of stone. The wagons were supplied by A S Nelson and Co of Glasgow, later Hurst Nelson.

The station lay to the south of the road overbridge, but the traffic was handled in an 80-foot long siding and loading dock, capable of handling eight open wagons built on the northern (Ramsey) side of the bridge. The siding was later locked by a patent Annett's Key, previously used at the Knockaloe branch junction on the Isle of Man Railway during the First World War.

The tramway was built on a descending gradient from the quarry to Peel Road of around 1 in 25. The route turned westwards out of the quarry, passing a stone crushing plant, then followed the northern side of the main Poortown road before sweeping slightly further north and hugging the edge of a field, before turning sharply north again to come alongside the three-foot gauge siding at Peel Road. The stone was tipped into wagons in the sidings. There was a stone horse trough, still visible today at the halfway point.

The tramway seems to have been very busy when first opened, with continuous movement of wagons throughout the day. Empty wagons were pulled back up to the quarry by horses. The traffic waned as in later years, with improvement to the roads, much of the stone was conveyed by motor vehicles. The line was closed just before the Second World War, and the tramway and three-foot gauge siding were both lifted in 1948.

The last train passed through Peel Road in 1967 and the wooden station building was later deliberately burnt down, and the site cleared. Today all that remains are a few decorative palm trees and the foundations of the platform.

A view from the bridge taken in 1992, shows the quarry siding area and the retaining wall, above which the tramway was laid. *Richard Kirkman.*

A general view of Peel Road station looking north towards St Germain's. The quarry siding lay on the opposite side of the bridge; the quarry tramway ran off the right of the picture, from the other side of the bridge. *Barry Edwards Collection*

ROLLING STOCK LIST

MANX ELECTRIC RAILWAY POWER CARS (3'0" Gauge)

No.	Built by	Year	Bogies	Motors	Car Type	No. of seats	Length	Width	Height	Notes
1	G F Milnes & Co. Ltd	1893	Milnes S3 [1]	2 x 25hp	Unvestibuled saloon	34	34'9" 10.59m	6'6" 1.98m	11'0" 3.35m	In service [2]
2	G F Milnes & Co. Ltd	1893	Milnes S3 [1]	2 x 25hp	Unvestibuled saloon	34	34'9" 10.59m	6'6" 1.98m	11'0" 3.35m	In service
5	G F Milnes & Co. Ltd	1894	Milnes S3 [1]	2 x 25hp	Vestibuled saloon	32	34'8" 10.56m	6'3" 1.90m	11'0" 3.35m	In service
6	G F Milnes & Co. Ltd	1894	Milnes S3 [1]	2 x 25hp	Vestibuled saloon	36	34'8" 10.56m	6'3" 1.90m	11'0" 3.35m	In service
7	G F Milnes & Co. Ltd	1894	Milnes S3 [1]	2 x 25hp	Vestibuled Saloon	36	34'8" 10.56m	6'3" 1.90m	11'0" 3.35m	In service
9	G F Milnes & Co. Ltd	1894	Milnes S3 [1]	2 x 25hp	Vestibuled saloon	36	34'8" 10.56m	6'3" 1.90m	11'0" 3.35m	In service [3]
14	G F Milnes & Co. Ltd	1898	Milnes S3	4 x 20hp	Cross bench open	56	35'5" 10.79m	6'3" 1.90m	10'6" 3.20m	Restored for 2018 In service
15	G F Milnes & Co. Ltd	1898	Milnes S3	4 x 20hp	Cross bench open	56	35'5" 10.79m	6'3" 1.90m	10'6" 3.20m	Stored
16	G F Milnes & Co. Ltd	1898	Milnes S3 [4]	4 x 20hp	Cross bench open	56	35'5" 10.79m	6'3" 1.90m	10'6" 3.20m	In service
17	G F Milnes & Co. Ltd	1898	Milnes S3	4 x 20hp	Cross bench open	56	35'5" 10.79m	6'3" 1.90m	10'6" 3.20m	Stored
18	G F Milnes & Co. Ltd	1898	Milnes S3	4 x 20hp	Cross bench open	56	35'5" 10.79m	6'3" 1.90m	10'6" 3.20m	In service
19	G F Milnes & Co. Ltd	1899	Milnes S3 [5]	4 x 20hp	Winter saloon	48	37'6" 11.43m	7'4" 2.23m	11'0" 3.35m	In service
20	G F Milnes & Co. Ltd	1899	Milnes S3 [5]	4 x 20hp	Winter saloon	48	37'6" 11.43m	7'4" 2.23m	11'0" 3.35m	In service
21	G F Milnes & Co. Ltd	1899	Milnes S3 [5]	4 x 20hp	Winter saloon	48	37'6" 11.43m	7'4" 2.23m	11'0" 3.35m	In service
22	McArds (Port Erin)	1992	Brill 27Cx	4 x 25hp	Winter saloon	48	37'6" 11.43m	7'4" 2.23m	11'0" 3.35m	Replacement [6] In service
23	MER Co. Ltd	1926	(Brill 27Cx)	(4 x 27.5hp)	Locomotive	—	34'6" 10.51m	6'3" 1.90m	10'0" 3.04m	Rebuild Stored [7]
25	G F Milnes & Co. Ltd/MER	1898	Brush Type D	[8]	Cross bench open	56	35'5" 10.79m	6'3" 1.90m	10'6" 3.20m	In service
26	G F Milnes & Co. Ltd/MER	1898	Brush Type D	[8]	Cross bench open	56	35'5" 10.79m	6'3" 1.90m	10'6" 3.20m	In service
27	G F Milnes & Co. Ltd/MER	1898	Brush Type D	[8]	Cross bench open	56	35'5" 10.79m	6'3" 1.90m	10'6" 3.20m	In service
28	ER&TCW Ltd	1904	Brill 27Cx [9]	4 x 25hp	Cross bench open	56	35'0" 10.66m	6'3" 1.90m	10'6" 3.20m	Stored
29	ER&TCW Ltd	1904	Brill 27Cx [9]	4 x 25hp	Cross bench open	56	35'0" 10.66m	6'3" 1.90m	10'6" 3.20m	Stored Restoration in Progress
30	ER&TCW Ltd	1904	Brill 27Cx [9]	4 x 25hp	Cross bench open	56	35'0" 10.66m	6'3" 1.90m	10'6" 3.20m	Stored
31	ER&TCW Ltd	1904	Brill 27Cx [9]	4 x 25hp	Cross bench open	56	35'0" 10.66m	6'3" 1.90m	10'6" 3.20m	Stored
32	UEC Co. Ltd	1906	Brill 27Cx	4 x 27.5hp	Cross bench open	56	35'0" 10.66m	6'3" 1.90m	10'6" 3.20m	In service
33	UEC Co. Ltd	1906	Brill 27Cx	4 x 27.5hp	Cross bench open	56	35'0" 10.66m	6'3" 1.90m	10'6" 3.20m	In service
34	IOMR	1995	Brush Type D	4 x 25hp	Diesel/Electric Locomotive	—	27'8" 8.43m	6'7" 2.00m	10'0" 3.04m	In service

Notes:
[1] Brush type D bogies and 4 x 25hp motors fitted in place of Milnes S3 in 1903
[2] Oldest electric tramcar in the world still in regular use on its original line.
[3] Became the Island's first illuminated tram in 1993 as part of the Year of Railways celebrations.

[4] Received Milnes S3 bogies and 2 x 25hp motors from car No.4 in 1899; Brush type D bogies and 4 x 25hp motors fitted in 1903.

[5] Nos 19-22 received Brill 27Cx bogies and 4 x 25hp motors from car Nos 29, 28, 30 and 31 respectively in 1904.

[6] Original car No.22 destroyed by fire at Derby Castle depot during the night of 30 September 1990. New body built by McArds of Port Erin and electrical repairs carried out by staff at Derby Castle. Re-entered service in May 1992.

[7] The original No.23, which borrowed bogies from No.17 when required, was damaged in a derailment in 1914 but not withdrawn until 1922. It was not broken up and in 1926 was rebuilt and now borrowed bogies from the more powerful No.33. Disused after 1944, stored at Laxey until superficially restored in 1978; restored to working order in 1983/4 and for 1993. Named *Dr R. Preston Hendry* at Derby Castle on 25 May 1992.

[8] Nos 24-27 entered service in 1898 as trailers Nos 40-43, fitted with 4 x 25hp motors by the MER in 1903.

[9] Nos 28-31 received Milnes S3 bogies and 4 x 20hp motors from car Nos 20, 19, 21 and 22 respectively in 1904.

MANX ELECTRIC RAILWAY TRAILER CARS (3'0" Gauge)

No.	Built by	Year	Bogies	Car Type	No. of seats	Length	Width	Height	Notes
36	G F Milnes & Co. Ltd	1894	Milnes S2	Cross bench open	44	29'0" 8.83m	6'1" 1.85m	9'0" 2.74m	Stored
37	G F Milnes & Co. Ltd	1894	Milnes S2	Cross bench open	44	29'0" 8.83m	6'1" 1.85m	9'0" 2.74m	In service
40	English Electric Co. Ltd	1930	Milnes S1	Cross bench open	44	28'8" 8.73m	6'5" 1.95m	9'7" 2.92m	In service [1]
41	English Electric Co. Ltd	1930	Milnes S1	Cross bench open	44	28'8" 8.73m	6'5" 1.95m	9'7" 2.92m	In service [1]
42	G F Milnes & Co. Ltd	1903	Milnes S3	Cross bench open	44	28'6" 8.68m	6'5" 1.95m	9'5" 2.87m	In service
43	G F Milnes & Co. Ltd	1903	Milnes S3	Cross bench open	44	28'6" 8.68m	6'5" 1.95m	9'5" 2.87m	In service
44	English Electric Co. Ltd	1930	Milnes S1	Cross bench open	44	28'8" 8.73m	6'5" 1.95m	9'7" 2.92m	In service [1]
46	G F Milnes & Co. Ltd	1899	Milnes S1	Cross bench open	44	28'8" 8.73m	6'5" 1.95m	9'10" 3.0m	In service
47	G F Milnes & Co. Ltd	1899	Milnes S1	Cross bench open	44	28'8" 8.73m	6'5" 1.95m	9'10" 3.0m	In service
48	G F Milnes & Co. Ltd	1899	Milnes S2	Cross bench open	44	28'8" 8.73m	6'5" 1.95m	9'10" 3.0m	In service
49	G F Milnes & Co. Ltd	1893	Milnes S1	Cross bench open	44	28'9" 8.76m	6'3" 1.90m	9'2" 2.79m	In service
50	G F Milnes & Co. Ltd	1893	Milnes S1	Cross bench open	44	28'9" 8.76m	6'3" 1.90m	9'2" 2.79m	Stored
51	G F Milnes & Co. Ltd	1893	Milnes S1	Cross bench open	44	28'9" 8.76m	6'3" 1.90m	9'2" 2.79m	In service
52	G F Milnes & Co. Ltd	1893	Milnes S1	Cross bench open	44	28'9" 8.76m	6'3" 1.90m	9'2" 2.79m	Body removed 1947 [2]
53	G F Milnes & Co. Ltd	1893	Milnes S1	Cross bench open	44	28'9" 8.76m	6'3" 1.90m	9'2" 2.79m	Stored
54	G F Milnes & Co. Ltd	1893	Milnes S1	Cross bench open	44	28'9" 8.76m	6'3" 1.90m	9'2" 2.79m	Stored, Restoration in Progress.
55	ER&TCW Ltd	1904	Brill 27CxT	Cross bench open	44	29'4" 8.94m	6'5" 1.95m	9'4" 2.84m	In service
56	ER&TCW Ltd	1904	Brill 27CxT	Cross bench open	44	29'4" 8.94m	6'5" 1.95m	9'4" 2.84m	In service [3]
57	ER&TCW Ltd	1904	Brill 27CxT	Unvestibuled saloon	32	32'9" 9.98m	6'9" 2.05m	10'8" 3.25m	In service
58	ER&TCW Ltd	1904	Brill 27CxT	Unvestibuled saloon	32	32'9" 9.98m	6'9" 2.05m	10'8" 3.25m	In service Fitted with Illuminations for MER125 in 2018
59	G F Milnes & Co. Ltd	1895	Milnes S2	Unvestibuled saloon	18	22'2" 6.75m	6'9" 2.05m	10'10" 3.30m	In service
60	G F Milnes & Co. Ltd	1896	Milnes S1	Cross bench open	44	28'9" 8.76m	5'9" 1.75m	8'7" 2.62m	In service
61	UEC Co. Ltd	1906	Brill 27CxT	Cross bench open	44	29'4" 8.94m	6'5" 1.95m	9'4" 2.84m	In service
62	UEC Co. Ltd	1906	Brill 27CxT	Cross bench open	44	29'4" 8.94m	6'5" 1.95m	9'4" 2.84m	In service

Trailer car numbering.
Trailers are listed here in current numerical order. These are the numbers they have carried since 1906 when the final power cars were delivered. Before 1906 many of the trailers were re-numbered, some several times when it was necessary to release numbers for new power cars. As an example of this, the first three trailers started life as 11-13, then became 23-25, then 28-30 and finally 49-51.

Notes:
[1] Replacements for the trailers destroyed in the Laxey fire were ordered in 1930. Although seven were destroyed, insurance only provided for three trailers and a replacement shed.
[2] Body removed in 1947, chassis still in use as a wiring flat fitted with a scissor lift.
[3] Rebuilt with wheelchair access and fittings to carry disabled passengers. Re-entered service in 1995.

SNAEFELL MOUNTAIN RAILWAY POWER CARS (3'6" Gauge)

No.	Built by	Year	Bogies	Motors	Car Type	No. of seats	Length	Width	Height	Notes
1	G F Milnes & Co. Ltd	1895	Milnes Special	4x 25hp	Vestibuled Saloon	46	35'7" 10.85m	7'3" 2.20m	10'4" 3.16m	New bogies and control equipment 1977. In service
2	G F Milnes & Co. Ltd	1895	Milnes Special	4x 25hp	Vestibuled Saloon	46	35'7" 10.85m	7'3" 2.20m	10'4" 3.16m	New bogies and control equipment 1977/78. In service
3	G F Milnes & Co. Ltd	1895	Milnes Special	4x 25hp	Vestibuled Saloon	46	35'7" 10.85m	7'3" 2.20m	10'4" 3.16m	New bogies and control equipment 1977/78. Destroyed in runaway incident 30 March 2016. Replica expected
4	G F Milnes & Co. Ltd	1895	Milnes Special	4x 25hp	Vestibuled Saloon	46	35'7" 10.85m	7'3" 2.20m	10'4" 3.16m	New bogies and control equipment 1978/79. In service
5	H Kinnan (Ramsey)	1971	Milnes Special	4x 25hp	Vestibuled Saloon	48	35'7" 10.85m	7'3" 2.20m	10'4" 3.16m	Replacement on original chassis. New bogies and control equipment 1978/79. In service
6	G F Milnes & Co. Ltd	1895	Milnes Special	4x 25hp	Vestibuled Saloon	46	35'7" 10.85m	7'3" 2.20m	10'4" 3.16m	New bogies and control equipment 1978/79. Body dismantled 2018. Replica under construction

Notes:
Passenger Cars:
As built these cars had unglazed windows; glazed sliding windows were fitted by April 1896. The lack of ventilation, when all windows were closed in sunny but windy weather, resulted in clerestory windows being fitted during the winter of 1896/97.
The seating capacity was increased to 48 by the addition of two single seats, one at each end backing onto the bulkhead.

CIVIL AVIATION AUTHORITY RAILCARS (3'6" Gauge)
(For use on the Snaefell Mountain Railway)

No.	Builder	Date	Builder No.	Length	Width	Height	Wheel Arrangement	Weight	Notes
1	D. Wickham Ware, Herts	1951	5864	9'5" 2.87m	5'7" 1.70m	7'9" 2.36m	4-wheel	2t 10cwt	Sold to IOMR 1977. Spent many years stored at Laxey SMR depot. Now Preserved at Stratfold Barn Railway
3	D. Wickham Ware, Herts	1977	10956	12'9" 3.88m	7'8" 2.35m	8'1" 2.47m	4-wheel	3t 0cwt	In service Owned by IOM Railways
4	Wickham Rail Suckley, Worcestershire	1991	11730	13'4" 4.06m	7'8" 2.35m	8'6" 2.47m	4-wheel	4t 0cwt	In service

STEAM RAILWAY LOCOMOTIVES (3´0˝ Gauge)

Steam Locomotives

No	Name	Builder	Date	Builder's No.	Type	Length over Beams	Width	Coupled Wheel Diameter	Cylinders	Weight	Notes
1	Sutherland	Beyer Peacock	1873	1253	2-4-0T	21´0˝ 6.40m	6´9˝ 2.06m	3´9˝ 1.14m	11˝x18˝ 28x46cm	17t 12cwt	Stored, On display in Port Erin Museum
3	Pender	Beyer Peacock	1873	1255	2-4-0T	21´0˝ 6.40m	6´9˝ 2.06m	3´9˝ 1.14m	11˝x18˝ 28x46cm	17t 12cwt	Sold (Off Island) 1978 [1]
4	Loch	Beyer Peacock	1874	1416	2-4-0T	21´0˝ 6.40m	6´9˝ 2.06m	3´9˝ 1.14m	11˝x18˝ 28x46cm	17t 12cwt	In Service
5	Mona	Beyer Peacock	1874	1417	2-4-0T	21´0˝ 6.40m	6´9˝ 2.06m	3´9˝ 1.14m	11˝x18˝ 28x46cm	17t 12cwt	Stored Douglas Cosmetic restoration in progress
6	Peveril	Beyer Peacock	1875	1524	2-4-0T	21´0˝ 6.40m	6´9˝ 2.06m	3´9˝ 1.14m	11˝x18˝ 28x46cm	17t 12cwt	Stored, On display in Port Erin Museum [2]
7	Tynwald	Beyer Peacock	1880	2038	2-4-0T	21´0˝ 6.40m	6´9˝ 2.06m	3´9˝ 1.14m	11˝x18˝ 28x46cm	17t 12cwt	Dismantled 1946 [3]
8	Fenella	Beyer Peacock	1894	3610	2-4-0T	21´0˝ 6.40m	6´9˝ 2.06m	3´9˝ 1.14m	11˝x18˝ 28x46cm	17t 12cwt	Stored Douglas
9	Douglas	Beyer Peacock	1896	3815	2-4-0T	21´0˝ 6.40m	6´9˝ 2.06m	3´9˝ 1.14m	11˝x18˝ 28x46cm	17t 12cwt	Stored Douglas
10	G H Wood	Beyer Peacock	1905	4662	2-4-0T	21´0˝ 6.40m	6´9˝ 2.06m	3´9˝ 1.14m	11˝x18˝ 28x46cm	20t 10cwt	Rebuild in progress
11	Maitland	Beyer Peacock	1905	4663	2-4-0T	21´0˝ 6.40m	6´9˝ 2.06m	3´9˝ 1.14m	11˝x18˝ 28x46cm	20t 10cwt	In service
12	Hutchinson	Beyer Peacock	1908	5126	2-4-0T	21´0˝ 6.40m	6´9˝ 2.06m	3´9˝ 1.14m	11˝x18˝ 28x46cm	20t 10cwt	Rebuild in progress
13	Kissack	Beyer Peacock	1910	5382	2-4-0T	21´0˝ 6.40m	6´9˝ 2.06m	3´9˝ 1.14m	11˝x18˝ 28x46cm	20t 10cwt	In service
14	Thornhill	Beyer Peacock	1880	2028	2-4-0T	21´0˝ 6.40m	6´9˝ 2.06m	3´9˝ 1.14m	11˝x18˝ 28x46cm	17t 12cwt	Formerly MNR No.3 Withdrawn 1958 Privately preserved on the Island, rebuild in progress
15	Caledonia	Dubs & Co.	1885	2178	0-6-0T	22´0˝ 6.71m	6´10˝ 2.08m	3´3˝ 0.99m	13˝x20˝ 33x51cm	23t 11cwt	Formerly MNR No.4 In service
16	Mannin	Beyer Peacock	1926	6296	2-4-0T	21´0˝ 6.40m	7´2˝ 2.18m	3´9˝ 1.14m	12˝x18˝ 30x46cm	23t 9cwt	Stored Douglas Assessment for return to steam in progress

Diesel Locomotives and Railcars

No.	Name	Builder	Date	Builder's No.	Length	Width	Height	Wheel Arrangement	Weight	Notes
17	Viking	Schoema Germany	1958	2175	20´0˝ 6.10m	7´2˝ 2.20m	8´10˝ 2.70m	4-wheel	21t 0cwt	Withdrawn Stored Douglas [4]
18	Ailsa	Hunslett Engine Co	1994	LD9342	20´5˝ 6.23m	5´7˝ 1.71m	8´2˝ 2.49m	4-wheel		In service
19		Walker/ GNR(I)	1949	79789	41´3˝ 12.56m	7´6˝ 2.28m	9´11˝ 3.02m	Bogie Railcar		Stored Douglas [5]
20		Walker/ GNR(I)	1950	83149	41´3˝ 12.56m	7´6˝ 2.28m	9´11˝ 3.02m	Bogie Railcar		Stored Douglas [5]
21		MP & ES	2013	550				Bogie Locomotive		Stored
		Motorail Ltd	1959	22021 /59	7´5˝ 2.26m	4´0˝ 1.21m	4´6˝ 1.37m	4-wheel	4t 20cwt	In service. Purchased from B&S Massey, Openshaw, Manchester
		Motorail Ltd	1966	40s280	7´5˝ 2.26m	4´0˝ 1.21m	6´0˝ 1.82m	4-wheel	4t 20cwt	In service. Purchased from NCB Kilnhurst
22		Wickham Ltd T27	1956	7442	8´0˝ 2.43m	5´7˝ 1.70m	6´10˝ 2.08m	4-wheel		In service. Purchased [6] from Lochaber Railway
23		Wickham Ltd T27a	1961	8849	8´0˝ 2.43m	5´7˝ 1.70m	6´10˝ 2.08m	4-wheel		In service. Purchased [7] from Lochaber Railway

Notes:

[1] Displayed in the Manchester Museum of Science and Industry as a sectionalised exhibit.

[2] Cosmetically restored by the Isle of Man Steam Railway Supporters Association and now in Port Erin Museum.

[3] Property of the Isle of Man Railway and Tramway Preservation Society. At Southwold railway, Suffolk.

[4] Purchased from Germany in 1992 for works duties.

[5] Purchased from County Donegal Railway in 1961, both railcars have been partially rebuilt. The original cab bodies on both were built by Speakman (Coachbuilders) Ltd.

[6] New to the Lochaber Railway 30/5/1956 as their HW6/8-1. Renumbered W6/11-1 c1962. Withdrawn and stored at Possil Park (Glasgow) c1973 and sold to the IOMR in May 1978.

[7] New to the Lochaber Railway 10/2/1961 as their W6/11-3. Withdrawn and stored at Possil Park c1973 and sold to the IOMR in May 1978.

STEAM RAILWAY PASSENGER COACHES (3'0" Gauge)

No.	Built by	Year	Coach Type	No. of Seats	Length	Width	Height	Notes
C1	MRCW Saltley	1873/4	4w 2nd with Guard/HB	20	16'6" 5.02m	7'0" 2.13m	9'4" 2.84m	Body to F64 in 1912 Body on display in Peel
F6	Brown Marshalls	1876	Bogie Brake Composite	42	35'0" 10.66m	7'0" 2.13m	9'4" 2.84m	Sold to Mr Peter Rampton 1975
F9	Brown Marshalls	1881	Bogie Brake Composite	60	35'0" 10.66m	7'0" 2.13m	9'4" 2.84m	In service
F10	Brown Marshalls	1881	Bogie Brake Composite	60	35'0" 10.66m	7'0" 2.13m	9'4" 2.84m	In service
F11	Brown Marshalls	1881	Bogie Brake Composite	60	35'0" 10.66m	7'0" 2.13m	9'4" 2.84m	In service
F15	Brown Marshalls	1894	Bogie Brake Composite	42	35'0" 10.66m	7'0" 2.13m	9'4" 2.84m	In service
F18	Brown Marshalls	1894	Bogie Brake Composite	50	35'0" 10.66m	7'0" 2.13m	9'4" 2.84m	In service
F21	MRCW Saltley	1896	Bogie Brake Composite	42	35'11" 10.94m	7'0" 2.13m	9'4" 2.84m	Sold to WHR, then to Ireland. Returned to IOM 1998. Now stored Partially restored
F25	MRCW Saltley	1896	Bogie Brake 3rd	60	35'0" 10.66m	7'0" 2.13m	9'4" 2.84m	Stored
F26	MRCW Saltley	1896	Bogie Brake 3rd	60	35'0" 10.66m	7'0" 2.13m	9'4" 2.84m	In service
F27(ii)	Isle of Man Railways	2013	Kitchen/Generator & Guard Van	—	35'0" 10.66m	7'0" 2.13m	9'4" 2.84m	In service Dining Train kitchen car
F28	MRCW Saltley	1897	Bogie Luggage Van	—	35'0" 10.66m	7'0" 2.13m	9'4" 2.84m	Stored
F29	MRCW Saltley	1905	Bogie Vestibule Open 3rd	32	36'11" 11.25m	7'0" 2.13m	10'3" 3.12m	In service Dining Train
F30	MRCW Saltley	1905	Bogie Vestibule Open 3rd	32	36'11" 11.25m	7'0" 2.13m	10'3" 3.12m	In service Dining Train
F31	MRCW Saltley	1905	Bogie Vestibule Open 3rd	32	36'11" 11.25m	7'0" 2.13m	10'3" 3.12m	In service Dining Train
F32	MRCW Saltley	1905	Bogie Vestibule Open 3rd	32	36'11" 11.25m	7'0" 2.13m	10'3" 3.12m	In service Dining Train
F35	MRCW Saltley	1905	Bogie Vestibule Open 1st/3rd	41	36'11" 11.25m	7'0" 2.13m	10'3" 3.12m	In service Dining Train
F36	MRCW Saltley	1905	Bogie Vestibule Open 1st/3rd	41	36'11" 11.25m	7'0" 2.13m	10'3" 3.12m	Royal saloon Port Erin Museum
F37	Hurst Nelson	1899	Bogie Guard Brake 1st/3rd	40	35'6" 10.82m	7'1" 2.32m	10'0" 3.04m	Former MNR No. 16(ii) Sold to Mr Peter Rampton 1975
F38	Hurst Nelson	1899	Bogie Brake 3rd	40	35'6" 10.82m	7'1" 2.32m	10'0" 3.04m	Former MNR No. 17(ii) Sold to Mr Peter Rampton 1975
F39	Bristol & South Wales RW Co	1887	Bogie Guard Brake 3rd	32	30'0" 9.14m	7'2" 2.18m	9'6" 2.89m	Former MNR No.17, later 15(ii) Used as Camping coach 1968-?. In service
F43	MRCW Saltley	1908	Bogie Guard Brake 3rd	30	37'0" 11.27m	7'0" 2.13m	10'0" 3.04m	Stored
F45	MRCW Saltley	1913	Bogie Guard Brake 3rd	50	36'11" 11.25m	7'0" 2.13m	10'1" 3.07m	In service
F46	MRCW Saltley	1913	Bogie Guard Brake 3rd	50	36'11" 11.25m	7'0" 2.13m	10'1" 3.07m	In service

F47	MRCW Saltley	1923	Bogie Brake 3rd	60	36'11" 11.25m	7'0" 2.13m	10'1" 3.07m	In service
F48	MRCW Saltley	1923	Bogie Brake 3rd	60	36'11" 11.25m	7'0" 2.13m	10'1" 3.07m	In service
F49	MRCW Saltley	1926	Bogie Guard Brake 3rd	40	37'00" 11.27m	7'0" 2.13m	10'0" 3.04m	In service
F54	MRCW Saltley (Frame)	1923	Bogie Guard Composite	50	34'2" 10.41m	7'0" 2.13m	9'4" 2.84m	Body broken up Replica body 1997. In service
F62	MRCW Saltley (Frame) with Bodies A1 & B1	1926	Bogie Composite	60	34'2" 10.41m	7'0" 2.13m	9'4" 2.84m	In Service
F63	MRCW Saltley (Frame) with Bodies B6 & B10	1920	Bogie 3rd	60	33'2" 10.10m	7'0" 2.13m	9'4" 2.84m	Restoration to service. in progress
F66	MRCW Saltley (Frame) with Bodies B11 & B15	1920	Bogie 3rd	60	33'2" 10.10m	7'0" 2.13m	9'4" 2.84m	Chassis exchanged with F64 and body rebuilt 1979. Body Stored on Island
F67	MRCW Saltley (Frame) with Bodies B23 & C14	1922	Bogie3rd	60	33'2" 10.10m	7'0" 2.13m	9'4" 2.84m	Body Stored on Island
F68	MRCW Saltley (Frame) with Bodies A9 & C13	1909	Bogie Composite	60	34'2" 10.41m	7'0" 2.13m	9'4" 2.84m	Sold to Phyllis Rampton Narrow Gauge Railway Trust 1975, now owned by VORR Earmarked for Vale of Rheidol Railway Museum at Aberystwyth
F74	MRCW Saltley (Frame) with Bodies A11 & C11	1921	Bogie Composite	60	34'2" 10.41m	7'0" 2.13m	9'4" 2.84m	Stored
F75	MRCW Saltley (Frame) with Bodies A12 & C9	1926	Bogie Saloon	60	34'2" 10.41m	7'0" 2.13m	9'4" 2.84m	On display in Port Erin Museum
N40	Swansea Wagon Company	1879	6w 1st	42	30'0" 9.14m	6'9" 2.05m	9'6" 2.89m	Formerly MNR No 1, then IMR F40 Sold to Mr Rampton, 1975
N41	Swansea Wagon Company	1879	6w 1st	42	30'0" 9.14m	6'9" 2.05m	9'6" 2.89m	Formerly MNR No 2, then IMR F41 Body became mess hut at Douglas shed in 1964. Chassis Scrap Manx Metals, Ballasalla 1974/75
N42	Swansea Wagon Company	1879	6w Composite	60	30'0" 9.14m	6'9" 2.05m	9'6" 2.89m	Formerly MNR No 3, then IMR F42 Stored, Property of IOMR&TPS At Southwold Railway, Suffolk
N45	Swansea Wagon Company	1879	6w 3rd Guard	60	30'0" 9.14m	6'9" 2.05m	9'6" 2.89m	Formerly MNR No 6, then IMR F45 Privately preserved on the railway.
N51	Swansea Wagon Company	1879	6w 3rd	60	30'0" 9.14m	6'9" 2.05m	9'6" 2.89m	Formerly MNR No 14, then IMR F51 Sold to Phyllis Rampton Narrow Gauge Railway Trust 1975, now owned by VORR Earmarked for Vale of Rheidol Railway Museum at Aberystwyth

DOUGLAS HORSE TRAMWAY CARS (3´0˝ Gauge)

No.	Built by	Year	Car Type	No. of seats	Length	Floor Width	Overall Width	Height	Notes
1	G C Milnes Voss & Co Ltd	1913	S/D Saloon	30	24´8˝ 7.51m	6´4˝ 1.94m	6´7˝ 2.0m	9´11˝ 3.02m	In service
11	Starbuck C&W Co	1886	Toastrack	32	22´9˝ 6.93m	5´4˝ 1.62m	6´8˝ 2.03m	9´6˝ 2.89m	Stored
12	G F Milnes & Co Ltd	1888	Toastrack	32	22´9˝ 6.93m	5´4˝ 1.62m	6´8˝ 2.03m	9´6˝ 2.89m	In service
13	MRC&W Co. Ltd Saltley	1883	Double Deck	42	22´6˝ 6.85m		6´0˝ 1.82m	10´8˝ 3.25m	From South Shields 1887 Renumbered 14 in 1908 [1]
18	MRC&W Co. Ltd Saltley	1883	Double Deck	42	23´1˝ 7.03m	6´1˝ 1.85m	6´4˝ 1.93m	10´8˝ 3.25m	From South Shields 1887 Converted to S/Deck in 1903-6 Back to D/Deck 1988/9. In service
21	G F Milnes & Co Ltd	1890	Toastrack	40	24´8˝ 7.51m	5´4˝ 1.62m	6´11˝ 2.09m		In service
22	G F Milnes & Co Ltd	1890	Toastrack	32	22´5˝ 6.83m	5´5˝ 1.65m	6´10˝ 2.08m	9´9˝ 2.79m	Withdrawn 1978. used as Tram shop at Derby Castle. Now at Jurby Transport Museum
27	G F Milnes & Co Ltd	1892	Winter saloon	30	24´5˝ 7.44m	5´10˝ 1.77m	6´6˝ 1.98m	9´2˝ 2.79m	In service [2]
28	G F Milnes & Co Ltd	1892	Winter saloon	30	24´5˝ 7.44m	5´10˝ 1.77m	6´6˝ 1.98m	9´2˝ 2.79m	Withdrawn, Sold for £2800 Saturday 27 August 2016
29	G F Milnes & Co Ltd	1892	Winter saloon	30	24´5˝ 7.44m	5´10˝ 1.77m	6´6˝ 1.98m	9´2˝ 2.79m	In service [2]
32	G F Milnes & Co Ltd	1896	Toastrack	32	21´8˝ 6.60m	5´4˝ 1.62m	6´10˝ 2.08m	8´7˝ 2.61m	In service
33	G F Milnes & Co Ltd	1896	Toastrack	32	21´8˝ 6.60m	5´4˝ 1.62m	6´10˝ 2.08m	8´7˝ 2.61m	Withdrawn, Sold for £1200 Saturday 27 August 2016
34	G F Milnes & Co Ltd	1896	Toastrack	32	21´8˝ 6.60m	5´4˝ 1.62m	6´10˝ 2.08m	8´7˝ 2.61m	Withdrawn, Sold for £1300 Saturday 27 August 2016. Fitted with Nissan Cabstar chassis & Mercedes C180 petrol engine
36	G F Milnes & Co Ltd	1896	Toastrack	40	24´11" 7.59m	5´4˝ 1.62m	6´10˝ 2.08m	8´7˝ 2.61m	In service
37	G F Milnes & Co Ltd	1896	Toastrack	32	21´8" 6.60m	5´4˝ 1.62m	6´10˝ 2.08m	8´7˝ 2.61m	Withdrawn, Sold for £1100 Saturday 27 August 2016
38	G F Milnes & Co Ltd	1902	Toastrack	40	24´5" 7.44m	5´5˝ 1.65m	6´11˝ 2.10m	8´7˝ 2.61m	In service
39	G F Milnes & Co Ltd	1902	Toastrack	40	23´0˝ 7.01m	5´4˝ 1.65m	6´11˝ 2.10m	8´9˝ 2.67m	Withdrawn, Sold for £1800 Saturday 27 August 2016
40	G F Milnes & Co Ltd	1902	Toastrack	40	24´5˝ 7.44m	5´4˝ 1.62m	6´10˝ 2.08m	8´11˝ 2.72m	Withdrawn, Sold for £1000 Saturday 27 August 2016
42	G C Milnes Voss & Co Ltd	1905	Toastrack	40	24´8˝ 7.51m	5´5˝ 1.65m	7´0˝ 2.13m	9´1˝ 2.77m	In service
43	United Electric Car Co. Ltd	1907	Toastrack	40	24´6˝ 7.46m	5´5˝ 1.65m	6´11˝ 2.10m	8´10˝ 2.69m	In service
44	United Electric Car Co. Ltd	1907	Toastrack	40	24´6˝ 7.46m	5´5˝ 1.65m	6´11˝ 2.10m	8´10˝ 2.69m	In service [3]
45	G C Milnes Voss & Co Ltd	1908	Toastrack	40	25´0˝ 7.62m	5´6˝ 1.67m	7´0˝ 2.13m	8´6˝ 2.59m	In service
47	G C Milnes Voss & Co Ltd	1911	Toastrack	40	25´1˝ 7.64m	5´5˝ 1.65m	7´0˝ 2.13m	8´9˝ 2.66m	Withdrawn 1978 Stored,
49	Vulcan Motor & Engineering Co Ltd	1935	Saloon/Toastrack Convertible	27/34	25´6˝ 7.77m	5´7˝ 1.70m	6´11˝ 2.10m	8´6˝ 2.59m	Withdrawn 1980 Privately Owned on IOM

Notes:

[1] Left the Island in 1955, later displayed at the Museum of British Transport, Clapham, returning for the centenary celebrations of 1976 and now on display in the Manx Museum, Douglas.

[2] Originally built without platform vestibules, which were added in 1895.

[3] The Royal car, having been used on several occasions to convey members of the Royal family.

UPPER DOUGLAS CABLE TRAMWAY CARS (3´0˝ Gauge)

Car No.	Built by	Year	Bogies	Car Type	No. of seats	Length	Width	Height	Notes
72/73	G F Milnes & Co. Ltd	1896	Milnes	Cross bench	38	30´0˝ 9.14m	5´7˝ 1.70m	9´0˝ 2.74m	[2]

DOUGLAS HEAD AND MARINE DRIVE TRAMWAY CARS (4´8½" Gauge)

Car No.	Built by	Year	Chassis	Motors	Car Type	No. of seats	Length	Width	Height	Notes
1	Brush [1]	1896	Lord Baltimore No 2	Westinghouse 2x25hp	Double Deck	75	29´5˝ 8.96m	7´4˝ 2.23m	14´4˝ 4.36m	Preserved at Crich, Derbyshire

[1] Brush Electrical Engineering Co. Ltd

GROUDLE GLEN RAILWAY LOCOMOTIVES (2´0˝ Gauge)

Steam Locomotives

Name	Builder	Date	Builder No	Type	Length over Beams	Width	Coupled Wheel Diameter	Cylinders	Weight	Notes
Sea Lion	W G Bagnall	1896	1484	2-4-0T	10´9˝ 3.28m	4´2˝ 1.27m	1´2˝ 0.36m	4˝x7˝	4t 12cwt	In service
Polar Bear	W G Bagnall	1905	1781	2-4-0T	11´0" 3.35m	4´2˝ 1.27m	1´3˝ 0.38m	5˝x7˝	5t 10cwt	Preserved in working order at Amberley Chalk Pits Museum.
Annie	Richard Booth Isle of Man	1998		0-4-2T	10´10" 3.30m	4´2˝ 1.27m	1´4˝ 0.41m	5˝x7˝	4t 0cwt	In service [1]
Brown Bear	GGR/NBR Engineering	2019	1	2-4-0T	11´0" 3.35m	4´2˝ 1.27m	1´3˝ 0.38m	5˝x7˝	5t 10cwt	in service
Otter	NBR Engineering	2019	006	0-4-0ST						In Service

Electric Locomotives

No.	Name	Builder	Date	Builder's No.	Length	Width	Height	Wheel Arrangement	Weight	Notes
	Polar Bear	Alan Keef	2006	313	9´7˝ 2.93m	4´2˝ 1.27m	6´4˝ 1.94m	4-wheel	4t 0cwt	Replica, In service

Diesel Locomotives

No.	Name	Builder	Date	Builder's No.	Length	Width	Height	Wheel Arrangement	Weight	Notes
1	Dolphin	Hunslet Engine Co.	1952	4394	8´11˝ 2.72m	3´5˝ 1.04m	5´0˝ 1.52m	4-wheel	5t 0cwt	In service [2]
2	Walrus	Hunslet Engine Co.	1952	4395	8´11˝ 2.72m	3´5˝ 1.04m	5´0˝ 1.52m	4-wheel	5t 0cwt	In service [2]

Notes:
[1] Replica of locomotive built by W G Bagnall in 1911 (Works No. 1922) for the Gentle Annie Tramway in New Zealand.
[2] Built for Tilbury Contracting & Dredging Co Ltd. Sold in 1957 to Twickenham Sand and Gravel Co for use at their Feltham terminal, transferring in 1960 to a gravel pit system adjacent to Farnborough North (SR) station. Sold in 1969 to Mr B J Weeks for use at the Doddington House Railway near Chipping Sodbury and arrived on the Isle of Man in 1983 following closure of the Doddington system.

GREAT LAXEY MINES RAILWAY LOCOMOTIVES (19″ Gauge)

Steam Locomotives

Name	Builder	Date	Builder No.	Type	Length over Beams	Width	Coupled Wheel Diameter	Cylinders	Weight	Notes
Ant (ii)	Great Northern Steam	2004	20	0-4-0T	8′7″ 2.62m	2′6″ 0.76m	1′2″ 0.36m	4 x 6in	2 Tons	Replica
Bee (ii)	Great Northern Steam	2004	21	0-4-0T	8′7″ 2.62m	2′6″ 0.76m	1′2″ 0.36m	4 x 6in	2 Tons	Replica

Electric Locomotives

Name	Builder	Date	Builder No.	Type	Length	Width	Wheel Diameter		Weight	Notes
Wasp	Clayton Equipment	1973	B0152	4 wheel Battery Electric	7′8″ 2.35m	2′3″ 0.69m	1′2″ 0.36m			

Acknowledgements

The Authors would like to thank all the photographers who have made images available for inclusion in this volume. Thanks are also due to the staff of Isle of Man Transport, Manx National Heritage Library, Groudle Glen Railway, Laxey Mines Railway, The Orchid Line and Crogga Estate. Thank you to Miles and Linda Cowsill of Lily Publications for the freedom afforded to the Authors in the content of the book and to Ian Smith for his superb design. Our wives Irene and Christina have given their unstinting and generous support, as ever. We hope that the reader will enjoy this celebration of the railways of the Isle of Man.

— Barry Edwards and Richard Kirkman

Bibliography

Basnett Stan (2008): Trains of the Isle of Man – The Ailsa Years (Lily Publications)
Basnett Stan (2008): Trains of the Isle of Man – The Twilight Years (Lily Publications)
Basnett Stan (2009): Trains of the Isle of Man – Post Nationalisation (Lily Publications)
Basnett Stan (2010): Trams of the Isle of Man – 1946-Present Day (Lily Publications)
Boyd James (1993): The Isle of Man Railway vol I (Oakwood Press)
Boyd James (1994): The Isle of Man Railway vol II (Oakwood Press)
Boyd James (1996): The Isle of Man Railway vol III (Oakwood Press)
Carter Capt. Stephen (2003): Douglas Head Ferry & the Port Soderick Boats (Twelveheads Press)
Easdown Martin (2018): Cliff Railways, Lifts and Funiculars (Amberley Publishing)
Edwards Barry (1993): The Railways and Tramways of the Isle of Man (Oxford Publishing Company)
Edwards Barry (1995): The Snaefell Mountain Railway 1895-1995 (Midland Publishing Ltd)
Edwards Barry (1996): The Isle of Man Steam Railway (B&C Publications)
Edwards Barry (1998): The Manx Electric Railway (B&C Publications)
Edwards Barry (1999): Isle of Man Railways Locomotive, Tram and Rolling Stock Directory (B&C Publications)
Edwards Barry (2010/15): Trains & Trams of the Isle of Man (Lily Publications)
Edwards Barry (2018): One Horse Power, The Douglas Bay Horse Tramway since 1876 (Lily Publications)
Goodwyn Mike (1993): Manx Electric (Platform 5)
Hendry Dr R Preston & Hendry R Powell (1978): Manx Electric Railway Album (Hillside Publishing)
Hendry Dr R Preston & Hendry R Powell (1979): Narrow Gauge Story (Hillside Publishing)
Hendry Dr R Preston & Hendry R Powell (1980): Manx Northern Railway (Hillside Publishing)

Hendry Robert (1993): Rails in the Isle of Man – A Colour Celebration (Midland Publishing)
Hobbs George (2014): Stops Along the Manx Electric Railway (Loughtan Books)
Hobbs George (2015): By Whing to Port Soderick (Loughtan Books)
Hobbs George (2015): Manx Electric Railway Past & Present (Loughtan Books)
Hobbs George (2019): Power, Poles & Platelaying – Keeping the MER on Track (Loughtan Books)
Jones Norman (1994): Isle of Man Tramways (Foxline Publishing)
Jones Norman (1994): The Isle of Man Railway (Foxline Publishing)
Kennedy Adrian (2021): Rails across the Isle of Man in the 1950s (Unique Books)
Kirkman Richard & van Zeller Peter (1993): Isle of Man Railways; a celebration (Raven Books)
Manx National Heritage (1993): Industrial Archaeology of the Isle of Man
Manx Transport Heritage Museum (2018): The Peel to Knockaloe Railway 1915 to 1920
Pearson Keith (1970): Isle of Man Tramways (David & Charles)
Pearson Keith (1977): Cable Tram Days (Douglas Cable Car Group)
Pearson Keith (1992): One Hundred Years of the Manx Electric Railway (Leading Edge)
Pearson Keith (1999): The Douglas Horse Tramway (Adam Gordon)
Phillips Howard (2004): Particularly Peel (The Manx Experience)
Scarffe Andrew (2004): The Great Laxey Mine (Manx Heritage Foundation)
Scarffe Andrew (2014): The Railways and Tramways of Laxey (Mannin Media)
Scarffe Andrew (2020): Snaefell – A Mountain and a Railway (Isle of Man Transport)
Smith David M (1989): The Groudle Glen Railway (Plateway Press)
Turner Keith (1999): Pier Railways & Tramways of the British Isles (Oakwood Press)
Turner Keith (2002): Cliff Railways of the British Isles (Oakwood Press)